1850
MEZZ

GW00982623

Evidence in Arbitration

Evidence in Arbitration

By

Marvin Hill, Jr.
Associate Professor of Industrial Relations
Northern Illinois University

and

Anthony V. Sinicropi
Professor of Industrial Relations
University of Iowa

The Bureau of National Affairs, Inc., Washington, D.C.

Copyright © 1980
The Bureau of National Affairs, Inc.
Second Printing June 1981
Third Printing June 1985

Library of Congress Cataloging in Publication Data

Hill, Marvin
Evidence in arbitration.

Includes index.

1. Arbitration and award—United States.
2. Evidence (Law)—United States. I. Sinicropi, Anthony V., joint author.
II. Title.

KF9085.H46   347.73'9   80-15508
ISBN 0-87179-336-9

Printed in the United States of America
International Standard Book Number: 0-87179-336-9

Contents

1

Introduction

Arbitrators are divided as to how problems of evidence ought to be handled with respect to the record or the hearing. One school of thought is that, since arbitration is essentially a private fact-finding proceeding, the arbitrator is not bound by any formal rules of evidence and should not be required to make on-the-spot decisions with regard to the materiality, competency, or relevancy of evidence, be it in the form of testimony or exhibits. Consequently, absent a directive by the parties to observe legal rules of evidence, arbitrators may conduct the hearing with a commonsense notion of what is important in resolving the case and thus accept all evidence offered by the parties. An example of this view is illustrated by Arbitrator William E. Simkin:

> One of the fundamental purposes of an arbitration hearing is to let people get things off their chest, regardless of the decision. The arbitration proceeding is the opportunity for a third party, an outside party, to come in and act as a sort of father confessor to the parties to let them get rid of their troubles. . . . Because I believe so strongly that that is one of the fundamental purposes of arbitration, I don't think you ought to use any rules of evidence. You have to make up your mind as to what is pertinent or not in the case. Lots of times I have let people talk for five minutes, when I knew all the time that they were talking it had absolutely nothing to do with the case—just completely foreign to it.[1]

Thus it is argued that the arbitrator should accept all information into the record and weigh its significance during his subsequent deliberations.

Another school of thought is that the arbitrator, while not bound by federal or state rules of evidence, should nevertheless make judgments at the hearing based upon these con-

1

cepts. The notion here is that a "commonsense" criterion only redefines the basic problem. The advocates are still left to determine what commonsense rules are applicable in resolving the dispute. Arguably, evidentiary rulings made at the hearing not only apprise the parties of the standards being used but also force the parties to direct their attention to the issues at hand. Moreover, such an approach eliminates irrelevant material from the record. The arbitrator may then feel less compelled to direct time in his opinion and award to discussing his reasons for excluding such evidence.

Without commenting on the merits of either position, it is clear that numerous problems regarding the introduction of evidence in the proceedings are constantly challenging the arbitrator. As a result, the arbitrator is inevitably required to make evidentiary rulings and determinations either at the hearing or in his subsequent opinion and award.

Although it may be unsound to attempt to prescribe a fixed set of procedural rules comparable to judicially adopted rules of evidence,[2] still the arbitrator should possess a working knowledge of the basic considerations underlying the traditional rules of evidence. This position is reflected by the following statement of the Chicago Area Tripartite Committee of the National Academy of Arbitrators:

> We believe it is fundamental, however, to the proper conduct of an arbitration hearing that the arbitrator himself be familiar with and fully understand the rules of evidence. These rules by and large govern what evidence is to be admissible and the weight to be attached to evidence. The rules are based on many generations of judicial experience. They have as their primary objective the search for truth and generally the seeking to confine evidence so as to remove confusion, irrelevancy and manufactured facts. The significant consideration to bear in mind in relation to these rules is that they all have an underpinning of reason. They are not whimsical or arbitrary. Their objective is to encourage the process of unemotional and objective reasoning with the sole purpose to get at the truth.[3]

The purpose of the materials that follow is to provide a general overview of some of the difficult problems in the evidence area the practitioner will encounter in preparing and presenting a case in arbitration. Advocates of the arbitral process should understand what evidence is worth so that they can effectively prepare a case and, more important, adequately rebut irrelevant or prejudicial evidence. Likewise, a working knowledge of evidence is important to the arbitrator as a means of providing standards to guide him in rendering an award that is not based on incomplete and immaterial considerations. Moreover, the Pittsburgh Area Tripartite Committee has noted:

> Parties have a right to know what general standards an arbitrator uses in this critical determination of what evidence is worth. It has been suggested that properly understood legal rules of evidence have their foundation in reason, common sense, and necessity, and that perhaps the rules for the admissibility of evidence in court trials may be re-molded into rules for weighing evidence by arbitrators, even if no evidence is absolutely excluded as inadmissible. . . . It is difficult to imagine that the legal rules of evidence which have evolved over centuries could not yield helpful suggestions for use by arbitrators and participants in arbitration cases.[4]

The Authors note that this text on evidence is not intended to institutionalize or subject labor arbitration to rigid evidentiary requirements, but only to alert the practitioner to the major problems likely to be encountered in preparing and presenting a grievance for arbitration.

2

Types of Evidence

In general there are two fundamental types of evidence: direct evidence and circumstantial evidence. Direct evidence is evidence which proves a proposition directly, provided by an "eye witness" to a specific event. To cite an example, assume that an employer suspects that employee X is stealing company property. After a careful investigation the employer discovers two colleagues of X who relate to the employer that both observed X placing company property in X's lunch box. Furthermore, one of the employees tells the employer that he saw X leaving the premises with the lunch box containing the stolen property and placing it in his auto. In such a case, testimony by both employees that they saw X place such property in his lunch box would be direct evidence. Similarly, testimony by an employee that he observed X place the box containing the property in X's auto would be direct evidence tending to prove that X in fact was guilty of theft.

Circumstantial evidence is evidence which raises an inference with respect to some fact other than the testimony which is offered as evidence to the truths of the matters asserted. Using the above example, suppose that the employer cannot produce an employee who will testify that X was seen placing company property in his lunch box. Nevertheless, it is known that the specific property alleged to have been stolen was in the room prior to X's entry. In addition, the property was missing immediately after X left. Finally, X was seen running from the premises after leaving the room. Although there is no direct evidence that it was X who stole the property, such facts—the presence of the property in the room immediately before X's departure and X's "flight" from the premises—are circumstantial facts which, in most instances, will arguably be admitted and considered by an arbitrator.

4

It is important to stress that when circumstantial evidence is offered, the trier of fact must draw inferences from that evidence as it relates to the event or proposition that the employer (or union) is attempting to prove (e.g., X stole property). It should not be concluded, however, that because circumstantial evidence depends upon such inferences that it is necessarily suspect, or that an arbitrator will not accord it great weight. To the contrary, numerous arbitrators, similar to courts of law, have fully credited circumstantial evidence.[1] Indeed, as summarized by one arbitrator, circumstantial evidence is essentially a form of direct evidence, and accordingly may be entitled to greater weight than an "eye-witness" account:

> Many times direct, eyewitness proof is valueless, for it is not uncommon for the eyewitness to be in error. No witness plans to be in a location of an accident or other occurrence. While the occurrence he witnesses happens, he is caught up in a train of action which becomes a part of the fabric and background of his own existence. The difficulty occurs when we interpret what we see. We do not live in a vacuum, our general background, education, training and other factors entering into the making of our personality are brought into play to transform the raw electrical impulses of our body chemistry into meaningful thought. It is this process of interpretation which makes one decide that what he sees has meaning, and as our backgrounds vary so does this interpretative process whereby we "see" the same thing differently.
>
> For this reason so-called circumstantial evidence has great validity. Circumstantial evidence is merely the taking of known facts, determining if they raise reasonable inferences or concepts concerning the occurrence under investigation. We do the same thing with "circumstantial evidence" that the eyewitness does with the message his optic nerves send to his brain.
>
> Therefore, known circumstances surrounding the questionable event, merely another term for circumstantial evidence, are fit into a pattern so that we can reconstruct the event involved. The question, therefore, is not whether circumstantial evidence is valid, but what does it mean.[2]

Arbitrator Joseph Jenkins, in *Lone Star Steel Co.*,[3] stated that circumstantial evidence is often far more persuasive than direct testimony, particularly where action "in the nature of a conspiracy" is involved.

SUMMARY—The labor or management practitioner is cautioned not to dismiss a case or otherwise agree to an adverse settlement in a grievance dispute merely because of the absence of direct evidence. Circumstantial evidence is viewed by both courts and arbitrators as a fully probative device. As cited by one court, "Circumstantial evidence is merely direct evidence indirectly employed."[4] Absent other considerations, labor arbitrators will generally accord equal validity to both direct and circumstantial evidence. The practitioner, however, must still be sensitive to the particular problems inherent in proving a case using either direct or circumstantial evidence. The central problem relating to direct evidence is generally one of credibility of the testifying witness, while most problems of relevancy arise when circumstantial evidence is introduced.[5] It is important that the advocate recognize the problems associated with each type of evidence so that unreliable or irrelevant evidence is not admitted or, alternatively, if it is admitted, the problems are called to the attention of the arbitrator.

3

Relevance and Materiality in Evidence

Arbitrator Russell Smith has declared that the most important criterion of admissibility of proffered evidence is relevance.[1] In litigation courts require evidence to be probative of a material issue before it may be admitted. Unlike the judicial system, however, arbitrators rarely deny the parties the opportunity to present evidence on the basis that it is immaterial or irrelevant. Rather, arbitrators will generally admit the evidence "for what it may be worth." Still, it is important to understand the concepts of relevancy and materiality in order to effectively argue and object when a party attempts to prove his case using evidence which is clearly immaterial or irrelevant.

The concept of relevancy is not an inherent characteristic of any item of evidence but exists only as a relation between an item of evidence and the issue(s) asserted in a case. For example, assume that an employer is attempting to establish that employee X stole property, and produces a witness who testifies that X was observed running from the "scene of the crime." There is an issue with respect to the relevance of this testimony. If it can be said that this *fact* renders the issue which the employer is attempting to prove (theft of property by X) probable (or not probable), then the evidence is said to be relevant. As stated in the Federal Rules of Evidence, " 'relevancy' means evidence having any tendency to make the existence of any fact that is of consequence to the determination of the action more probable . . . than it would be without the evidence."[2] It is not expected that every witness or each exhibit "can make a home run" with the arbitrator before evidence may be deemed relevant. The standard under the Federal Rules is only "more probable . . . than it would be without the evidence." Accordingly, if testimony or exhibits arguably have *any* tendency to make the existence of the fact or issue to be proved more probable than not, the criterion for relevancy is established.

Once it is established that the evidence is relevant, it will generally be admitted regardless of its form unless the arbitrator finds some policy reason for its exclusion. Many of the traditional standards adopted by arbitrators for excluding relevant evidence will be subsequently discussed. At this point, however, it is noteworthy that in a close case concerning the relevancy of evidence, arbitrators invariably side with the view that the evidence should be received. In this regard the late Dean Harry Shulman has observed:

> The more serious danger is not that the arbitrator will hear too much irrelevancy, but rather that he will not hear enough of the relevant. Indeed, one advantage frequently reaped from wide latitude to the parties to talk about their case is that the apparent rambling frequently discloses very helpful information which would otherwise not be brought out.[3]

Similarly, the West Coast Tripartite Committee has asserted that it may be advisable, within limits, to admit all evidence notwithstanding questions of relevancy:

> On occasion, evidence will be proffered which recognizedly has no probative value but which should nonetheless be admitted, because to exclude it would be too damaging to confidence in the efficacy of the grievance procedure among unsophisticated participants in the arbitration. Some call this therapy evidence, and we are willing to admit it so long as the therapy itself does not become traumatic.[4]

Somewhat related to the issue of relevancy, questions of materiality involve the specific issue a party will be attempting to establish. Where evidence is relevant to a proposition of fact, but that proposition is not relevant to the issue before the arbitrator, the evidence is immaterial. For example, the fact that a grievant does not regularly attend services on Sunday goes to no material issue in a discharge for producing too many defective parts.[5] The fact that the grievant attends Sunday services would arguably be admissible as relevant evidence where the issue before the arbitrator is whether the grievant had a valid excuse for refusing overtime work on Sunday. In general, if the issue to which the evidence goes is not a material issue, it will command little (if any) weight by a trier of fact.

SUMMARY—It is reasonable for the labor or management advocate to assume that if testimony or exhibits offered at an arbitration hearing go toward establishing an issue deemed by the arbitrator to be material, and if the evidence is probative of that issue (i.e., the issue is rendered more probably true, or untrue, than it would be absent the evidence), it will generally be admitted and given appropriate weight. The practitioner should note, however, that even if evidence is relevant and material, it may still be excluded for policy reasons. For example, the evidence may be a prior offer to settle the dispute. Moreover, even if evidence does not satisfy the standards of materiality and relevancy, chances are excellent that the arbitrator will admit it "for what it is worth," a posture that may not be undesirable considering the overall function of the grievance procedure.

Although most evidence is likely to be admitted, notwithstanding objections involving relevancy, the advocate is still advised to test all pieces of evidence against this standard. Such an exercise should facilitate the formulation of those issues relevant to the arbitration. More important, such a test will clarify the relationship that each bit of evidence has upon the ultimate resolution of the case and will force the advocate to examine the reasons why a particular piece of evidence is being introduced. In addition, it should alert the proponent to relevancy-type objections that might be made at the hearing.

4

Quantum and Burden of Proof

Quantum of Proof

"Quantum of proof" is essentially the quantity of proof required to convince a fact finder to resolve or adopt a specific fact or issue in favor of one of the advocates. The quantity of proof required by a trier of fact to prefer one party over the other is, of course, a function of the individual arbitrator. As a result, it is impossible to state when a requisite degree of belief is established in the mind of a neutral.

Within the context of specific cases, however, arbitrators have over the years developed tendencies to apply different standards of proof according to the particular issue disputed. Often indicative of the arbitrators' overall philosophy of the function of the grievance arbitration mechanism, these tendencies are the subject of this analysis.

It has been suggested that the most useful way to think of the quantum of proof is to think in terms of variable degrees of caution. The West Coast Tripartite Committee has reasoned that an arbitrator may wish, on balance, to be more persuaded than not ("preponderance") in many cases; pretty certain in some others ("clear and convincing"); and completely convinced in yet others ("beyond a reasonable doubt").[1]

In cases involving moral turpitude, or where the charges are in their nature criminal, there is a definite division of opinion among arbitrators as to the degree of proof required. Support for the "beyond a reasonable doubt" rule is advanced by Arbitrator Howard Block:

> On the quantum of proof necessary to sustain an accusation of theft, arbitrators are virtually unanimous that the proof offered

10

must be beyond a reasonable doubt. Arbitrator Harold M. Somers has written the most oft-quoted explanation for the imposition of such a stringent standard of proof.

". . . discharge for stealing involves an unfavorable reflection on the moral character of the employee which is almost impossible to erase and which will seriously hamper if not altogether prevent his getting a job elsewhere in his line of work and will even hurt innocent members of his family. He and they are branded for life. The Company has a very heavy obligation in such a case. It carries the burden of proving beyond a reasonable doubt—in its own conscience as well as before an arbitrator—that the employee committed the offense of stealing."[2]

Arbitrator Burton Turkus has stated the applicable principle as follows:

The proof upon which the discharge is predicated, when grievous misconduct involving moral turpitide . . . is the basis, should establish guilt thereof beyond a reasonable doubt.

In other types of overt misconduct such as (a) illegal strikes . . . (b) refusal to perform job assignments . . . (c) fighting and (d) other offenses likewise constituting a breach of peace inside the plant or other challenge to the authority of management and its right to maintain morale, discipline, and efficiency in the work force, the requisite quantum of proof may not fall short of a clear and convincing demonstration of the commission of the offense. . . .[3]

Other arbitrators, however, have concluded that a standard of proof less than that required by criminal law is acceptable in arbitration cases:

Those who are prone indiscriminately to apply the criminal-law analogy in the arbitration of all discharge cases overlook the fact that employer and employee do not stand in the relationship of prosecutor and defendant. It cannot be emphasized too often that the basic dispute is between the two principles to the collective bargaining agreement, that is, the company and the union. At stake is not only the matter of justice to an individual employee, important as the principle is, but also the preservation of the collective bargaining relationship. . . .

The one thing we may be sure of is that, if the arbitrator is familiar with the facts of industrial life and understands that his function is creative as well as purely adjudicative, he will not evaluate the evidence solely on the basis of rigid standards of absolute proof or presumptions of innocence.[4]

Similarly, Robert Gorske has stated:

The standard of proof in civil litigation when commission of a crime is directly in issue is proof by a preponderance of the evidence. . . . An employer who could successfully sue an employee for an intentional conversion of the employer's property should probably not be required to retain the individual in his employ merely because a case cannot be proven beyond a reasonable doubt.[5]

Arbitrator Russel A. Smith, in the much quoted *Kroger Co.* decision, enunciates a "clear and convincing" standard even where the misconduct involves a kind recognized and punished by the criminal law:

> In general, arbitrators probably have used the "preponderance of the evidence" rule or some similar standard in deciding fact issues before them, including issues presented by ordinary discipline and discharge cases. However . . . it has been held that where the alleged "cause" for disciplinary action or discharge is misconduct of a kind recognized and punished by the criminal law, the employer must meet a higher standard of proof. . . . [I]t seems reasonable and proper to hold that alleged misconduct of a kind which carries the stigma of general social disapproval as well as disapproval under accepted canons of plant discipline should be clearly and convincingly established by the evidence.[6]

Finally, Arbitrator C. William Stratton in *Day & Zimmermann* rejected a criminal standard of proof citing the following rationale:

> I believe that proof "Beyond a Reasonable doubt" in a criminal case is actually in layman's terms more akin to clear and convincing proof. In the trial of criminal cases the court usually instructs the jury that a reasonable doubt is more than just a slight question in the mind of the juror but must be a doubt based on some flaw in the prosecution's case which makes the juror honestly question whether or not the prosecution has proved the defendant guilty. There is another standard of proof which is used in civil cases which is known as "Proof by a preponderance of the evidence." This means that after considering the evidence the tryer of the facts whether it be a judge or jury forms the opinion that it is more likely that the event occurred or that the thing was done than it did not occur or was not done. Proof by a preponderance of the evidence is not sufficient in the arbitration case where an employee has been charged with an act which would ordinarily be considered a crime. However, it is this arbitrator's opinion that proof by clear and convincing evidence is sufficient to insure that the employee has been given the benefit of any favorable testimony on his behalf or lack of sufficiency in the employer's case.[7]

It is important to caution the advocate that it is difficult to ascertain a true picture of the quantum of proof actually required by a particular arbitrator in a specific case merely by reference to prior decisions. As noted by one arbitrator:

> When an arbitrator writes that the company or union has proved a particular point "by a preponderance of the evidence," he may be implying the conscious application of a standard of proof; much more likely, however, he is simply using an expression which comes trippingly off the tongue and which has no real connection with the degree of proof he will require in future cases of the same type.[8]

Moreover, there is always the possibility that the arbitrator rendered an award not based on factors cited in the opinion. This is not to say that the advocate should not conduct research on the standard of proof that an arbitrator professes to apply in a specific case. A careful review of the decisions may provide critical insights into an arbitrator's reasoning process. A judgment can then be made how specific issues, facts, and other evidence are likely to relate to the standard of proof applied. While the authors recognize that a mere reading of opinions may provide an incomplete or even incorrect picture, still there is no substitute for conducting an in-depth analysis of relevant cases written by the arbitrator.

Burden of Proof

"Burden of proof" is a judicial concept often applied in an arbitral setting that designates what party has the obligation of establishing by evidence the ultimate fact or issue to be proved. Within the arbitration context it is useful to consider the burden of proof as containing two separate components: (1) the initial burden of going forward with the evidence, and (2) the burden of persuading the fact finder concerning the ultimate resolution of some fact or issue.

A review of published decisions indicates that the burden of proof may depend upon the nature of the issue, the specific contract provision, or a usage established by the parties.[9] As a general practice, however, in disciplinary cases the burden is on management both to proceed first with its evidence and to prove employee guilt or wrongdoing.[10] Of the various rationales utilized by arbitrators to justify the imposition of the burden of proof upon the employer, Gorske cites the following:

> [S]ince discharge is the most severe penalty an employer can impose, being the equivalent of "economic capital punishment," he must bear the burden of justifying such serious move;

(2) since the reasons for the employer's disciplinary action are peculiarly within his own knowledge, he must carry the burden of demonstrating their adequacy, otherwise the employee would be unreasonably obligated to prove the "universal negative," i.e., that he was guilty of no offense of any kind at any time; (3) it is "consistent with the American tradition that a person should not be considered a wrong-doer until proof establishes his guilt"; (4) the imposition of the burden of proof on the employer is justifiable as merely an "extension of scientific management to industrial relations"; (5) the existence of "just cause" for discharge is in the nature of an affirmative defense, therefore the burden rests on the party asserting it; (6) a "just cause" provision in the agreement, in view of circumstances peculiar to industrial relations, requires the Company, when challenged, to retrace the process and convince an impartial third person that the facts acted upon warranted the action taken. . . .

Gorske concludes that

[w]hatever the rationale adopted . . . it seems quite clear that the universal rule in grievance arbitration is that the employer must carry the burden of proof of "just cause" in a discharge case. This unanimity is rather heartening, and suggests that, even in a field so amorphous as industrial relations, some principles have such obvious validity that they will be accepted and applied with uniformity by a wide variety of personalities in a great diversity of situations. The consistency of arbitral opinion on this point seems to suggest the existence of an emerging and evolving system of industrial jurisprudence.[11]

While it is generally held by arbitrators that the burden of proceeding first to establish just cause for discharge is placed upon the employer, exceptions to this rule are found. For example, in refusing a union request that the employer present its evidence first as to whether the grievant had been discharged for just cause, Arbitrator R. H. Morvant stated:

Arbitration hearings were never intended to be courts of Law, nor should they be conducted in such a manner. Excessive legalism or stern, strict formality in arbitration hearings are beyond the desires and understanding of the majority of the participating parties.[12]

In nondisciplinary cases, the general rule is that the charging party would proceed first at the hearing and subsequently prove his case.[13]

Not infrequently after establishing a *prima facie* case (i.e., presentation of evidence, sufficient in quality and quantity to warrant a ruling by the arbitrator in favor of the presenting party),[14] the union will allege the existence of factors that undermine the *prima facie* case of the employer. For example, employer X discharges employee Y for theft of company property. At the hearing the grievant does not deny the charge, but instead alleges that he should not have been discharged since the employer has a policy of not discharging employees for a first offense of theft. In such cases arbitrators will generally require the party alleging discrimination (or some other mitigating factor) as a defense to prove such mitigating or discriminatory circumstances.[15] Thus, in *Linear, Inc.*,[16] Arbitrator Alexander Frey held that

> [i]n a discipline case that initial burden is on the employer to prove that the grievant misconducted himself in a manner warranting discipline. If the employer sustains this burden, then the burden shifts to the union to establish, if it seeks to have the arbitrator award a lesser penalty, that the discipline imposed is overly severe. In other words, once the employer has convinced the arbitrator that some penalty is justified, the employer's judgment as to the extensiveness of the penalty should not be decreased unless the union persuades the arbitrator that under the circumstances the penalty is unreasonable.[17]

Similarly, in *Georgia Kraft Co.*,[18] the arbitrator ruled that in determining whether an employee violated a contract rule in refusing to perform required overtime work, the employer does not bear the burden of proving "just cause" after it has demonstrated that a legitimate company rule containing a discharge penalty was violated, subject, however, to the union's right to demonstrate that the rules were improperly applied or, given special circumstances, that the penalty was unreasonable.

SUMMARY—This chapter has focused on the various positions taken by arbitrators with regard to the burden and quantum of proof. As can be observed, the pattern is well established as to which party is expected to proceed as the moving party. In most disciplinary cases it is management's task to proceed as the moving party; in cases where discipline is not at issue, the union is expected to assume the role. Exceptions to these patterns are indeed rare and occur only for good reason. As for the burden or quantum of proof, the experience is not standardized; arbitrators have in fact announced differing standards, depending upon the particular conduct at issue.

Consistent with the policy favoring the settlement of labor disputes by arbitration,[19] the courts have generally refused to review the merits of an arbitrator's award. This includes refusing to review an award on the basis that the arbitrator applied an incorrect standard of proof. Thus, in *Meat Cutters v. Neuhoff Bros.*,[20] the Fifth Circuit held that, where the agreement did not define the standard of proof (the only relevant provision was that an employee may be discharged for proper cause), the arbitrator did not exceed his authority by imposing upon the employer the burden of proving the grievant's guilt "beyond a reasonable doubt." Reversing a lower court decision, the court of appeals noted that the quantum selected was consistent with the general arbitral practice under similar agreements where the discharge involves criminal intent or moral turpitude. The court further reasoned that while the standard might be offensive to judicial thinking, the court is nevertheless obligated to recognize that an arbitration proceeding is not a judicial proceeding and that the standard applied by the arbitrator should not warrant overturning the award.

Finally, when discussing the concept of "burden of proof" in the arbitral setting, it should be stressed that all arbitrators may not find the concept very useful in the decision-making process. Arbitrator Edgar Jones, Jr., in a recent address to the National Academy of Arbitrators, offered the following thoughts on the role of burden of proof in decisional thinking:

> In this process of making up my mind, however, I have not found the time-honored legal "burden of proof" very helpful. It is, after all, an act of judgment to decide that a party has not "borne the burden"; the "burden" formula, therefore, is only one of inquiry, not conclusion. I have no quarrel with a trier who finds it a decisionally helpful thinking aid; it is important to be aware, however, that the formula has at least the potential of obscuring, even masking, the actual mental process of deciding to the "yes" or the "no" to the claimant. Furthermore, I also have the perception that one has to be cautious about prematurely turning to "burden of proof" ideas in the course of decisional thinking. It is susceptible to self-indulgent use to foreshorten the persistence in puzzlement, itself often enough an unpleasant and irksome experience, which sometimes is necessary in order to break out of the underbrush of contention and loose ends of circumstance that clutter up and obscure the route of the trier to this reconstruction of events. As with legal conceptual reasoning in general, the relief supplied by invocation of the concept of "burden of proof" is experienced because further painful attention to the dilemma of irresolution has thereby been obviated; the need to be concerned about analysis has thereby been removed.[21]

5

The Examination of Witnesses

Oaths

The American Arbitration Association's Voluntary Rules of Labor Arbitration provide that an arbitrator may, in his discretion, require witnesses to testify under oath and, if required by law or requested by either party, shall do so.[1] Otherwise, there is no requirement that witnesses be sworn before giving testimony.

Required Perception

Before a witness testifies to a matter of fact, an arbitrator may require that evidence be introduced which is sufficient to support a finding that the person testifying has personal knowledge of the matter. This foundation requirement may be furnished by the witness himself. For example, an advocate may wish to solicit the testimony of an eyewitness to an altercation involving the grievant. The foundation requirement may merely consist of a statement by the witness that he was present and actually observed the event. As an alternative, testimony by another witness that certain individuals were present, including the eyewitness, would also suffice.

One reason for this requirement is to avoid testimony based upon accounts provided by persons not present at the hearing. Statements by a witness that something is true because others have so told the testifying witness is suspect evidence. As will be noted in Chapter 6, such testimony is a gross form of hearsay and not a reliable basis upon which to base a decision.

Opinion and Expert Testimony

A general rule often endorsed by both the judicial and arbitral community is that witnesses should testify to facts and
not opinions. As applied, however, this tenet is subject to
many exceptions and it is expected that an arbitrator will not
exclude opinion evidence unless it would absolutely be of no
value in the ultimate resolution of the grievance. An extreme
example is the witness who testifies how the grievance should
be decided. More common occurrences include testimony by a
witness concerning what he thinks the contract means, or testimony by a company official that an employee was intoxicated. While such testimony may escape objection, a party
is advised to use its witnesses to develop the facts most con-
ducive to a particular interpretation and not to render opinions on the ultimate issue before the arbitrator.

When the issue before the arbitrator is related to some sci-
ence, profession, or occupation beyond the competence of the
average layman, an "expert" may be used. Thus, arbitrators
have received and credited expert testimony from physicians,
polygraph examiners, psychiatrists, and handwriting experts.[2]
In such cases, however, it is generally required that the advocate calling the expert satisfy the arbitrator that the expert's
qualifications and skills are sufficient to lend a professional
opinion on the matter at issue. This may be accomplished by
reference to the witness's education, training, experience, or
professional reputation.

Mode and Order of Examination

Direct Examination

Direct examination is the process of questioning witnesses by the calling party. Leading questions (i.e., questions
that "beg" the answer) are generally not encouraged on direct
examination of a witness except as may be necessary to develop his testimony. When a party calls an adverse party, however, interrogation may be by leading questions.[3]

The bias against leading a witness on direct examination
is the concern that it may put in the mouth of a witness an
assertion that may not necessarily conform to the witness's
knowledge. Thus, the Chicago Area Tripartite Committee has
stated that leading questions should be discouraged on issues

of fact that are central or close to the crucial issue. On non-controversial matters, however, such as the employee's background, job position, functions, etc., the arbitrator is encouraged to permit leading questions.[4]

Cross-examination

The opportunity to cross-examine a witness is viewed as an essential safeguard of the accuracy and completeness of testimony and, as noted by Professor Cleary, common law judges have insisted that the opportunity is a right and not a mere privilege.[5] Arbitrators have been particularly sensitive to ensuring that the parties have an adequate opportunity to cross-examine witnesses and have cited this concern in excluding hearsay evidence.[6]

Traditionally the federal courts have limited the scope of cross-examination to matters testified to on direct examination, plus matters bearing upon the credibility of the witness.[7] Moreover, leading questions are permitted when cross-examining witnesses.

Various reasons have been advanced in the federal sector to justify the rule of limiting the scope of cross-examination. Most important is the notion that a practice of limited cross-examination promotes the orderly presentation of the case. In the arbitral forum, the Chicago Committee, while taking the position that the scope of cross-examination should not be restricted to the scope of direct examination, urges that when the cross-examination appears to be getting into irrelevant matters, and objection is made, the arbitrator should accordingly discourage and shut off such examination.[8] Arbitrator Trotta has taken a similar position that cross-examination in arbitration need not be restricted in scope except in the following circumstances: (1) the questions clearly have no relevance to the issue; (2) the witness is not competent to respond; (3) improper tactic, abuse, or intimidation is present; (4) the questions are complex or repetitious.[9]

Since a major function of cross-examination is to afford an opportunity to elicit answers which will impeach the credibility of a witness, cross-examination for impeachment purposes is not limited in scope to matters brought out in direct examination.[10] Again, in the arbitral forum the general rule is that a party is free to cross-examine about any subject relevant to any issue disputed in the case, subject only to checks on intimidation of witnesses or questions that have no bearing on the issue.

Order of Interrogation

Rule 26 of the American Arbitration Association, in relevant part, provides:

> The Arbitrator has discretion to vary the normal precedure under which the initiating party first presents its claim, but in any case shall afford full and equal opportunity to all parties for presentation of relevant proofs.[11]

Absent a contractual provision mandating a specific order of presentation, the usual order of proof in a discharge case requires the employer to proceed first with its case;[12] otherwise, the party initiating the grievance will have the obligation to proceed first and subsequently prove his case.

While the arbitrator's control of the order of proofs will generally not be disturbed by a reviewing court,[13] when prejudice to one of the parties can be demonstrated the award may be vacated. In *Harvey Aluminum v. Steelworkers,*[14] an arbitrator refused to credit testimony of a witness because it was not offered as part of the union's case in chief but rather as rebuttal evidence. The court, in remanding the case, noted that no evidentiary rules were announced by the arbitrator prior to the hearing. Had the arbitrator announced at the commencement of the proceeding that the rules of evidence would be applied, the court stated, a different result might have been reached. As it is, the court held that the procedure adopted by the arbitrator denied the union a fair hearing.[15]

Writings Used to Refresh Memory

Not infrequently a witness will refer to notes or other writings while testifying at an arbitration. This procedure is generally permissible, subject to making the writings available to the other party upon request.[16]

Exclusion of Witnesses

Excluding or sequestering witnesses is recognized as a proper means of discouraging and exposing fabrication, inaccuracy, and collusion.[17] When the outcome of a dispute is likely to rest on an ultimate determination of the credibility, a party may request that those witnesses expected to testify be sequestered. Under the rules of the American Arbitration Association,[18] the arbitrator has the power to require the exclusion of any witness during the testimony of other witnesses. Since the rules provide that a person having a direct interest in the arbitration is entitled to attend the hearing, an arbitrator is not expected to exclude the grievant, especially in a discharge case.[19]

Interrogation by the Arbitrator

Section 5 of the Code of Professional Responsibility for Arbitrators, in relevant part, provides:

> An arbitrator may: encourage stipulation of fact; restate the substance of issues or arguments to promote or verify understanding; question the parties' representatives or witnesses, when necessary or advisable, to obtain additional pertinent information; and to request that the parties submit additional evidence, either at the hearing or by subsequent filing.[20]

Consistent with the Code of Professional Responsibility, the degree of involvement or the assertiveness of the arbitrator in the interrogation of witnesses varies. An extreme example of this principle is described below.

Where an employer displayed reluctance to call one unit employee to testify against another, Arbitrator David Keefe, in *Kelsey-Hayes*[20a] called the employee as his own witness so that she could be at the union's disposal for cross-examination (the employer had unsuccessfully attempted to introduce a written statement of the employee but the arbitrator had ruled it hearsay). When the employee failed to appear at the hearing room, the arbitrator, accompanied by representatives from both sides, proceeded to the plant site to interview the employee. Although the employee refused to talk with the representatives present, she did agree to talk privately with the arbitrator. The representatives gave their consent and Arbitrator Keefe, in private conversation with the employee, discovered that she refused to testify because of physical fear of reprisal. She asserted that she had threats conveyed to her from the grievant through a third party. The meeting was subsequently opened to the partisan representatives, and the employee and the informant were eventually persuaded to testify at the hearing. Based on that testimony, the grievant was then assessed an additional 30-day suspension for threatening the witness.

Against a claim by the union that the arbitrator was instrumental in uncovering evidence upon which the employer relied in suspending the grievant and that it was improper for the arbitrator to launch his own investigation, Arbitrator Keefe, in sustaining the additional suspension, reasoned as follows:

> The Umpire had called these witnesses because the integrity of the arbitration process was imperilled if the accusation against the Grievant had substance and, on the other side of the coin, the Grievant, if falsely accused, would have been absolved of all charges against him and made whole.[20b]

Failure to Receive Evidence

It is clear that the arbitrator, as judge of the relevancy and materiality of all evidence, has discretion to exclude evidence which he deems to be clearly immaterial.[21] Similarly, there is no requirement that an arbitrator must hear all evidence, even if arguably relevant, from any and all witnesses that a party might desire to have testify. The arbitrator's mandate is only to conduct a hearing consistent with notions of due process and the latter concept does not require that an arbitrator provide a forum to all witnesses who may have something to say. Both arbitrators and courts have recognized that the arbitrator has a legitimate interest consistent with overall fairness to refuse to countenance unnecessary delays in the presentation of evidence and the completion of the hearing.

Thus, in *Warehouse Union v. Greater Living Enterprise*,[22] a federal district court held that an arbitrator did not abuse his discretion in refusing to grant an employer a one-day continuance in order to obtain additional witnesses. Finding no act of misconduct on the arbitrator's part, the court noted that the arbitrator did in fact offer to subpoena the additional witnesses subject, however, to the requirement that they testify that same day. The court further stated that the need for additional witnesses could well have been anticipated by the employer prior to the date of the hearing.

Likewise, in *Teamsters v. Narragansett Co.*,[23] a federal court found no violation of due process considerations when an arbitrator refused to allow an employer the opportunity to call additional witnesses in support of a contention that a discharge was for just cause. Stating that "an award will not be vacated because of an erroneous ruling by arbitrators, which does not affect the fairness of the proceeding as a whole,"[24] the court found no procedural infirmity when the arbitrator refused to hear additional testimony, at least after a finding by the court that no pertinent or material evidence was excluded as would otherwise render the proceeding unjust or unfair to the employer.

In yet another decision on the subject, a federal district court affirmed the proposition that an arbitrator need not receive all relevant evidence, especially where the hearing has been closed.[25] In *Shopping Cart* v. *Food Employees*,[26] the arbitrator refused to hear testimony of a handwriting expert offered one week after the hearing was closed. Although the court, in dictum, stated that if the evidence had been offered at the hearing the arbitrator would have been required to hear it, the arbitrator's concern with the necessity for completing the hearing and not permitting it to drag on indefinitely was considered of sufficient importance to warrant sustaining the award.[27]

Where the parties agreed not to call witnesses but rather to submit their controversy by briefs, a New York court vacated an arbitrator's award for failing to consider evidence where it was shown that the arbitrator rendered his award without reading the employer's reply brief.[28] The court rejected an offer by the arbitrator to reopen the hearing since, under the Rules of the American Arbitration Association,[29] an arbitrator has power only to reopen the hearing before the award is issued. Thus, the only "cure" as seen by the court was a new arbitration before another arbitrator.

Arbitration in the Absence of a Party

Situations arise where a party may withdraw from the hearing and thus fail to produce any witnesses in support of its case. In such cases, unless otherwise provided by statute, an arbitrator may proceed with the hearing on an *ex parte* basis.[30]

6

Evidentiary Standards Applicable in the Arbitral Setting

Use of Presumptions in Labor Arbitration

Declaring that " 'presumption' is the slipperiest member of the family of legal terms, except its first cousin, 'burden of proof,' " Professor Cleary defines "presumption" as "a standardized practice, under which certain facts are held to call for uniform treatment with respect to their effect as proof of other facts."[1] The West Coast Tripartite Committee has stated that presumptions are not regarded as "evidence," but are viewed solely as analytical devices to aid in determining the facts from the evidence presented.[2] In the arbitral and judicial settings, presumptions have come into existence primarily because fact-finders have believed that, *absent evidence to the contrary,* reason, logic, and human experience render the existence of one fact probable once another fact has been proven. Thus, to cite an example, Arbitrator Geissinger, in *FMC Corp.,*[3] held that evidence that obscene phone calls were made from the grievant's home was sufficient to support a presumption of fact (or inference) that the calls were instigated by the grievant:

> It is a well-established legal principle that a "presumption of fact" is a logical and reasonable conclusion of the existence of a fact, not presented by direct evidence as to the existence of the fact itself, but inferred from the establishment of other facts from which, by the process of logic and reason, based upon human experience, the existence of the assumed fact may be concluded. There must be a rational connection between the proved fact and the fact presumed.

24

Under the circumstances of this case there is no basis whatever upon which to reach the conclusion that someone other
than the grievant made or was responsible for making the calls.[4]

It is important to note that the use of presumptions in both
the legal and arbitral setting is generally only a means of shift-
ing the burden of producing evidence to the party against
whom the presumption operates.[5] In other words, if fact Y is
generally one that is presumed to follow from fact X, the party
against whom the presumption operates has the burden of producing evidence sufficient to overcome the presumption. Absent such evidence, fact Y will stand.

Some presumptions commonly recognized in the arbitral
forum are cited below. It should be stressed, however, that the
list, noted by Owen Fairweather in his comprehensive text,
Practice and Procedure in Labor Arbitration, is not exhaustive
and that other presumptions may be recognized within the
context of a specific factual setting.

Presumption That Notices That Are Mailed Are Received

When it can be demonstrated that a letter has been mailed
by U.S. mail, it is presumed to have been received within a
reasonable time by the addressee.[6] This presumption has particular relevance in discharge cases where the contract calls
for notice of disciplinary action to be given the union. Proof
that notice was mailed would, other considerations being
equal, be sufficient to support the inference that such notice
was given.

Presumption That Documents That Are Delivered Are Authorized

Not infrequently the collective bargaining agreement will
call for the employer or union to issue a written response during the processing of a grievance. Similarly, in connection
with other industrial functions, representatives of either the
employer or union may deliver documents to the other party.
In such cases there is a recognized presumption that writings
that are published or delivered by representatives of the employer or union are authorized.[7] Accordingly, arguments that
a delivered writing was not authorized by upper echelons of
management or labor organizations must be supported by com-

petent evidence before the presumption is dismissed by a fact-finder. The practitioner should keep in mind that arbitrators may legitimately apply agent-principal concepts in resolving disputes whether a representative was authorized to make specific statements (deliver documents) on behalf of management or labor. Thus, it is possible for an agent (e.g., union steward) to bind the principal (union executive board) if a third party (employer) could reasonably believe that the agent possessed *apparent authority* to so act. This is true even though in the matter contested *actual authority* was never given or otherwise expressly denied.

Presumption of Knowledge of Plant Rules

Decisions of arbitrators have established a general pattern by which the employer's disciplinary action may be judged. Arbitrator Daugherty has described one criterion as follows: "Did the employer give the employee forewarning or foreknowledge of possible or probable disciplinary consequences of the employee's conduct?"[8] Noting that arbitrators have cited this criterion when reversing disciplinary action, employers have invariably posted or otherwise issued plant rules governing behavior at the workplace. Once plant rules have been issued or posted, arbitrators have held that employees' knowledge of such rules may be presumed. Thus, Arbitrator Robert Howlett has stated:

> [I]n the arbitrator's opinion a conscious remembering of a rule at the time an act is taken is not necessary in order that a discharge may be for proper cause. If such were the rule every discharge could be reversed by the testimony of the grievant (necessarily a subjective test) that he did not remember the rule which he was violating at the time he did so. The test with respect to a rule clearly communicated to employees must, of necessity, be determined by objective evidence. Unless strong reason is shown, every employee should be charged with knowledge of rules clearly communicated, whether he actually remembers them or not.[9]

Similarly, arbitrators have held that employees are presumed to know established past practices.[10]

Presumption That Facts Reported in Unchallenged Prior Disciplinary Warnings Are Correct

Owen Fairweather, in *Practice and Procedure in Labor Arbitration*,[11] cites an arbitral opinion by McCoy in support of the proposition that unchallenged facts relating to prior disciplinary proceedings are presumptively correct.

> Some companies have a system of personnel reports on employees that go into their personnel file. For example, if a man does a negligent piece of work, for which he ought to receive a warning, do you make out a slip, and give him a copy, and send a copy to the labor relations office?
>
> I have ruled in other arbitrations that where a company does have that system they cannot bring into evidence any previous offenses to help justify a subsequent disciplinary layoff or discharge unless a written record was made of the previous offense.
>
> In addition, if under such a system a man has a chance to file a grievance to take such a reprimand off his record then the employee cannot claim that he did not engage in the conduct reported in the reprimand warning, unless he has filed such a grievance. In other words, if a man deserves a warning and is given it and is given a slip reporting the offense and doesn't protest it with a grievance, then at a subsequent hearing it must be taken as an admitted offense. In such a case, there is no need for testimony about the prior incident. . . .
>
> This is the only way that I can see to keep a hearing concerning a discipline or discharge case from becoming a hearing about a thousand incidents.[12]

Presumption That a Dispute Is Arbitrable

Against a backdrop of well-established federal labor policy favoring arbitration as the means of resolving disagreements under a collective bargaining agreement,[13] arbitrators, when confronted with challenges to their jurisdiction, have adopted the stance that disputes are presumptively arbitrable. Similarly, the Supreme Court has established a strong presumption favoring arbitrability. Thus, in *Warrior & Gulf Navigation Co.*[14] the Court declared:

> [T]o be consistent with the congressional policy in favor of settlement of disputes by the parties through the machinery of arbitration . . . [a]n order to arbitrate the particular grievance should not be denied unless it may be said with positive assurance that the arbitration clause is not susceptible of an interpretation that covers the asserted dispute. Doubts should be resolved in favor of coverage.[15]

Judicial Notice

The usual method of establishing the facts of a particular case is through the testimony of witnesses or the production of exhibits. If, however, some facts are outside the area of reasonable controversy, the advocate need not proceed through witnesses and exhibits. Rather, in those select instances where a high degree of indisputability exists, a trier of fact may dispense with the necessity of requiring formal proof and take "judicial notice" of such facts.

It is generally conceded that the concept of judicial notice applies in the arbitral forum. The New York Tripartite Committee has stated:

> 1. Arbitrators should take judicial notice of any facts or law which the courts of law would generally notice. (These would include: (a) specific facts so notorious as not to be the subject of reasonable dispute; and (b) specific facts and propositions of generalized knowledge which are capable of immediate and accurate demonstration by resort to easily accessible sources of indisputable accuracy.)
>
> 2. Considerations of fairness would seem to require that: (a) the parties notify the arbitrator and each other of facts concerning which they desire the arbitrator to take notice; or (b) in the absence of such notification, the arbitrator advise the parties of facts concerning which he will take notice.[16]

SUMMARY—The doctrine of judicial notice is one of common sense. The theory is that, where a fact is generally known by all reasonably intelligent people in the community capable of accurate and ready determination by resort to sources whose accuracy cannot reasonably be questioned, it would not be good sense to require formal proof.[17] As applicable in arbitration, however, caution must be taken in requiring that the fact at issue be beyond reasonable controversy before judicial notice is taken. A legitimate objection should warrant the proponent of a fact to establish through witnesses or exhibits the matter proposed.

Best-Evidence Rule

As noted in *McCormick,* the "best evidence rule" may be summarized as follows: "In proving the terms of a writing, where the terms are material, the original writing must be produced unless it can be shown to be unavailable for some reason other than the serious fault of the proponent."[18] Historically, the basic reason for the rule has been the central position which the written word has occupied in the law. Additionally, the rule has also been viewed as a protection against mistaken or fraudulent admissions as well as a protection against intentional or unintentional misleadings which could occur through the introduction of selected portions of a comprehensive writing to which a proponent has no access.

While there are admittedly few problems in this area,[19] the rule may have a particular applicability in situations involving the authenticity of exhibits. For example, there may be a dispute with respect to the specific time that an individual starts his shift. In this respect an actual time card may be better evidence than a company memo, and thus subject to the "best evidence" rule.

While the rule technically requires the offering of an original writing (the terms of which are relevant in the particular case), the present day copying by various photographic and other processes has become so technologically advanced that one may consider the copies as if they were "duplicate originals." Thus, absent other compelling reasons, the arbitrator may properly admit such copies into the record notwithstanding objections citing the best-evidence rule.

SUMMARY—In the arbitral setting, concepts of "best evidence" will generally be applicable in the case where more reliable evidence is available, yet the advocate fails to make use of the better evidence. In such a case, the mere failure, absent a satisfactory explanation, may, as declared by the West Coast Tripartite Committee, "have evidentiary weight adverse to the profferer of the lesser valued proof."[20] As such, the advocate is advised to use the most reliable evidence available, irrespective of its form, in order to avoid "best evidence" concerns.

Medical Evidence

There are numerous occasions where an issue of medical fact will control the outcome of the arbitration hearing. For example, an employee, when discharged for excessive absenteeism may, as a defense, allege that a serious medical problem is the cause and introduce a statement from his personal physician which indicates that the grievant has been under the physician's care for a serious illness. Moreover, there may be situations where conflicting medical evidence will be presented to the arbitrator, as in the case where there is disagreement between the company doctor and the grievant's personal physician concerning whether the grievant is physically able to resume work.

Medical Evidence as Hearsay

In general, arbitrators will presume that expert medical evidence is correct,[21] although an arbitrator will probably accord greater weight to oral testimony of a doctor than to a written statement or a physician's affidavit.[22] Arbitrators have recognized, however, the hearsay nature of written statements of physicians if offered to prove the truth of the matter asserted in the statement. Still, in recognition of the difficulty of a busy doctor taking time to attend a hearing and the cost involved, a doctor's certificate will generally be admissible notwithstanding hearsay concerns. The Chicago Area Tripartite Committee has declared that, while such evidence should be admissible, there is no guarantee that it will be credited to the extent that it would be if the physician were present:

> There are occasions where the medical issue may become the central point of the case and here the arbitrator must be quite careful in determining whether the statement should be admitted. In general, the committee would admit the certificate of the doctor with the qualification that, absent the opportunity for cross examination, such evidence is entitled to less weight than medical evidence given in person by a doctor.[23]

This is especially true where medical fact is at the very heart of the issue, such as the case where the parties are litigating whether an individual is permanently disabled, as opposed to a case where the issue is whether an employee has a valid excuse for missing work and relies upon a doctor's statement as proof of illness.[24]

Conflicting Medical Evidence

More troublesome, noted Arbitrator John Sembower, is the fact that too often an element of "mere contest" creeps into a medical case to the extent that "it degenerates into an unworthy trial by battle between so many medical experts on one side saying one thing, and so many on the other saying the opposite."[25] In this regard, consider the following fact situation:

In July 1953, the grievant developed a pain in her left shoulder and consulted her personal physician, who found that she required surgery for the removal of scar tissue. The grievant was operated upon on August 13, and was released from the hospital on August 17. Subsequently the doctor who performed the surgery submitted an "Attending Physician's Report" to the company stating, among other things, that the grievant's condition would enable her to return to work on October 26. Thereafter she presented a statement indicating that she would not be able to return to work until November 2. On October 6 she was examined by a company doctor who found the surgical scar well healed and concluded that she was able to return to work on October 12. Preferring to rely on her own doctor's advice, the aggrieved did not report for work on the 12th and was accordingly terminated.[26]

If the opinions of the grievant's and the employer's doctors conflict, an arbitrator may not attempt to resolve the conflict but, rather, may uphold the employer if the medical advice was relied upon in good faith. As stated by Arbitrator Saul Wallen,

> The proper use of this power will be evident if the facts in a particular case show that management's action was taken in good faith, was based on reasonably adequate medical testimony and evidence, and was not taken against a background that would indicate a discriminatory purpose. If these facts exist, there is a presumption of validity that favors the plant physician's medical testimony. This presumption arises out of the fact that the plant physician has a knowledge of both the employee's health and the job conditions. On the other hand, if in a given case there is evidence that management's good faith is lacking, that its physician's conclusions are not well supported by the medical findings, or that there are circumstances surrounding the case tending to support a claim of discrimination, then there would be grounds to set management's action aside or at least cause the case to be submitted to impartial medical inquiry.[27]

Arbitrator James Doyle has expressed a similar view in *Hughes Aircraft Co.:*[28]

> It is axiomatic that the initial judgment in matters of this kind belongs to management. The judgment of the plant physician is entitled to great weight. He is conversant with the requirements of the occupation involved and the risks inherent in such work. It is generally held that where there is a conflict in the views of

qualified physicians, whose veracity there is not reason to question, the Company is entitled to rely on the views of its own medical advisers.[29]

Likewise, in an arbitration of a discharge of an employee who intentionally concealed his back problem on an employment application, Arbitrator Robert Meiners, in *Chanslor-Western Oil Co.*,[30] held irrelevant the statement of the grievant's back problems as "insignificant." The arbitrator ruled that the grievant's statement of no previous back trouble related to a material matter concerning employment, and thus the employer, who made the final decision of who was hired, could properly discharge the grievant notwithstanding the grievant's personal physician's diagnosis.

However, in the fact situation cited above (*International Harvester*,)[31] Arbitrator Harry Platt did not credit the medical opinion of the company's physician:

> The company's position, in the circumstances of this case, cannot be sustained. An employee who has been operated upon and who is receiving post-operative medical care from a personal physician certainly has every right to rely on that doctor's advice and instructions respecting the date he should return to work. But, here, the aggrieved is terminated precisely because she insisted on observing the medical advice of her own doctor. Generally speaking, the Company is, of course, also entitled to rely on the advice of its doctors; but where there are differences between the company doctor's conclusion and an employee's doctor's conclusion as to when an employee may safely return to work after an operation, it would seem that in all fairness to the employee whose job is at stake, an effort would be made to reconcile the differences. . . . Instead of attempting to reconcile the differences, the Company imposed a termination. . . . Under the circumstances of this case, I find that the aggrieved did have a legitimate reason for her absence. . . .[32]

SUMMARY—While it has been suggested in some arbitration awards that no lay arbitrator should undertake to pass on the justifiability of a discharge for medical reasons,[33] it is clear that health and medical issues are frequently placed before the arbitrator. Arbitrator David Miller suggests that in evaluating expert medical evidence it is important to distinguish medical *fact* from medical *opinion*:

> By medical *fact*, I mean objective data gathered by some recognized laboratory or clinical procedure, or by some accepted process of empirical measurement, for example, weight, temperature, pulse rate, blood pressure, or conditions such as a frac-

ture, swelling, sugar in the urine, and dilation of the pupils. Medical *opinion*, on the other hand, consists of conclusions and implications drawn by a doctor from a given set of medical facts. The pertinent difference is that an *opinion*, even though objectively given, is not susceptible to the same kind of before-hand tests and proofs which apply in a search for *facts*.[34]

Miller suggests that an arbitrator, faced with the problem of evaluating medical evidence, consider the following points:

1. Conflict in medical *fact*, as opposed to medical opinion, is generally susceptible to resolution by approved methods of observation or some laboratory or clinical procedure. When an arbitrator is unable to resolve an important conflict in fact to his satisfaction, he should make every effort to persuade the parties to engage a third qualified medical expert to ascertain the facts and report his findings.

2. Conflict in medical *opinion*, as opposed to medical fact, is not generally susceptible to objective resolution by referral to a third expert, where the opposing opinions are each shown to be supported by a recognized body of medical authority. The arbitrator must then look to resolution of the case by application of appropriate standards of equity and fairness rather than force himself into choosing between two apparently legitimate schools of medical thought.

3. The arbitrator need not defer to the opinion of a medical witness whose judgment on the matter goes beyond the scope of his professional expertise. In accepting such evidence, the arbitrator should recognize its limitations and weigh it accordingly in deciding the issue before him.[35]

When considering evidence of medical fact or medical opinion it is important that the arbitrator is satisfied that the evidence is in fact authentic medical evidence.[35a] Frequently an employee will obtain a writing from a nurse or a physician's assistant and introduce it at the hearing as medical evidence. This is especially common when the employee claims that he had a valid excuse for missing work. The advocate should be prepared to demonstrate that the evidence is in fact bona fide medical evidence, and not a mere forgery or other substitute.

A review of the cases indicates that arbitrators are most receptive to crediting medical evidence that is (1) of a current nature, (2) in a form that leads to cross-examination, and (3) based on observation over a period of time, as opposed to "one-time" medical advice. It is also clear that arbitrators are more receptive to crediting medical evidence, notwithstanding the absence of the physician at the hearing, where the medical issue is only "collateral" to the case. Although the employer is presumptively entitled to rely upon the advice of medical advisers, medical evidence is accorded greater weight to the extent that it is directed to the specific work requirements of the employee's job, rather than to the physical fitness of a particular individual. Finally, arbitrators generally require that the grievant be given fair notice and opportunity to overcome the medical evidence of the employer before a decision is made that adversely affects the employment status of the individual.[36]

Evidence and the Past Record of an Employee

The treatment of an employee's past work record when offered as evidence has varied among arbitrators, especially in discipline and discharge cases where records of past behavior have been offered by both employers and unions in any number of contexts.[37]

Past Disciplinary Record to Assess Propriety of Discipline

By far the most common use of an employee's work record is to justify the degree of discipline imposed. This is especially true in discharge cases where employers have recognized that evidence of progressive discipline will often establish that the grievant was accorded prior opportunity to reform his pattern of behavior. Similarly, it is not uncommon for unions to cite the good record of an employee when contesting that a particular penalty is too severe.

Absent a specific contractual provision to the contrary, arbitrators will consider evidence of the grievant's past work record when the propriety of the penalty is at issue.[38] Arbitrator Pollard has cited "the common practice in industry of considering a man's record in deciding what penalty to attach to any given infraction of discipline," and the "inherent reasonableness of letting a man's record help decide the penalty for such infraction."[39] Likewise, Arbitrator Larkin is on record as supporting an examination of an employee's entire work record when determining whether discipline is appropriate in a particular case:

> The Arbitrator is often asked to weigh an employee's past good record and thus decide in favor of leniency in disciplining him.

It follows that he may also take into account the employee's past conduct in determining whether more severe discipline is within reason.[40]

Particularly troublesome is the case where the record of employment with a previous employer is introduced, or where the employer offers a "stale" record. Except for the first case (the employer may have been aware of the prior employment record before the employee was hired), arbitrators will generally admit the evidence, although less weight will be accorded dated records, or records where the offenses are "bunched" toward the beginning of the record.[41]

Arbitrators have also disagreed as to the weight to be given prior disciplinary incidents that are unrelated to the specific charge at issue, although when considering past misconduct *as it relates to the penalty assessed*, a distinction is generally not made between related and unrelated incidents.[42]

Past Record to Establish Innocence or Guilt or Likelihood That Employee Acted in Conformity With Record

When the grievant's employment record is introduced to establish the innocence or guilt of the grievant or the likelihood that the grievant acted in conformity with his past record, arbitrators are in disagreement concerning the weight to be accorded such evidence. Arbitrator Robben Fleming offers the following examples illustrative of the problems facing arbitrators:

> A bus driver is disciplined for negligent driving. He denies the charge, and the company offers to show that the driver has had three accidents of a similar nature during the past year and must now be considered "accident prone."
> An employee is discharged for drinking, gambling, or pilferage on the job. He denies the charge, and the company wishes to show that he was given a disciplinary layoff for the same reason during the past year, and has been warned on two other occasions.
> The same basic facts as in examples one and two, except that the previous occurred while employed by a previous employer, or were offenses against the civil or criminal law.[43]

In all cases the clear purpose of offering the past record of an employee is to suggest to the arbitrator the likelihood that an employee with a past record has, in fact, committed the present offense. Professor Fleming suggests that a majority of arbitrators will admit and credit the evidence where the present offense has a functional relationship to the past offense, for example, the "accident prone" driver. Thus, in *Butler Mfg. Co.,*[44] Arbitrator Welch concluded that past absenteeism of an employee indicates that he will probably never be able to work regularly.

Arbitrator W. Wirtz cites the example where the key issue was whether the grievant was intoxicated when she reported for work. She and the plant guard disagreed about this, and the employer offered to support its case by proffering a record of two previous, and recent, acknowledged instances of this grievant's reporting "under the influence."[45] Reflecting the view of another arbitrator, Bert Luskin, that use of similar offenses as evidence of the commission of a current offense is "poppy-cock,"[46] Arbitrator Wirtz held that the evidence should not be admissible for the cited purpose.

In his self-styled "confessions of an arbitrator," Allan Dash focused on the subtle complexities of the issue:

> The use of a record of a prior similar offense as evidence that the grievant has committed the one at issue before me is, I suspect, a procedure of which I have been guilty on a number of occasions. It seems to me that an employee who has been warned or disciplined on a number of prior occasions for the use of violent, insubordinate or threatening language is prone to continue in that vein in the future (somewhat like a person whose ordinary speech is punctuated by frequent oaths). Thus, if there is a denial that a grievant before me has made a certain insubordinate or threatening statement, I believe that I am somewhat persuaded by his past uses of such language as evidence of his guilt in the immediate case. I feel that I am also sometimes persuaded in doubtful cases that an employee with slipshod work habits has been responsible for the most recent one of which he is accused if his record shows unprotested warnings and prior disciplinary actions for the same type of improper work habit. Thus, if there is a question as to which of two employees has been responsible for bad work that has led to disciplinary action against one employee, I suppose I have resolved the question of doubt against the employee whose past record shows evidence of bad work.[47]

Exclusion of Past Record Where Grievant Is Not Given Notice of Contents

Where an employee is not given notice of adverse incidents an arbitrator may accord little, if any, weight to an employee's record, since the preferred procedure is one that provides for immediate discipline or notice to the employee of the offense with which he is charged.[48] Thus, in *Consolidated Vultee Aircraft*,[49] Arbitrator R. A. Dwyer excluded evidence of prior alleged infractions of company rules where the employer did not notify the employee at the time that such infractions occurred. The arbitrator made it clear that while the employer could maintain any records it so desired, it could not use evidence of rule infractions to justify a subsequent discharge where no notice was given to the disciplined employee at the time the alleged violation occurred.

Unless otherwise stated on the termination notice, a similar problem may occur where the union claims that an employer may not justify a discharge citing the past record of an employee, even though the employee may have been notified of each incident cited in the record. In his text, Professor Smith cites the case of an employee who was discharged for insubordination and the use of profane language against a supervisor. In the arbitration proceeding, the employer sought to justify the discharge by evidence of past misconduct of the dischargee. The union objected to the use of the employee's work record on the ground that the employer was bound by the language of the termination notice which stated the cause of the discharge. In ruling on the objection, Arbitrator Louis Belkin declared:

> The question of the use of the employee's past work record by the company in making the determination to discharge him is one which has several ramifications. In the opinion of the undersigned it would be inconceivable that the company do anything else. We have here a matter of equity and fairness. In order to be fair and equitable the totality of an employee's record, good or bad, must be weighed. This would certainly be applicable where the record is good. It must also apply where the opposite is true. It must also apply insofar as an arbitrator is concerned.
>
> . . .
>
> This does not mean nor is it intended to mean that the union is barred from asserting its claim that the notice shows that the company's use of the employee's work record is an after-thought. The union may offer proof, if it can, that when the employee was discharged the foreman did not know of his past record and thus only the immediate incident was in his mind. It may offer proof, if it can, that this is the first time an employee's record of absenteeism or tardiness was used in a discharge for insubordination.

These, however, are matters of evidence going to motivations. They are matters of proof and issues for argument. They do not and cannot obviate the requirement and necessity for viewing the whole record of performance.[50]

Likewise, arbitrators have excluded evidence of past incidents *when used as a cumulative or contributing item for sustaining a discharge* where punishment has already been assessed. Thus, Arbitrator Keltner, in *Libby, McNeill, & Libby, Inc.,*[51] found that an employer could not use a past incident of insubordination as additional evidence to sustain a discharge since the record indicated that the grievant had already been punished for his refusal to follow orders.

Evidence of Grievant's Conduct After Imposition of Discharge but Before Arbitration Hearing

Ordinarily postdischarge conduct is not relevant to the question of just cause. However, where events giving rise to the discharge are determined to be of a continuous nature, postdischarge evidence may indeed be admitted and credited by arbitrators. Arbitrator Bernard Cushman considered a postdischarge suicidal gesture and subsequent hospitalization of the grievant as "an integral part of the events which led to the discharge," and thus evaluated it in connection with the totality of the grievant's conduct prior to and after the discharge.[52] Arbitrators have also considered rehabilitation programs commenced after incidents precipitating discharge to be relevant when reviewing the severity of discipline.[53]

Past Records and Credibility of Grievant

Frequently an advocate will introduce the past record of the grievant for the purpose of undermining or supporting his credibility as a witness. While issues of credibility will be discussed in another section,[54] suffice it to state that arbitrators will generally consider employment records as one factor in the overall decision to credit the testimony of a particular witness. The advocate must take care, however, to ascertain the purpose for which the record is being offered. For example, if the contract contains a clause prohibiting the introduction of an employee's past record (or otherwise limiting the applicable time period beyond which records are not to be used), an individual should not be permitted to show that the grievant has been disciplined in the past merely by alleging that the record is being offered only to attack the credibility of the witness.

SUMMARY—Although the treatment of an employee's past work record has varied widely among arbitrators, the following considerations should prove useful when assessing the weight an arbitrator is likely to assign an employee's work record:

1. With respect to considerations of progressive discipline, Arbitrator David Miller has declared:

> The application of progressive discipline (oral warning, written warning, suspension, discharge) is considered by many arbitrators to be a necessary element of fair discipline. This does not mean, of course, that all violations of reasonable policies must go through the progression of penalties. Discharge for a first-time serious offense, such as assault, insubordination, possession of a dangerous weapon, etc., may be upheld. If it can be shown that discipline for an offense (such as sleeping on the job) has been inconsistently applied among employees or erratically applied to a worker (leading the worker to think that there is no established standard of conduct), then the employer's use of past record is weakened.[55]

2. An arbitrator will invariably assign greater weight to a current record than to a dated record, or to prior unrelated events. An important exception, as cited by Arbitrator Miller, would be in the case where the employer specifically notified the worker that hiring or continued employment would be predicated on no repetition of undesirable conduct.[56]

3. When evidence of past misconduct is offered for the purpose of inferring that the grievant committed a present offense, it will generally be admitted and credited, provided notice is given to the grievant at the time of the alleged offense. As stated by Professor Fleming, such evidence should be given weight only insofar as (a) there is a clear relationship between the kinds of offenses involved, and (b) the events have taken place within a reasonable span of time.[57] Thus, an employee's accident record would not be relevant in a discharge for insubordination, while it would be important if the charge involved reckless operation of a forklift.

4. Arbitrators will generally consider the employee's past work record when justifying the severity of the penalty. Again, the weight to be given such evidence will depend on (a) the

relationship between the kinds of offenses, and (b) the relevant time period involved.

5. Finally, when evidence of past misconduct is offered for the purpose of impeaching the credibility of the grievant, it will generally be received. Robben Fleming further notes that unless the grievant has already put in evidence of his good character, evidence of his past offenses should not be received until the record contains more than a *pro forma* showing with respect to the offenses charged.[58]

Evidentiary Value of Arbitrators' Awards

Although arbitration awards involving different parties but similar issues are not considered to have precedential force,[59] nevertheless many rules and principles involving the application and interpretation of language commonly found in collective bargaining agreements have evolved from published awards. The result has been the formulation of an industrial common law capable of providing guidance for uniform solutions to common problems. Accordingly, parties will frequently offer the awards of other arbitrators in support of a desired resolution of a disputed grievance.

In certain industries, such as coal and steel, parties' reliance on past arbitration awards is extensive. While such past decisions are not binding, they do have a strong persuasive value since they often become part of the industry tradition and are used to clarify disputed contract terms.

Giving authoritative force to prior awards when a similar issue arises *(stare decisis)*, however, is to be distinguished from refusing to permit the merits of the same event or incident to be relitigated *(res judicata)*. As stated by one commentator,[60] when a prior arbitrator has rendered an award in a dispute between the same employer and the same union, the precedential effect of the prior award moves from that of *stare decisis* to that of *res judicata*. In general, issuance of an arbitration award bars any subsequent court action on the merits of the same event.[61] Likewise, arbitrators have recognized and applied *res judicata* concepts where the *same* parties are involved and the *same* issue was presented in an earlier arbitration.[62] In such cases it is often held that adherence to prior awards is desirable in order to maintain stable labor-management relations, the necessity for finality, and the need for consistency in contractual interpretation. As cited by Arbitrator Whitley McCoy in *Pan American Refining Corp.*:[63]

> But where, as here, the prior decision involves the interpretation of the identical contract provision, between the same company and union, every principle of common sense, policy, and labor relations demands that it stand until the parties annul it by a newly worded contract provision.[64]

In those situations where an award is not offered for its *res judicata* effect, but rather for purposes of merely supporting an advocate's position, an arbitral decision involving different parties but a similar issue may have great force. In this respect Arbitrator Maurice Merrill has declared:

> As to arbitral decisions rendered under other contracts between parties not related to those in the case at hand, usefulness depends upon similarity of the terms and of the situations to which they are to be applied. They must be weighted and appraised, not only in respect to these characteristics, but also with regard to the soundness of the principles upon which they proceed. Certainly, an arbitrator may be aided in formulating his own conclusions by knowledge of how other men have solved similar problems. He ought not to arrogate as his own special virtues the wisdom and justice essential to sound decision . . .[65]

While there is no application of precedent similar to that mandated in the judicial system, the advocate should not overlook the value and effect of past arbitral awards. Fundamental notions of fairness can strongly influence an arbitrator seeking to arrive at an equitable result. If the advocate can paint a reliable picture of the fairness and rationality of a position and then support that argument with one or more arbitral decisions which arrive at the result advocated, an arbitrator may be more inclined to adopt the view proposed than would otherwise be the case if the position advocated had little or no arbitral support.

When relying upon precedent it is advised to cite only cases which stand for the proposition being argued. To do otherwise may be an invitation to the arbitrator to discredit the proposed theory entirely. The following hierarchy of precedential sources is offered for consideration in drafting arguments in an arbitration case:

(a) An earlier case construing essentially the same facts involving the same language decided by the same arbitrator (a rare occurrence except in cases involving umpires).

(b) An earlier case involving analogous facts and an analogous contract clause decided by a different arbitrator construing the same contract.

(c) An earlier case decided by the same arbitrator construing a different contract involving analogous facts and contract language.

(d) An earlier case decided by a different arbitrator involving different but analogous contract language and facts.

(e) An authoritative proposition cited in a recognized treatise or labor relations publication.[66]

Exclusionary Rules

While the strict rules of evidence as applied by the courts are not applicable in the arbitral forum, certain evidence will in most circumstances not be credited because of its suspect or unreliable nature.

Hearsay Evidence

Introduction —One of the most difficult evidentiary problems facing a fact-finder concerns the disposition of hearsay evidence. In the traditional court setting hearsay will be excluded in civil and criminal cases unless some exception can be applied. While labor arbitrators are not constrained by the same rules of evidence that are followed by the courts, a competent arbitrator will invariably discount some types of hearsay consistent with conducting a fair and adequate hearing.[67] Accordingly, this section will introduce the practitioner to selected problems dealing with hearsay evidence which are likely to be encountered when preparing and presenting a case for arbitration.[68]

Definition of Hearsay—Professor Cleary, in his text on evidence,[69] states that "too much should not be expected of a definition. It cannot furnish answers to all the complex problems of an extensive field (such as hearsay) in a sentence. The most it can accomplish is to furnish a helpful starting point for discussion of the problems, and a memory aid in recalling some of the solutions."[70] Noting this caveat, "hearsay" may be defined as a statement other than one made by the declarant while testifying at the hearing and offered in evidence to prove the truth of the matter asserted. Under the above definition, hearsay may take an oral or written form, or it may be in the form of conduct.

Hearsay as a Three-Part Process—It is useful to consider hearsay as the following process:

(1) *A "statement" or an "assertion" or "conduct"*

(2) *Made or done by someone other than a testifying witness* and

(3) *Offered in evidence to prove the truth of the matter asserted.*

As an aid in understanding the nature of hearsay, the following examples are offered as illustrative of the above process:

1. *"The Absent Accuser"*— Jack Jones was discharged for allegedly taking company property. At the arbitration hearing Sam Sack is called to testify on behalf of the company. When questioned about the theft, Sack testifies: "Sally told me that she saw Jones take company property."

Discussion: Sack's testimony as to what Sally said is clearly hearsay if offered to establish (1) that a theft took place, (2) that Jones was responsible, or (3) that it was in any respect as stated by Sack. Applying the three-part process we note that Sally, who is an "out-of-court declarant," has made an "assertion" that Jack has taken company property. Moreover, it appears that the company is offering the testimony to "prove the truth of the matter asserted" (i.e., that the grievant in fact stole the property). Consequently the statement of the witness is hearsay and thus is highly suspect.

The reasons why the statement of the witness for the employer is suspect are that the validity of Sally's statement depends on a number of factors, which include the following:

1. It depends on how good Sally's eyesight was, or on how close she was to the grievant when she allegedly observed the grievant taking the property. In other words, there may be serious problems with Sally's perception.

2. Also important is how good Sally's recollection was when she spoke to the witness. Perhaps it was another employee and not the witness. Perhaps it was another

employee and not the grievant whom Sally observed. Thus problems of *memory* arise.

3. It depends on whether Sally, who is not testifying at the hearing, has any reason to lie about the grievant. Sally may not be a credible witness because of prior contacts with the grievant (Jack may have broken a date with Sally). In other words, there are problems with the *veracity* and *sincerity* of the person making the "out-of-hearing" statement.

4. Finally, the validity of Sally's assertions depends on how good Sally was at reporting the incident to others. Sally's account of the incident may have consciously or unconsciously produced disparity between the picture that she has given and what actually happened. Sally's language may not have accurately conveyed the true facts, thus giving rise to problems of *articulateness*.

In the above example, the inherent problems of the evidence offered by Sack are all concerned with its *reliability*. Sally's statements were not made under oath, or in a formal hearing, nor was Sally available for cross-examination to test for the presence of the hearsay risks or dangers: perception, memory, veracity, and articulateness. In the example cited, any reliance based on Sack's testimony would deprive the grievant of the chance to test whether the "out-of-court" declarant was lying, misremembering, or just reporting ineptly. It is this lack of opportunity for cross-examination that is the main justification for the exclusion of hearsay. As stated by Chancellor Kent:

> Hearsay testimony is from the very nature of it attended with . . . doubts and difficulties and it cannot clear them up. "A person who relates a hearsay is not obliged to enter into any particulars, to reconcile any contradictions, to explain any obscurities, to remove any ambiguities; he entrenches himself in the simple assertion that he was told so, and leaves the burden entirely on his dead or absent author. . . ."[71]

2. *"The Silent Declarant"*—At the arbitration hearing, the union, attempting to prove that the grievant was an efficient and competent lathe operator, offered the testimony of a fellow employee who stated that "no employee had ever complained about the grievant's work."

Discussion: In the cited example, according weight to the *absence* of statements by out-of-court declarants involves risks similar to those of accepting statements of out-of-court declarants. The employees whose noncomplaints (assertions) are offered are in the same position as the out-of-court declarant Sally was in the first example. In both cases the evidence is clearly offered to prove the truth of the matter asserted. The union, in the "Silent Declarant" case, is offering "non-statements" to establish, first, that the noncomplaining employees believed that the grievant was a good lathe operator, and, second, that they believed so because the grievant was in fact a good operator. However, this type of evidence is suspect. Although the noncomplaining employees may have believed the grievant was competent, the belief may have been carelessly formed and not based on first-hand information. Moreover, the employees may actually have believed that the grievant was a poor worker, but may have foregone complaining to management in order to avoid trouble with the grievant or his colleagues. It is for these reasons the practitioner should recognize that assertions by "silent declarants" are suspect as hearsay and thus may be accorded little weight by an arbitrator. However, there are exceptions to the above rule as the next example illustrates.

3. *"The Silent Grievant"*—After numerous complaints by supervisors that company tools had been disappearing from the shop, the personnel director placed a non-bargaining unit employee in the shop for purposes of conducting an investigation. During the second week of the investigation, the grievant was observed placing tools in his lunch box. When confronted with the evidence by management, the grievant remained silent. At the hearing the employer introduced the testimony of the personnel director regarding the grievant's silence in the face of the accusations.

Discussion: Unless some public policy considerations would dictate otherwise, admissions by a party-opponent are not within the hearsay rule.[72] The reason for this exception is that if a person's statement is offered against him, he cannot validly complain that he has no opportunity to cross-examine himself.

A similar case is presented where an admission is inferred from the conduct or the absence of conduct by the grievant. In the above example the grievant's silence in the face of an accusation *to which one would normally respond* is offered as an implied admission of the correctness of the charge. While the accusation itself is not offered in a hearsay capacity, the absence of a response would technically be hearsay (similar to the case cited in example 2).

Without unduly commenting on the weight that an arbitrator is likely to give the "non-assertion" of a grievant,[73] it is important to stress that if the silence of the grievant is considered an admission, it is not considered hearsay and accordingly may be given appropriate weight.

> 4. *Conduct as Hearsay*— The grievant was discharged for making a racial slur to her supervisor. At the hearing, the employer introduced the testimony of the personnel director that the grievant's supervisor had reported the incident to management. In addition, the employer introduced the supervisor's written report of the incident. The union, citing the hearsay rule, requests the arbitrator to exclude the testimony of the personnel director as well as the supervisor's written report.

Discussion: The above example illustrates the importance of identifying the issue in resolving hearsay problems. If the supervisor's conduct (reporting the incident) is offered to prove the truth of the matter at issue (that the grievant made a racial slur), the conduct is clearly hearsay. Likewise, if the written report is offered as evidence that a slur was made, hearsay concerns are present. However, if the evidence is offered to prove some other issue, for example, that the supervisor made a report, or that she *believed* that a racial slur was made (state-of-mind), then the evidence is not hearsay. In the latter case the practitioner must take care to establish that the state of mind of the supervisor is relevant to a material issue in the case. Otherwise there is the danger that a party-opponent will attempt to circumvent the hearsay problems of written reports of incidents by merely asserting that the evidence is introduced to establish the "state-of-mind" of the person testifying.

> 5. *"The Trustworthy Breathalizer"*—The employer discharged the grievant for intoxication on company proper-

ty based upon the results of a breath test which was administered by a company nurse. The union requests the arbitrator to exclude the testimony of the employer with respect to the results of the test on the ground that this evidence is clearly hearsay.

Discussion: Not infrequently arbitrators will be confronted with evidence generated from machines (e.g., polygraph; computer) or some other device (breathalizer; Naline test for narcotics use). Questions arise whether the reports of the results of such tests should be excluded as hearsay evidence.

Although such evidence is technically hearsay, generally evidence of this type is not subject to the traditional problems characteristic of hearsay evidence. Machines, unlike some humans, lack a conscious motivation to tell falsehoods, and because the workings of such machines can be explained by witnesses who are subject to cross-examination, there appears to be little problem with allowing such evidence into the record (at least with respect to hearsay concerns). In admitting such evidence, however, the practitioner must be satisfied that the party relying upon the results of such tests has fully established the accuracy and procedures characterizing the tests.

6. *Business Records and Hearsay Objections*—Employee Jones is dismissed from employment because of excessive absenteeism. At the arbitration hearing the employer offers the time cards (compiled by a trusted employee in the personnel department). Jones objects, citing the cards as hearsay.

Discussion: Entries in business books or computerized entries may be offered in various situations, although in most cases the entry is offered to prove the truth of some matter at issue. For example, the employer introduces a time card to prove that the grievant punched out early, or a phone bill is offered to prove that a call was made. In such cases the evidence is clearly hearsay, although evidence of this type is usually "great hearsay" and courts and legislatures have recognized an exception for regularly kept business records.[74] In general, a writing, contemporaneously made in the regular course of a business, by a person with personal knowledge of the entrant (or based on the reports of others who themselves possessed knowledge of the event), will be admissible as long as the record is sufficiently authenticated (i.e., it must be shown to be genuine).

7. *"The Spontaneous Declarant"*—The grievant was denied a sum of money for an alleged job-related accident. As evidence that the grievant was indeed injured on the job, he notes to the arbitrator that when he fell against a machine, everyone heard him yell, "My arm is broken." The employer moves to have the testimony excluded as self-serving hearsay.

Discussion: The grievant's testimony in the cited example, while clearly "self-serving," may nevertheless withstand hearsay objections under an "excited utterance," or res gestae exception.[75] The theory for allowing an exception for excited utterances is that circumstances may produce a condition of excitement which temporarily stills the capacity of reflection. For this reason, a person who makes spontaneous declarations while under the stress of an excited event will not have the time to fabricate the facts surrounding the event. Although this exception has been criticized on the ground that excitement impairs accuracy of observation as well as elimination of conscious fabrication, the exception finds judicial and arbitral support.[76]

Conclusion—In the arbitral forum virtually every hearing will contain problems concerning the introduction and consideration of hearsay evidence. As noted by Arbitrator Updegraff:

In arbitrational hearings, hearsay testimony is very freely received. Indeed, in many instances the record seems to consist of little else. Much of this stems from the reluctance of employers to bring more than the minimum of employees from their duties to the hearing and from the efforts of union officers and spokesmen to proceed without the evidence of men and women who would prefer to be earning their usual income in the usual way and who may dislike participating in a controversy.[77]

While there are no hard and fast rules followed by arbitrators when hearsay is introduced at the hearings, the advocate should nevertheless be cognizant of the following considerations:

1. The historic exclusion of hearsay evidence has been based on the commonsense notion of justice that the party

against whom evidence is offered should have an opportunity to cross-examine the actual speaker to whom the statement is attributed. Yet hearsay objections only apply to "out-of-court" statements *offered to prove the truth of what was said.* This important distinction has been noted by *American Jurist* as follows:

> The hearsay rule, however, does not operate, even apart from its exceptions, to render inadmissible every statement repeated by a witness as made by another person. It does not exclude evidence offered to prove the fact that a statement was made or a conversation was had, rather than the truth of what was said. Where the mere fact that a statement was made or a conversation was had is independently relevant, regardless of its truth or falsity, such evidence is admissible as a verbal act.[78]

Accordingly, it is important for the advocate to evaluate all evidence from the above perspective and to take care that a party-opponent will not attempt to circumvent the rule merely by stating that the evidence is not offered for its truthfulness.

2. Merely because evidence is determined to be hearsay does not ensure that the evidence will not be credited by a neutral. For example, there is nothing to prevent an arbitrator from "taking for what it is worth," testimony or exhibits that 30 employees (not present at the hearing) complained about the behavior of the grievant. Moreover, under certain fact situations it may not be unreasonable for an arbitrator to conclude that such testimony, while admittedly hearsay, is "great hearsay" and thus should be considered when rendering an award.[79] While the above fact situation may not be an exceptional case, the practitioner is cautioned that care should be taken to ascertain what evidence is hearsay so that, at minimum, the arbitrator is reminded to proceed with caution.

3. Similarly, even though evidence (otherwise classified as hearsay) comes within a recognized exception to the hearsay rule, there is no guarantee that such evidence will be admitted or, if admitted, credited by an arbitrator. The exceptions cited provide only that the evidence is not inadmissible under the hearsay rule. It may still be excluded for lack of relevancy or even because of some overriding policy reason.

4. In discussing the rationale why formal rules of evidence are not followed in arbitration hearings, Arbitrator Bowles made the following observation:

> No doubt the reason that the parties and the Arbitrator are not limited by the formal rules of evidence in an arbitration is the belief that rigid conformity to strict rules of evidence would tend to make the proceeding too technical and unreasonably restrict the parties from offering proofs that enable the Arbitrator to more fully grasp the labor relations situation, properly evaluate the problem, and render a just award.[80]

Although the rules of evidence are not strictly followed, the arbitrator is, nevertheless, charged with providing a fair and adequate hearing.[81] As such, when confronted with hearsay, the arbitrator can generally be expected to follow the suggestion of the West Coast Tripartite Committee:

> Unless corroborated by truth-tending circumstances in the environment in which it was uttered, it (hearsay) is unreliable evidence and should be received with mounting skepticism of its probative value as it becomes more remote and filtered. If a witness can testify at the hearing and does not, his statements outside the hearing should be given no weight, indeed, should even be excluded if there appears to be no therapeutic, nonevidentiary reason to admit it.[82]

5. Finally, even when the arbitrator credits hearsay evidence, it is reasonably clear that the party adversely affected will have little, if any, subsequent recourse in the courts. For example, in *Instrument Workers v. Minneapolis-Honeywell Regulator Co.*,[83] a federal district court rejected a claim by the union that an award sustaining a discharge should be set aside. The union did not argue that hearsay evidence is inadmissible, but rather argued that in the present case there was "too much of it." Finding that the arbitrator had evidence on which to make his award, the court went on to state:

> Although the rules of evidence exclude hearsay in a trial at law, the exclusion is not because hearsay is entirely without probative value. It has been said with some justice that the characterization of evidence as hearsay is in reality simply a criticism of the weight that should be given it. In an arbitration the parties have submitted the matter to persons whose judgement they trust, and it is for the arbitrators to determine the weight and credibility of evidence presented to them without restrictions as to the rules of admissibility which would apply in a court of law.[84]

Parol Evidence

Introduction—Parol evidence is any evidence whether oral or in writing which is extrinsic to the written contract and not incorporated therein by reference. Technically the parol evidence rule is not a rule of evidence but a substantive rule of contract interpretation which forbids the use of extrinsic parol to "add to," "vary," or "alter" the written agreement. Thus, it has been described:

> The parol evidence rule, as it is now universally recognized, is not a rule of evidence but is one of substantive law. It does not exclude evidence for any of the reasons ordinarily requiring exclusion, based on the probative value of such evidence or the policy of its admission. The rule as applied to contracts is simply that as a matter of substantive law, a certain act, the act of embodying the complete terms of an agreement in a writing (the "integration"), becomes the contract of the parties. The point then is, not how the agreement is to be proved, because as a matter of law the writing is the agreement. Extrinsic evidence is excluded because it cannot serve to prove what the agreement was, this being determined as a matter of law to be the writing itself.[85]

The parol evidence rule has applicability in the area of labor relations when one (or both) of the parties are introducing evidence which, if given weight, will alter the terms of the written contract. In this respect it is important for the advocate to understand the nature of the parol evidence rule and when it is likely to be applied.

Application of the Rule—Initially it is important to stress that the rule is only applicable when the parties intend that the written agreement is the final and complete integration of all the terms of the contract. If, for whatever reason, the parties do not intend the written agreement to be the final integration of the bargain, then the parol evidence rule is not applicable. It should be noted, however, that a finding that the parties have not intended the agreement to be the final integration of all the contractual terms does not mean that the evidence at issue will therefore be admissible, as certain types of evidence may still be excluded under other "rules" (e.g., hearsay; evidence of offers of settlement prior to arbitration). Again, the important point to stress is that if the writing at issue was not intended to be the final integration of the agreement, even evidence that varies or contradicts the written document will not be subject to valid parol evidence objections.

What if it is determined that the writing in issue was intended to be a final "integration"? This, of course, may be an issue for an arbitrator to determine. One party may allege that the agreement was not intended to be the final, complete integration of the bargain and introduce documents and other memoranda supplementary to the agreement. Accordingly, an arbitrator will have to determine whether such evidence should be credited.

One way to ascertain whether a written agreement was intended to be the complete integration of the bargain would be by direct reference to the agreement itself. For example, the agreement may contain a "completeness of agreement" clause, otherwise known as a "zipper" clause. Common examples include:

> This agreement supercedes and cancels all previous agreements between the Board and Teacher's Council and constitutes the entire agreement between the parties, and concludes collective bargaining for its term.[86]

> The parties agree that they have bargained fully with respect to all proper subjects of collective bargaining and have settled all such matters as set forth in this Agreement.[87]

> This agreement constitutes the entire collective bargaining agreement between the parties as to wages, hours and conditions of employment.[88]

Furthermore, the agreement may contain an explicit admonition or limitation on the arbitrator precluding him from adding to, subtracting from, or changing the parties' agreement.

> The Arbitrator, in his opinion, shall not amend, modify, nullify, ignore, or add to the provisions of the agreement.[89]

While the rule prohibits the use of extrinsic evidence to "add to," "detract from," or "vary" the terms of a written contract that on its face is apparently integrated and complete, if parol is used to resolve some ambiguity in the agreement, the evidence will be received and given appropriate credit. The problem for the arbitrator, of course, is determining when contract language is clear and unambiguous. As noted by Professor Nolan, language does not become ambiguous merely because the parties disagree over the meaning of a phrase, for that would only encourage them to contest the clearest provision in the hope of a favorable arbitration award.

> The test most often cited is that there is no ambiguity if the contract is so clear on the issue that the intentions of the parties can be determined using no other guide than the contract itself. This test borders on a tautology, however, for it comes perilously close to a statement that language is clear and unambiguous if it is clear on its face. Perhaps a better way of putting it would be

to ask if a single, obvious and reasonable meaning appears from a reading of the language in the context of the rest of the contract. If so, that meaning is to be applied.[90]

Where contractual language is found to be clear and unambiguous, it will generally be applied without recourse to other indications of intent. As declared by one arbitrator:

> [T]he Arbitrator is confronted with the question of on which evidence does he rely in attempting to ascertain the mutual intent of the parties: (1) the plain, clear and unambiguous language which the parties incorporated in their Agreement supposedly to express their mutual intent, or (2) parol evidence concerning the bargaining history and intent of the bargaining parties, and past practice in applying this contract language, to indicate an intent contrary to that indicated by the plain and unambiguous language of the Contract?
>
> If there is any one principle of contract interpretation upon which arbitrators are agreed, it is that where no ambiguity exists in the language of the contract, then the obvious intent of the Contract language governs and must be enforced; that the contracting parties must be presumed to have known what they were doing when they adopted the language which they did to express their bargaining intent; that parol evidence cannot be relied upon to defeat the obvious intent of clear and unambiguous contract language; and that when the language of the Agreement is sufficiently clear as to enable the Arbitrator to reasonably ascertain the intent of that contract language, that ends the Arbitrator's inquiry and he must enforce the apparent intent of the words of the Agreement.[91]

Thus, it is expected that the parties will introduce prior agreements, drafts of bargaining proposals, and even evidence of the intent of a particular negotiator in an effort to clarify ambiguity. Again, assuming a bona fide issue of ambiguity[92] (which, in the final analysis, will ultimately be determined by the arbitrator), evidence extrinsic to the written agreement will not be excluded by operation of the parol evidence rule.

Statements Made Prior to and Contemporaneous With the Written Agreement—It is important to note that the parol evidence rule applies only to statements made prior to or contemporaneous with the written agreement. Additional agreements made subsequent to the written contract (even though the written contract states that the present document is the final agreement and all others are excluded) will not be subject to a successful parol objection. In this respect the West Coast Tripartite Committee has stated:

> There is a general principle which seems . . . to distinguish past
> practice cases from those cases in which "intent" evidence,
> contemporaneous or antecedent to execution of an agreement
> and extrinsic to it, is proffered to vary or contradict the terms of
> the agreement. It is the basic idea in contract law that parties
> can amend an earlier agreement by later conduct (oral, written,
> or otherwise) so long as it is not in conflict with an agreed and
> operative mechanism for amendment. It is also a basic element
> of the parol evidence rule that the rule is inapplicable where the
> issue is whether an earlier agreement has been altered by sub-
> sequent conduct.[93]

An application of this principle is found in *Kaiser Aluminum & Chemical Corp.*[94] In that case Arbitrator John Sembower ordered an employer to reinstate a day labor rate for a group
of employees where it was demonstrated that the rate had
been paid for a four-year period subsequent to the negotiation
of the collective bargaining agreement. Alleging error in paying the rate, the employer discontinued payment because
there was no provision in the contract authorizing such payment. Although the agreement provided that the parties were
without the power to alter, waive, or amend any of the provisions without the written consent and approval of both the
union and employer, the arbitrator nevertheless found that the
employer's conduct operated against unilaterally making a
change.

Likewise, in *Keene Corp.*,[95] Arbitrator Robert Williams
recognized that an oral agreement could indeed operate to alter a term or condition of the written contract. The arbitrator
cautioned, however, that such an oral agreement must be specific and definite to be enforceable. "A vague and ambiguous
understanding where the parties have differing recollections
of its content is not enforceable. An Arbitrator would not
know what to enforce."[96]

**Allegations of Fraud, Duress, or Mistake and the Refor-
mation of Contracts**—Finally, it should be noted that parol is
admissible even where an unambiguous, integrated, written
agreement is operative if there is a bona fide issue of fraud,
duress, or mistake. Thus, in *Kennecott Copper,*[97] Arbitrator
Abernethy, citing *Williston on Contracts,* declared that "if the
meaning of the contract is plain, the acts of the parties cannot
prove an interpretation contrary to the plain meaning." Yet
the arbitrator observed:

On the other hand the Arbitrator should not enforce the obvious intent of patently erroneous language which the record establishes is clearly contrary to the reasonable expectations of the contracting parties. Hence it is appropriate to consider the evidence introduced by the Company to ascertain whether it does unmistakably establish error in the contract language adopted.[98]

Likewise, the Chicago Tripartite Committee has endorsed receipt of parol evidence by an arbitrator where there has been a mutual mistake in the preparation of the agreement which is contrary to what the parties have intended.[99] Since the arbitrator is granted authority to interpret the agreement as the parties have intended it, evidence of prior understandings and communications may survive parol objections.

SUMMARY—The importance of the parol evidence rule is simply that proffered oral or written evidence of prior or contemporaneous negotiations will generally not be admitted (or if admitted, not credited) in order to vary or contradict the terms of a written contract which the parties have intended to be the final integration of their agreement. As observed by the Chicago Committee, what is involved in the application of the rule is not an evidentiary standard, but an issue concerning the arbitrator's jurisdiction.[100] Since the arbitrator is without authority to vary the parties' agreement, he or she should not accept or credit evidence that would clearly alter the bargain. It must be remembered, however, that until an arbitrator interprets the agreement, it cannot be known whether there is an inconsistency between it and other agreements, oral or written, prior or subsequent. Accordingly, it is expected that the following issues would be relevant to the labor advocate: (1) Have the parties made a contract? (2) If so, did the parties intend that it be the final integration of their bargain? (3) Is the bargain clear? (4) Does the written agreement represent what was actually bargained? and (5) Was the agreement amended, discharged, or otherwise modified by a subsequent agreement or a course of conduct clearly evidenced by the parties?

Offers of Settlement or Compromise

During the process of negotiations prior to arbitration, it is expected that compromise efforts to resolve grievances will be made. For example, in disputes involving the discharge of an employee pursuant to a just cause provision in the agreement, a party may request that the arbitrator consider that the other side offered to settle the matter if the employee were reinstated without backpay. Similarly, during an arbitration a party may introduce writings containing offers to settle contractual claims for amounts less than that requested in the original grievance. A party may also argue that the writings contain a tacit admission by the other side that its position is not meritorious and thus should be considered by the arbitrator as material and relevant evidence.

Although such evidence may indeed be relevant in the above cases, it is a general tenet of arbitration that compromise efforts to settle a grievance will not be permitted to prejudice the party's case when the matter goes to arbitration.[101] It is recognized that during the process of negotiations compromise proposals will go further than a party considers itself bound to go on a strict interpretation of its rights. More important, a party might be reluctant to make compromise offers if it is known that any offer made could be introduced against that party as a tacit admission of the weakness of one's position. As stated by one arbitrator:

> Complete freedom of both parties to suggest and reject offers of settlement during grievance meetings is essential and should not be restricted or limited in any way by fear that such action will prejudice the rights of either party should the dispute be submitted to arbitration.[102]

The Pittsburgh Tripartite Committee has noted in this regard that

> [m]ost arbitrators and advocates agree that the exclusion rule should be absolute in arbitration cases. Successful solution of grievances short of arbitration is vital to the process. Anything which imperils this philosophy must be avoided. Additionally, parties normally have neither inclination nor skill sufficient to cloak their settlement offers protectively. There are many reasons why offers of settlement are made, and they do not necessarily imply that the offering party admits it was wrong.[103]

Finally, the Chicago Tripartite Committee has also concluded that an arbitrator should not receive offers of compromise:

> It is important to the disposition of grievances that the parties feel free to speak candidly and openly to each other and to make full disclosure of all relevant facts. An arbitrator who receives evidence of such statements, even though he takes such evidence with the usual admonition that it will receive only such weight as it may deserve, may do a disservice to the parties,

particularly if this evidence is relied upon in the decision. If the parties realize that what they say in the grievance procedure may be used against them, this may inhibit their presentation during the grievance procedure and result in the withholding of information that would lead to a settlement of the disputes. The parties to the labor-management and arbitrators have an obligation to make the grievance procedure as effective as possible. In one sense the success of the grievance procedure may be measured by the number of disputes that eventuate in arbitration.[104]

Offers of compromise, however, may properly be received when the relevant issue is whether a dispute had been settled in the lower stages of the grievance procedure.[105]

SUMMARY—It is not uncommon that in a labor arbitration a party will not object solely because of a lack of knowledge of what is objectionable. The West Coast Tripartite Committee has declared that the arbitrator may well regard negotiations for settlement in the earlier stages of the grievance procedure as so desirable the he himself may be expected to interpose an objection and inform the advocates why this evidence would not be heard.[106] While the Authors are reluctant to assert that in no case should an arbitrator ever hear evidence of compromise offers,[107] it is clear that the integrity of the grievance procedure will be seriously undermined if such evidence is readily introduced and credited. As such, absent a compelling reason, such evidence should be summarily excluded.

Privileged Communication

A testimonial privilege effectively permits a witness to refuse to disclose certain types of information even though it may have relevance to the issue before the trier of fact.[108] At common law, judges recognized testimonial privileges to ensure that certain relationships would not be compromised by the disclosure of confidential communications. Thus, communications between husband-wife, priest-penitent, and lawyer-client were exempt from enforced disclosure. Similarly, privileges were recognized for holders of government secrets, as well as nondisclosure of the identity of informants. In the federal sector, testimonial privileges are to be developed by the federal courts "under a uniform standard applicable both in civil and criminal cases."[109] That standard mandates the application of the principles of common law; no standard list of privileged communications is catalogued in the federal rules.

The Voluntary Labor Arbitration Rules and the Code of Professional Responsibility are silent on the application of testimonial privileges in the arbitral forum. The New York Tripartite Committee, however, discusses the following privileges likely to be encountered in arbitration.

a. Physician-Patient

(1) Basically, a patient may claim as privileged his communications with his physician in any situation where such claim could be made in a court of law.

(2) An employee asserting a claim or defense based on a physical condition may assert the privilege. However, the consequences of nondisclosure are for the arbitrator to determine.

(3) The disclosure of the fact of a communication with a physician is not privileged, even though the content of a communication may be privileged.

(4) If an employee's employment or continued employment is, by contract, controlling practice, or company rule, conditioned on his physical condition, he may not claim the privilege.

(5) If an employee's employment or continued employment is not explicitly or implicitly, by contract, controlling practice, or a company rule, conditioned on his physical condition, he may claim the privilege.

Note: In the event that an employee desires, for some special reason, to avoid the general disclosure of his communication with his physician, the arbitrator may, at his discretion, limit such disclosure to selected representatives of the parties.

b. *Husband-Wife*—A confidential communication between spouses is privileged where a witness is, at the time of testifying, one of the spouses.

c. *Grand Jury*—A witness is privileged to refuse to disclose a communication made to a grand jury by a complainant or witness unless the findings of the grand jury have been made public by virtue of having been filed in a court or otherwise.

d. *Classified Information*—A witness who, in the course of his duties, acquired official information, such as classified information not open or disclosed to the public relating to the internal affairs of a government, is privileged to refuse to disclose such information. However, if the arbitrator has government clearance for access to such classified information, the privilege may not be claimed.

e. *Union and Employer Communications*—Intra-union and intra-employer communications are not privileged.

f. *Grievance Discussions*—Evidence concerning grievance discussions, other than offers of settlement or compromise, is not privileged unless the parties have explicitly agreed otherwise, (The labor members would limit such evidence to admissions and statements of position, unless the contract provides for some type of reporting of grievance discussions.)

g. *Witness-Attorney*—Communications between a union member testifying on behalf of a union and a union's attorney, or between a company employee and a company's attorney, are privileged.[110]

Arbitrators have also held that statements of mediators made during negotiations are privileged and cannot be admitted in any future dispute over the same issue.[111]

Finally, some courts have suggested that an employee may have some kind of privilege against disclosure of information that would otherwise be protected by the First Amendment if government action were present. In *Holodnak* v. *AVCO Corp.*,[112] a federal district court vacated an arbitrator's award, in part, because the arbitrator permitted inquiries to be made concerning the political views of the grievant, the books he read, and his personal background. The court found that such inquiries evidenced partiality on the part of the arbitrator. Similarly, the Supreme Court, in *Detroit Edison* v. *NLRB*[113] held that the NLRB abused its remedial discretion when it ordered an employer to deliver directly to the union copies of a test battery and employee-linked exam scores. Noting the "sensitivity of any human being to disclosure of information that may be taken to bear on his or her basic competence," the Court ruled that, where the employer promised examinees that their scores would remain confidential, absent employee consent to release the scores the employer's interest in preserving employee confidence in the testing procedure should be recognized.

7

Collateral Proceedings

Introduction

Rulings by courts and other administrative bodies are frequently offered in arbitration proceedings as indicative or even dispositive of an adopted position in a labor dispute. For example, an employee is discharged after an altercation with another employee on company property. Subsequent to his discharge, but prior to an arbitration hearing, the employee pleads guilty to criminal charges of assault and battery. At the hearing the employer offers the guilty plea as proof that just cause existed for the discharge. Citing another example, an employee is discharged after incurring a work-related injury. A claim is filed with the state accident commission and the employee is found disabled. Subsequently, a grievance is filed under the collective bargaining agreement. At the arbitration hearing the employer introduces the rulings of the industrial accident board as proof that the grievance is unfounded.

In ascertaining the weight that an arbitrator is likely to give the rulings of another administrative body, it is useful to consider the doctrines of collateral estoppel and res judicata as applied by the courts. "A common statement of the rule of collateral estoppel is that 'where a question of fact essential to the judgment is actually litigated and determined by a valid and final judgment, the determination is conclusive between the parties in a subsequent action on a different cause of action.' "[1] Judge Learned Hand, writing for the Second Circuit, wrote: "It is of course well-settled law that a fact, once decided in an earlier suit, is conclusively established between the parties in any later suit, provided it was necessary to the result in the first suit."[2]

Collateral estoppel, however, should be distinguished from res *judicata*. The latter doctrine, as cited by the Supreme Court,

> provides that when a court of competent jurisdiction has entered a final judgment on the merits of a cause of action, the parties to a suit and their privies are thereafter bound "not only as to every matter which was offered and received to sustain or defeat the claim or demand, but as to any other admissible matter which might have been offered for that purpose." [Citation omitted.] The judgment puts an end to the cause of action, which cannot again be brought into litigation between the parties upon any ground whatever, absent fraud or some other factor invalidating the judgment.[3]

Collateral Civil Proceedings: Findings of Industrial Unemployment Compensation Boards

The most common occurrence where evidence of rulings from other proceedings are offered at an arbitration hearing is where an employee has been discharged or reclassified for reasons of physical disability, makes a claim with an industrial accident board, and also contests the employer's decision through the grievance procedure. Arbitrators have recognized that an employee appearing before a workman's compensation body for adjudication of a claim is inclined to present himself in a manner that will be most effective in litigating the facts surrounding the industrial accident. Thus, in *Zellerbach Paper Co.*,[4] an employee was discharged after a California Workman's Compensation Board determined the employee was 56 percent permanently disabled. Arbitrator Arthur Stashower rejected the employer's argument that the disability rating of the compensation board was the controlling and final determination of the grievant's physical condition and capacity to perform work. Since a higher disability percentage claim would necessarily have the effect of jeopardizing the grievant's future employment, the arbitrator reasoned that the entire workman's compensation procedure would be undermined by allowing the employer to rely exclusively upon an independent, adversary proceeding as being the final and binding determination of the grievant's ability to perform work. While the arbitrator recognized that the same issues may be presented in both forums, he nevertheless concluded that a decision by one body cannot be determinative in the other.[5]

In *Kaiser Cement*,[6] Arbitrator Thomas Roberts chose not to give effect to a decision by the California Department of Employment that the grievant had been discharged for reasons other than misconduct. The employer dismissed the grievant for suspected theft and for refusing to permit a plant guard to examine materials in the employee's vehicle. Aside from the fact that the employment board was legally required to weigh evidence solely against the norm found in the California Unemployment Insurance Code, the arbitrator found that the collective bargaining agreement which creates the right to arbitrate grievances clearly anticipates the right to an independent adjudication free of any "estoppel" flowing from collateral administrative proceedings.[7] It is especially noteworthy, however, that in rendering the award, the arbitrator cited the fact that the Department of Employment's referee found the grievant guilty of "disloyalty" in not permitting the inspection.[8]

Arbitrator Howard Block, in *Sears, Roebuck & Co.*,[9] stressed that the functions and procedures of accident commissions or unemployment compensation boards are different from those in the arbitral forum, and thus there should be no functional incongruity in contradictory decisions of referee and arbitrator.[10]

Finally, Arbitrator Howard Fitch, in *Fawn Engineering Corp.*,[11] elaborated on the infirmities in accepting findings of employment commissions:

> The sworn testimony, as set forth in the transcript of the proceedings before the Commission were used in determining some of the facts in this arbitration hearing. This was especially important because the Company relied on it for most of its case. There are several faults that limit such use. There is no opportunity to personally examine and cross-examine the witnesses. Not all of the witnesses in the Commission's hearing were present before this arbitrator. Even more important to this decision, however, is the fact that not all of the witnesses before this arbitrator were heard by the examining officer for the Commission. . . . Whether they would have ruled differently if they had heard that additional testimony is unknown.[12]

Some arbitrators have found difficulty with allowing a grievant to reverse his position in the grievance procedure after successfully claiming incapacity before an industrial compensation commission. For example, in *Loma Corp.*,[13] an employee was reclassified to the job of janitor as a result of a back injury suffered some five months earlier. The reason for the late reclassification was that the employer did not receive knowledge of the severity of the injury until the day of a hearing before the Texas Industrial Accident Board where the grievant claimed a "sure disc" and argued for a 20- to 25-percent permanent disability. In sustaining the reclassification of the grievant, the arbitrator, on his own motion, applied the doctrine of collateral estoppel:

> [The company] neither during the hearing nor in its brief presented the argument of collateral estoppel. Nonetheless, the Arbitrator is inclined to agree with Lord Kenyon: "A man should not be permitted to blow hot and cold with reference to the same transaction, or insist, at different times, on the truth of each of two conflicting allegations, according to the promptings of his private interest." [Citation omitted.][14]

To rule otherwise, concluded the arbitrator, "would permit a man to have his cake and eat it too."[15]

In *Wheeling Steel Corp.*,[16] Arbitrator Mitchell Shipman found it difficult to square the grievant's statements before an industrial accident commission that he was disabled with his subsequent contentions that he was physically able to return to work. Unable to give greater evidentiary value and effect to the report of the grievant's doctor over that of the employer's physician, the arbitrator found "most persuasive" the grievant's workman's compensation claims.

In *Bettencourt v. Boston Edison Co.*,[17] the Court of Appeals for the Fifth Circuit upheld an arbitrator's award against a claim that it was in "manifest error of law" for the arbitrator to fail to treat the findings of Massachusetts' Industrial Accident Board as *res judicata* in a subsequent arbitration. In *Bettencourt*, an employee, after being injured on the job, was suspended and subsequently discharged when the employee did not receive proper clearance from the employer's medical department. After the Massachusetts board sustained his claim for workman's compensation, the union requested arbitration of the discharge. The arbitrator, in sustaining the discharge, found that the grievant had failed to appear at his suspension hearing and had offered no excuse for not doing so. Noting evidence that the employer had in the past treated similar cases as voluntary quits, the arbitrator ruled that the contract was not violated.

The court of appeals found no error of law where the arbitrator considered the *res judicata* argument and rejected it. The arbitrator found the scope of the two proceedings to be different, the discharge being based, in effect, not solely or even mainly on whether the grievant had sustained a compensable injury, but on the grievant's unsatisfactory pattern of conduct and dealings with the company concerning his employment following the alleged injury. Accordingly, the Fifth Circuit affirmed the lower court's grant of summary judgment in favor of the employer.

Collateral Criminal Proceedings

Certain employee conduct may, at the same time, constitute an offense punishable by law and a private industrial offense warranting disciplinary action at the place of employment. Generally the same concerns voiced by arbitrators in industrial accident or compensation cases are operative in those select instances where the results of criminal investigations are urged for their collateral estoppel or *res judicata* effect. In *ITT Continental Baking Co.,*[18] Arbitrator Ted High refused to credit evidence that the grievant was acquitted in a criminal proceeding growing out of the same events giving rise to his discharge. Ruling that an arbitrator who reviews a discharge case should not be bound by a judgment of conviction or acquittal, the arbitrator stressed the different standards of proof operative in the respective forums. While the employer need only prove its case by a preponderance of the evidence, proof in a criminal proceeding is to establish guilt beyond a reasonable doubt. In addition, the arbitrator noted that the employer has no control whatever over the proceedings before a court which are conducted by a prosecutor. Moreover, the company should have a right to review and evaluate the evidence itself in deciding whether disciplinary action is warranted. Finally, the arbitrator stated that his obligation is to decide the case only on the record before him, and not on the record before a court or some other body.[19]

In *Congoleum-Nairn, Inc.,*[20] Arbitrator J. C. Short reinstated an employee where it was shown that the employer sought to justify a discharge based on evidence that was the result of an unlawful search and seizure. In that case an employee was arrested at work after police conducted a gambling raid on plant premises. During the arbitration hearing, the union's attorney produced a court order suppressing (and returning to the grievant) evidence illegally seized at the plant. Accepting the employer's general proposition that there is a distinction between a criminal judicial proceeding and the arbitration process, the arbitrator nevertheless noted some situations where a decision by the judiciary would have evidentiary value in the arbitral forum:

> For one thing, if a court of competent jurisdiction were to find an employee guilty of criminal gambling activities on the premises of an employer this arbitrator would be inclined to accord considerable weight to such finding in an arbitration involving the discharge of the employee.[21]

An interesting aspect of this case involved the arbitrator's disposition of a constitutional-type challenge to the use of the illegally seized evidence.

> Principles embodied in the fundamental law of the land are not to be regarded lightly. Although the Fourth Amendment applies to governmental action, and not the unlawful seizure of private papers by private persons, we are not confronted in the instant case with a private seizure . . . but a situation where a private employer seeks to justify its disciplinary action almost entirely upon a tainted transaction, in the form of an adjudicated unlawful search and seizure by government action. . . . [T]he constitutional protection against unlawful search and seizure is of little value if evidence ordered suppressed may be recaptured by public authorities and used against an accused in a collateral arbitration proceeding without risking possible self-incrimination in a related judicial proceeding.[22]

Arbitrator David Dolnick reached a different result in *Aldens Inc.*[23] An employee was discharged after police discovered employer merchandise (clothing) in the trunk of the employee's car. Prior to an arbitration challenging the discharge, a criminal court found that the items of clothing were obtained as a result of an unlawful search and seizure. The charges against the employee were accordingly dismissed. At the arbitration hearing the grievant entered a motion that the company not be allowed to introduce any of the evidence suppressed by the court.

Stating that informality is a cardinal rule in an arbitration hearing, Arbitrator Dolnick first focused on the differences between forums:

> No criminal proceeding may be submitted to an Arbitrator whose selection and whose authority is derived solely from the provisions of the collective bargaining agreement. A penalty for engaging in a criminal act involves imprisonment and/or a fine prescribed by statute or ordinance. In a criminal proceeding the issue is whether an individual has violated a specific law. And if found guilty, he is punished as directed by law. . . .

An arbitration proceeding involves an alleged violation of one or more contractual provisions, the interpretation and application of these provisions, the alleged violation of a long established and accepted practice or any act arising out of the employer-employee relationship. And this is true in an issue of employee termination.[24]

The arbitrator further noted that although the Fourth and Fifth Amendments protect individuals against unlawful searches and seizure in the criminal sector, there is no definitive law whether evidence obtained by illegal search and seizure is admissible in civil cases. As such, exclusionary rules applicable in criminal cases do not automatically apply in arbitration proceedings.[25] Accordingly, in sustaining the discharge the arbitrator accorded no weight to the outcome of the criminal proceedings.

United Parcel Service, Inc.,[26] presents a situation where an employee was discharged for allegedly assaulting a supervisor. While the hearing was still in progress, the grievant was acquitted of a criminal assault charge growing out of the same incident that gave rise to his discharge. The arbitrator noted that the criminal system of trial by one's peers has built into it the community's prejudices and a host of other factors that make it different from industrial arbitration. When the parties bargained for the arbitration process, reasoned the arbitrator, they did not bargain for a jury of lay persons to render the decision and thus replace the arbitrator. Indeed, had the jury found the grievant guilty, the arbitrator noted, he would not have been justified in merely affirming the jury's decision, since an arbitrator is charged with making a judgment not as the grievant's peer, but rather as someone whose training and experience qualifies him to make such a judgment. While the arbitrator said that he would "take note" of the jury's decision, he nevertheless concluded that under the agreement he must make an independent determination as to the facts and applicable law.[27]

Conclusion

Consistent with arbitral opinion, the West Coast Tripartite Committee has concluded that the existence of criminal proceedings collateral to an arbitration hearing have no necessary consequence in an arbitration.

The standards of proof, the relevant policies at issue, the cast of judgment of the triers of fact, and the environment in which the respective hearings take place are sufficiently different to warrant the conclusion that a decision in one tribunal should not bind the other, although it should be admissible as relevant evidence.[28]

The Chicago Committee has likewise concluded that such evidence may be admitted if it relates to the original cause of discipline or discharge.[29]

While the overwhelming weight of arbitral opinion is that a decision in a civil or criminal forum will not be dispositive of the ultimate grievance in an arbitration proceeding, there are situations where an arbitrator may be receptive to crediting testimony given in another forum. In *Dunlop Tire & Rubber Corp.*,[30] Arbitrator Mills honored a company proposal that the depositions of two physicians in a pending workman's compensation case, when taken and transcribed, be submitted as part of the record in a present arbitration. In granting the request, the arbitrator noted the difficulty the parties experienced in securing the attendance of physicians in court and other adversary proceedings, the seriousness of the charge against the grievant, and the importance of the testimony in determining the outcome of the case. The arbitrator allowed this procedure on the assumption that both parties would be represented at the taking of the depositions.

In line with what appears to be the generally accepted view of courts and arbitrators, Arbitrator Sembower, in *Vulcan Mold & Iron Co.*,[31] permitted an employer to cross-examine a grievant regarding any statements made by him under oath in a workman's compensation proceeding. Holding that such statements may be used for impeachment purposes, the arbitrator reasoned that such evidence would be a proper safeguard against duplicity on the part of the grievant and at the same time provide him with the opportunity to explain or amplify his earlier statement.[32]

Although the results established in other forums will usually not be dispositive as to the ultimate resolution of the grievance before the arbitrator, facts or issues established in other proceedings may, under certain circumstances, be introduced and credited by an arbitrator. In those instances where a party is introducing testimony from another proceeding to establish credibility of testimony or consistency of evidence in the arbitral forum, arbitrators will generally credit such evidence and accord it proper weight. These instances should be distinguished from cases where a party is introducing the final outcome of another proceeding for its "summary judgment" effect. Rarely, if ever, will an arbitrator so credit the results of other proceedings collateral to the arbitral forum.

8

Problems of Evidence and Due Process Considerations

Source Problems and Evidentiary Considerations

Use of the Polygraph

The polygraph, commonly known as the "lie detector," is a machine that measures and records fluctuations in blood pressure, rate or respiration, and galvanic skin response. The theory behind the test is that the act of not telling the truth causes psychological conflict, conflict causes fear, and fear will bring about measurable physiological changes (blood pressure, respiration, and perspiration) which, in turn, will be detected and recorded by the polygraph machine. First invented in the 1920s by a medical student working part-time for the police department of the city of Berkeley, California, the polygraph in its early years was primarily used in law enforcement; however, the test is now becoming a more relied-upon method of screening applicants for employment and a security device for determining the truthfulness of employees suspected of misbehavior.

The admissibility of evidence obtained from the use of the polygraph is an issue which has occupied the attention of both arbitrators and advocates.[1] At the present time there is a split of authority among arbitrators with respect to the admissibility of evidence obtained from polygraph exams, with the overwhelming majority holding that the evidence should not be credited.[2] The following fact pattern focuses on the problems confronting arbitrators:

The employer discharged employees G, K, and R because of its conviction that all three grievants used their employment with the company to consciously and intentionally furnish telephone service from time to time in the creation of establishments to be used illegally by horse race bookmakers in carrying on illegal gambling. In addition, the company asserted that it discharged grievants K and R for refusing to cooperate with the company in an investigation of the matter by refusing to supply pertinent information, and refusing to submit to a lie detector test. Employee G did take a company-requested lie detector test, the result of which indicated that he was not telling the truth in denying complicity in the matter charged. At the hearing, the union requested that the arbitrator exclude the results of the polygraph. Moreover, the union argued that the arbitrator could not sustain the discharge of employees K and R for refusing to submit to such an exam.[3]

In holding that the results of such tests should not be admitted, Arbitrator Peter Carmichael noted the scientific unreliability of polygraph evidence:

> While this test may have diagnostic value in psychology, it probably could never be conclusive against an accused employee who . . . was shielded by the typical just-cause guarantee found in the contract here. The test presumes that a guilty person, in contrast to an innocent one, will be disturbed at the mention of features of his misdeed, and that his disturbance, as in pulse, breathing, blood pressure, and skin sensitivity, can be registered on an instrument contrived for that purpose, the polygraph. But an astute and sensitive subject of the test might so control himself as to give results indicative of either guilt or innocence . . . while the opposite type might seem to betray guilt though he was innocent. The plurality of causes that may be operative in motivation, attention, and association of ideas is too great or too uncertain in the great range of human faculty to allow a test like this to stand as proof beyond a reasonable doubt.[4]

Similarly, arbitrators have ruled that employees are not to be penalized for refusing to submit to such exams,[5] although there are cases which hold to the contrary.[6] In refusing to sustain a discharge, Arbitrator Ryder commented on the inaccuracy of the polygraph:

> An innocent individual may lack confidence in his emotional stability whereby he may believe warrantedly or unwarrantedly that such testing will show deception where there is none. Such an individual may refuse a testing as readily as may a guilty individual who desires to hide the truth. In many cases in-

nocent individuals will confidently submit to such testing. Other innocent individuals may reluctantly submit because of the implicit social threat in their refusing in the setting of a plant community. It appears that the polygraph has been an effective instrument in indicating deception in the heavy preponderance of cases. However, where there is employee refusal to give consent to such testing, the refusal, standing by itself and coupled or not coupled with the presence of factual material giving reasonable suspicion of culpability, *is not that kind of behavior that should be an offense* in and of itself. To punish for refusing to consent on the basis that this is lack of cooperation appears to supply an overtone of being required to self-incriminate, a proposition repugnant to Anglo-Saxon legal codes. (Emphasis in original.)[7]

In *Illinois Bell Telephone Co.*,[8] Arbitrator M. S. Ryder held that assessing discipline for "insubordination" due to a lack of cooperation has constitutional-type infirmities of compelled self-incrimination, "a proposition repugnant to Anglo-Saxon legal codes."

In *Meat Cutters* v. *Neuhoff Brothers Packers*,[9] the Fifth Circuit considered a case where a grievant had taken a lie detector test but had refused to take a second one. A second grievant took both tests. While the arbitrator admitted the tests into evidence, he nevertheless held that the tests could be used only to show that the employer had received certain statements from the grievants. The test results were not considered as evidence of guilt even though the collective bargaining agreement provided that the company could require polygraph tests of any employee suspected of theft of company property. The district court, in refusing to enforce the award, found that the arbitrator had exceeded his authority in that his refusal to consider the tests' results was nonrecognition of the collective bargaining agreement's provision that the employer reserved the right to require polygraph exams. The district court also found that the grievant's refusal to take the second test was itself proper cause for his discharge.

In reversing the district court, the Fifth Circuit stated that the collective bargaining agreement made no mention of the use of such tests in an arbitration proceeding, and to deny their use in one specific context did not render the contract provision meaningless. More important, the circuit court addressed the evidence problem:

Viewed as a question of admissibility of evidence the arbitrator has great flexibility and the courts should not review the legal adequacy of his evidentiary rulings. . . . This must particularly be so where the issue, the admission of lie detector tests, is one that even the courts have found debatable.[10]

Finally, the court ruled that the action by the district court in finding proper cause for discharge of the employee who failed to take the second test was singularly unwarranted. The court of appeals reasoned that every violation of the agreement cannot be presumed to be automatic grounds for discharge as distinguished from a lesser sanction. Accordingly, the court held that the award of the arbitrator must be reinstated and enforced.

Interestingly, some arbitrators have ruled that polygraph evidence may have more utility in verifying the truthfulness of testimony than in detecting unreliable testimony.[11] Thus, in *Brink's, Inc.,*[12] the arbitrator declared:

> "It has long been the view . . . that polygraph tests are more useful in verifying the truthfulness of testimony than in detecting its unreliability. From that point of view the term truth verifier would be more apt than lie detector.
>
> . . .
>
> "If the results of the polygraph test had verified the Grievant, great weight would have been given thereto."[13]

Finally, arbitrators may be more receptive to crediting polygraph evidence where consent was obtained either from the grievant or the parties to the proceeding. In this regard, Arbitrator Seward has stated:

> The courts have generally—indeed, almost universally—rejected polygraphic evidence unless offered with the consent of all parties concerned. Though arbitration proceedings are not controlled by the strict rules of evidence, wisdom suggests that the [arbitrator] should follow this judicial approach and admit polygraph evidence only if both the Company and Union agree.[14]

Some arbitrators, however, have questioned whether consent, either implied or expressed, can ever be voluntary in such circumstances. As noted by one arbitrator:

> The implicit social threat to an employee in the setting of a plant community were he to refuse to submit to lie detector testing where crimes have concededly been committed so compels consent that a guiltless but emotionally fearful employee has practically no choice but to consent.[15]

Arbitrator Edgar Jones is of the view that it would be improper for an arbitrator to relax the determination to assure fair procedures that are protective of employees solely because they have consented to a polygraph test or, by "stipulation," to the admission in evidence of such test results.[16] Unreliability, notes Jones, is not altered simply because an individual or the parties stipulate to be bound by it.

Some commentators have proposed that arbitrators should recognize polygraph evidence as an aid in resolving credibility disputes.[17] In *Bethlehem Steel*,[18] however, Arbitrator Seward rejected an employer's offer of an account by a polygraph examiner which, if credited, would have verified the truthfulness of an employee (not present at the hearing) who claimed an assault by the grievant. The arbitrator stated that the offered testimony (an account by an examiner of a series of conversations he had under controlled conditions with the assaulted employee) was "hearsay testimony," and thus subject to the doubts and reservations which usually attach to such testimony. Interestingly, the arbitrator focused upon the conditions under which the exam was administered. The union was not present when the test took place. In addition, it had no part in the selection of the examiner, in designating his task, or in paying him when he was finished. The arbitrator, in rejecting the evidence, concluded that both the examiner's report on the test results and his interpretation of those results, arranged for and conducted entirely apart from the grievance procedure, would be substantially immune to analysis, challenge, or useful cross-examination by anyone other than another polygraph examiner.

SUMMARY—In 1974, the staff of the Subcommittee on Constitutional Rights of the Senate Judiciary Committee concluded that "doubt must be cast upon the objectivity, accuracy, and reliability of the polygraph test."[19] Generally, arbitrators have taken the same position. The principal grounds for rejection of polygraph evidence are the scientific unreliability of the test, the invasion of privacy of the employees affected, and the Fifth-Amendment concern that employees should not be compelled to incriminate themselves. Such evidence is particularly suspect where the polygraph test is the primary evidence relied upon in the discharge of employees.

The practitioner who desires to make use of the results of polygraph tests is advised to satisfy the following conditions: (1) the test should be administered by a qualified examiner; (2) the exam should be administered promptly after the incident in question; (3) the test should be voluntary; and (4) the examiner and his record of the test should be available for cross-examination.[20] In addition, an arbitrator may be more receptive to crediting polygraph evidence where the results corroborate direct evidence of innocence, rather than establishing guilt.

It should be noted, however, that satisfaction of the above criteria is no guarantee that an arbitrator will consider the results of a polygraph test. Even if an arbitrator would otherwise be receptive to lie-detector evidence, numerous states have enacted legislation that either prohibits or severely limits the use of the polygraph in the employment context.[21] Thus, in those states that have addressed the matter, any issue concerning the use of such evidence may be removed from the arbitrator's discretion and controlled by statute.[22]

Use of Confessions

> Today, then, there can be no doubt that the Fifth Amendment privilege is available outside of the criminal court proceedings and serves to protect persons in all settings in which their freedom of action is curtailed in any significant way from being compelled to incriminate themselves.[22a]

The Fifth Amendment provides that an accused person cannot be compelled in a criminal case to be a witness against himself. The historical roots of this privilege were discussed by Mr. Justice Fortas in the case of In re Gault:[23]

> The privilege against self-incrimination is, of course, related to the question of the safeguards necessary to assure that admissions or confessions are relatively trustworthy, that they are not the mere fruits of fear or coercion, but are reliable expressions of the truth. The roots of the privilege are, however, far deeper. They tap the basic stream of religious and political principle because the privilege reflects the limits of the individual's attornment to the state and—in a philosophical sense—insists upon the equality of the individual and the state. In other words, the privilege has broader and deeper thrust than the rule which prevents the use of confessions which are the product of coercion because coercion is thought to carry with it the danger of unreliability. One of its purposes is to prevent the state, whether by force or by psychological domination, from overcoming the mind and will of the person under investigation and depriving him of the freedom to decide whether to assist the state in securing his conviction.[24]

As observed by Professor Fleming, in the arbitral setting the constitutional protection against self-incrimination presumably has little application except insofar as it may be a desirable principle in the interest of fair procedure.[25] Similarly, Willard Wirtz has stated that the privilege against self-incrimination enters into due process of arbitration but its relevance is a very special one:

> [T]here is a fairly clear consensus in the arbitral opinions that this privilege, established in the criminal law, has no place, at least as such, in the arbitration of grievance cases (invariably discharge or discipline cases). The importance of this point is accordingly, as an illustration of the fact that "due process of arbitration" is a distinct concept, similar in its approach and purposes to "due process of law," but entirely independent in the conclusion it reaches.[26]

While it is true that the strict "self-incrimination" protection offered by the Fifth Amendment is not applicable in the absence of government action, it is nevertheless clear that issues of self-incrimination are often present in labor arbitration, and the reported decisions indicate that arbitrators have often credited constitutional-type arguments in rendering awards.[27] In this respect consider the following problem:

> Grievant S was apprehended by the security force of Safeway Stores after leaving the store with two plugs of chewing tobacco in his pocket. S was subsequently taken to a small office in the corner of the store where security men took turns questioning him. While in the room S signed a statement acknowledging the fact that S stole two plugs of tobacco. The document contained an acknowledgment that it was read by S, and that the statement was true in every respect as well as a declaration that no threats of any kind were used in obtaining the statement.

In refusing to credit the confession, Arbitrator Arthur Jacobs stated:

> [T]he constitutional protection of the rights of the individual against self-incrimination is broad and is related to the question of the safeguards necessary to assure that admissions or confessions are reasonably trustworthy and are not the result of fear or coercion; that they are reliable expressions of truth.[28]

In *Thrifty Drug Stores Co.*,[29] Arbitrator Edgar Jones stated a trier of fact should proceed with caution when confessions are introduced. He noted that a consideration must be whether the statements are so tainted by the manner of their taking as to make it too speculative for a trier of fact to give them credence as evidence against those whom they would implicate.[30]

Similarly, Arbitrator Whitley McCoy justified a refusal by an employee to cooperate with an investigation[31] since it constituted an attempt by the employer to shift the burden of proof. Citing Fifth-Amendment concerns, the arbitrator reasoned:

> I know of no principle, or decided case, upholding a company's right to compel an employee, under pain of discharge, to admit or deny a rule violation or other offense. Such a principle would contradict all our Anglo-American principles, particularly the one that a man is presumed innocent until he is proven guilty, and that the burden of proof is on the one alleging an offense.[32]

An interesting case where the arbitrator credited the confessions of employees involved the alleged placing of sugar in the gasoline tank of a company supervisor's automobile. In that case, a Pinkerton investigator called each of the grievants into a company office for interviews. Each man was briefed as to who the investigators were, why they were there, and what the investigation was about. Each person was warned that he had a right to remain silent, that anything he said might be used against him in a criminal prosecution, and that his job was at stake. During the interviews the investigators claimed to have photographs of an employee putting sugar in the tank and suggested that the men might as well confess, though in fact no such picture existed. Indeed, the investigator conceded at the hearing that the statement was made as a trick by which to produce the confessions of the three grievants. Notwithstanding union objections, the arbitrator credited the confessions obtained by the Pinkerton investigator. However, while the statements of the grievants were given weight, the arbitrator, citing the decision in *Weirton Steel*,[33] stated that such statements are examined with care:

> "[A] confession without more, is ordinarily insufficient to establish the existence of what in law is termed the 'corpus delecti'— the substance of the alleged offense." Following this rule the questions of the voluntariness of the present statements, and of the truth of the matters related in them, must be decided in relation to other available evidence regarding the incident which led to the discharge.[34]

SUMMARY—At this writing probably the best statement that can be made with respect to the admissibility of a grievant's confession is that the weight to be accorded a confession will be assessed in the light of all the conditions under which it was obtained. When it can be demonstrated that a confession has been made out of fear or coercion, and is thus not a reliable expression of truth, an arbitrator can be expected to give it little weight, particularly where the employer offers little or no evidence other than a confession that an offense warranting discharge has taken place.

Although the Fifth-Amendment privilege against self-incrimination is not applicable in a nongovernmental setting,[35] the advocate is still advised to consider the due process standards that are traditionally applied in the criminal law setting. This is especially true where the alleged misconduct is of a kind that carries the stigma of general social disapproval. In such cases arbitrators have tended to require a high degree of proof, and thus may be more cognizant of the conditions under which a confession is obtained.[36]

It should not be concluded, however, that employers cannot interrogate employees for fear that any information derived will summarily be excluded by an arbitrator. As stated by the West Coast Tripartite Committee, "Interrogation of employees is a normal and vital prerogative of an employer." While it is to be favored, the committee nevertheless noted that "the concern of the arbitrator at the proffer of evidence of 'confessions' . . . will be for its reliability, and, in egregious situations, for its allowability in terms of fair play and reasonable privacy."[37] The committee concluded:

> Emotional strain at accusation and the latent fear of the power of an employer to cause criminal prosecution irrespective of guilt or innocence, render this kind of evidence unreliable, and unless it is demonstrated that reasonable safeguards were observed in the investigation, including the real opportunity for representation, evidence of employee admissions during interrogation should be deemed inadmissible.[38]

Illegally Obtained Evidence

Historically, the common law was not concerned with the means used to obtain evidence. Once material and competent evidence was obtained, the accused had no valid complaint or argument that because the means used were illegal the evidence should be excluded.[39] In *Weeks* v. *United States*[40] the Supreme Court reversed this trend by holding that any evidence obtained by federal officers in violation of the Fourth

Amendment[41] would be excluded in federal prosecution. Similarly, in *Mapp v. Ohio*,[42] the court ruled that the exclusionary rule was applicable to criminal proceedings in state courts. In support of this holding the Court found that other remedies against unreasonable searches, such as tort actions, had proven ineffective. Moreover, the Court cited the trend in the state courts where a majority of states had adopted the rule as a matter of state law. The Court concluded that the exclusionary rule, by removing the incentive to disregard the Fourth Amendment, constituted the only effective way to compel respect for the constitutional guarantee. Subsequently the *Mapp* analysis was extended to require exclusion of evidence obtained from the "fruit of official illegality."

Exclusion of Evidence by Arbitrators—In determining the applicability of the exclusionary rule in an industrial relations setting, it must be remembered that the constitutional protection which the *Mapp* decision extends to individuals is not operative in absence of state action.[43] As such, a search or seizure, no matter how outrageous, carried out by a truly private person is not subject to the Fourth Amendment's proscriptions, and anything incriminating derived therefrom can be admitted into evidence.

While the constitutional standards do not necessarily apply in the same way to private investigations where there is no agent of the state present, conceivably there are circumstances under which a private arbitration could be considered governmental action for purposes of invoking the constitutional protections. This would especially appear to be the case when the arbitrator is functioning in the public sector, or where the courts are called upon to enforce an arbitral award.[44] Notwithstanding the government action issue, Fleming suggests that it is more important to consider whether arbitrators ought to evolve a rule against the receipt of improperly obtained evidence simply because this would contribute to the fairness and integrity of the arbitration process.[45] In this regard, consider the following problem:

> Employee X was dismissed from the service of the company for violating a company rule which prohibited the possession by employees of a dangerous knife on the premises. The union protested the dismissal as unjustified since the knife was within the aggrieved employee's

locker and the company employed questionable means (opening X's locker and examining the contents of X's purse) in determining the guilt of the accused.

There is a split among arbitrators concerning the issue whether improperly obtained evidence should be admitted in an arbitration hearing. In the case cited in the above problem,[46] Arbitrator Lohman, in overturning a discharge, focused on the apparent invasion of the personal rights of the grievant:

> To the majority members of the arbitration committee, the adoption of the aforementioned procedure by the company guards represented a serious error in judgment and invaded the personal rights of the aggrieved. In certain respects, the tactic bordered on that of entrapment since the aggrieved's innocence of the company's objective or of her own rights placed her honesty and good will at the disposal of the company and caused her to incriminate herself. Such self-incrimination has long been outlawed by the basic law of the United States, specifically, under the Fifth Amendment of the Constitution and the precedent-making Supreme Court decisions in the noted Search and Seizure cases. . . .
>
> In the present case, the majority members of the arbitration committee are of the considered opinion that both the knowledge and possession of the knife by the company were brought about under highly questionable if not illegal procedures. Knowledge, even though incriminating, if acquired through such illegitimate procedures, is of questionable validity in bringing action against the individual. . . .
>
> . . . Under the circumstances, the majority members conclude that the evidence of the possession of the knife is inadmissible, and, consequently, the discharge of the aggrieved was unjustified.[47]

A similar approach was taken by Arbitrator Rankin Gibson:

> [T]he arbitrator finds that although all rights of a criminal defendant do not automatically extend to a grievant in every disciplinary case, e.g., absenteeism, incompetence, negligence, in those cases involving moral turpitude, such as theft, the privilege against self-incrimination and the protection against unreasonable search and seizure should be applied. Under these circumstances, the physical evidence obtained as a result of the unlawful search and seizure, as well as the testimony of the police officer who made the search and seizure, and the testimony of the Plant Manager who accompanied the police officer in making the unlawful search and seizure, should be suppressed, such testimony being the fruit of the poisonous tree of the illegal search.[48]

It is noteworthy that all practitioners do not share this view. One member of the Chicago Tripartite Committee declared:

> At the risk of seeming not to believe in civil rights, I think there is a distinct difference between the citizen in his relationship with his government and the employee in his activity and conduct on the premises of his employer. But when you get to the question of a forcible search of the person, I am a little less inclined to go along with . . . the forcible entry into the locker. I believe that a locker is the property of the company. The employee is only permitted to use it for certain periods of time.
>
> . . .
>
> . . . It certainly seems to me that it should be permissible to open a man's locker where you have reason to believe that he has used it for the keeping of stolen property. Under these circumstances I can see no reason why a man should be entitled to any protection that might be afforded him as a citizen in his relationship with his government.[49]

An interesting case concerning illegally obtained evidence involved the arrest of some employees who were charged with the theft and possession of cartons of clothing from the company. The criminal case was dismissed after a motion to suppress the evidence was allowed. The employees were subsequently discharged after the company received word from a bonding company advising the employer that bonds were being cancelled on the two grievants allegedly involved in the thefts. The arbitrator noted that it could validly be argued that the spirit of the constitutional prohibition against unreasonable search and seizure is violated when the fruits of what has been judicially determined to be an illegal arrest are nevertheless allowed to be considered by the company or an arbitrator in a discharge case. Nevertheless, the arbitrator credited the evidence which was suppressed due to the illegal arrest. Reasoning that there is an essential difference between the procedural and substantive rights of the parties, the arbitrator stated that constitutional principles may keep the grievants out of jail but they do not guarantee their jobs in the face of their employer's knowledge of dishonesty.[50]

Likewise, Arbitrator David Dolnick denied a motion to suppress illegally obtained evidence, stating that an arbitration hearing is not a criminal law case:

> An arbitration hearing is a civil proceeding. It is not a court of law. I do not derive my authority to hear and decide the issue in dispute from any statute, ordinance or law enacted by a legal-

ly constituted legislative body. . . . My authority is prescribed and limited by the applicable provisions in the collective bargaining agreement freely entered into by the parties.

With respect to the constitutional issue, Arbitrator Dolnick reasoned as follows:

> The fourth and fourteenth amendments to the United States Constitution protect individuals against unlawful search and seizure and self-incrimination respectively. Admissibility of evidence wrongfully obtained usually arises in criminal cases and generally in connection with evidence obtained by an illegal search and seizure. . . .
>
> But there are no real definitive court decisions on the question of whether or not evidence obtained by illegal search and seizure is admissible in civil cases. . . .
>
> . . .
>
> I get no clear guidance from the courts, I do not believe that I have the right, under these circumstances, to conclude that the merchandise found in grievant's automobile is inadmissible in evidence to determine whether or not it is the rightful property of the Company and whether or not it was illegally in the possession of the grievant.[51]

Perhaps the most comprehensive analysis for not excluding illegally seized evidence was provided by Arbitrator Lawrence Doppelt in *Commodity Warehousing Corp.*[52] In that decision an employer contacted police authorities and arranged for them to follow an employee (L) after he left the employer's premises. As a consequence, L was stopped "for speeding," and requested to open his trunk. He agreed, and the police discovered stolen meat. The police and the employer questioned L who, in turn, implicated himself and the grievant in the theft. A criminal complaint was issued against both men, but was subsequently dropped when the court ordered that all evidence against L be suppressed.

At the arbitration hearing L testified directly to the facts as cited. The grievant denied that he was involved in the scheme. Furthermore, the union moved to quash all evidence seized as a result of the illegal police search of L, as well as all evidence discovered as a result of the search. In support of this motion the union alleged that the evidence was secured as the result of an illegal search and seizure and was thus tainted and inadmissible under the Constitution.

In denying the motion, Arbitrator Doppelt stated that it was questionable whether the motion served any real purpose since the evidence that the union was trying to suppress was merely corroborative of other direct evidence (the testimony of L) properly before the arbitrator. More important, the arbitrator cautioned that neutrals should tread lightly when it comes to interpreting the exclusionary rules of evidence based on criminal and constitutional law. An arbitrator is chosen for his presumed expertise in matters pertaining to labor-management relations, and not as an expert on rules of evidence in criminal cases. To point this out, the arbitrator addressed the difficulty in attempting to apply rules of evidence:

> [T]he employer here says that the Fourth and Fourteenth Amendments would not, in any event, protect grievant because grievant was not himself the victim of an illegal search and seizure, and such Amendments are designed to protect the victim of an illegal search and seizure, not implicate third parties. . . . Thus, says the employer, evidence secured through an illegal search and seizure of L- may be used against grievant even if it cannot be used against L-. The union, on the other hand, says the Fourth and Fourteenth Amendments protect grievant as well as L- from evidence garnered through an illegal search and seizure of L-. This dispute points up the traps confronting a labor arbitrator when he attempts to resolve issues involving the interpretation of intricate rules of evidence applicable to criminal and constitutional law matters.

Finally the Arbitrator cited the different policies involved in criminal and arbitral proceedings:

> Criminal law pertains to vindicating the rights of society against individuals who have broken society's laws. In vindicating such rights, the individual must be protected against certain possible governmental abuses, and exclusionary rules of evidence help afford that protection. Labor arbitration, on the other hand, adjudicates the rights and responsibilities of employers, unions, and employees under a labor contract. It involves private disputes without any spectre of governmental excesses. It is doubtful whether all various evidentiary rules necessary to protect individuals against possible governmental abuses should automatically be applied in employer-employee relations matters which involve private disputes.
>
> . . .
>
> This is not to say that an employee does not have certain basic procedural and substantive due process rights under a contract requiring that an employee not be discharged except for "cause." Of course, he does, and arbitration cases are replete with examples of such. Indeed, such contract language implies the imposition of certain rights and duties on employers and employees. However, the rights accorded an employee are not necessarily the same as those granted individuals under exclusionary rules of evidence in criminal matters.[53]

SUMMARY—The Supreme Court has long held that evidence obtained in violation of the unreasonable search-and-seizure provisions of the Fourth Amendment is inadmissible in criminal cases, both in state and federal proceedings. It must be recognized, however, that there is no definite holding making the exclusionary rule applicable in civil proceedings. Nevertheless, when preparing a case for arbitration the advocate should be particularly careful of the means used to obtain evidence. While there is a difference of opinion whether the evidentiary rules developed in the criminal law sector should be applicable in industrial relations cases, an arbitrator may be reluctant to credit evidence if it can be demonstrated that it was obtained by means which if conducted by a government entity would be considered violative of the Fourth and Fourteenth Amendments.

In his comprehensive research on the subject, Professor Fleming found that arbitrators agree that a company may impose reasonable rules as to the search of one's person and property where such rules are made a condition of employment. Furthermore, Fleming found that arbitrators would permit employers to use evidence obtained without the knowledge or consent of the employee if it is obtained from company property (e.g., a locker), even if the property is momentarily under the control of the employee. Although exclusionary rules are not automatically applicable in the arbitral proceeding, Fleming notes that few, if any, arbitrators would permit the employer to use evidence obtained by breaking and entering an employee's personal property, even though the property is located on plant premises.[54]

Evidence Acquired Through the Use of Movie, Television, or Recording Equipment

Arbitrators have upheld the use of closed-circuit television for surveillance purposes against claims that such surveillance is an infringement of employees' basic right of privacy.[55] For example, in *FMC Corp.*,[56] Arbitrator Richard Mittenthal, in upholding management's right to install closed-circuit cameras, stated:

> The right of privacy concerns an individual's right not to have his statements, actions, etc., made public without his consent. But this serves only to protect him against the publication of his private statements or private actions. It should be evident that an employee's actions during working hours are not private ac-

tions. Management is properly concerned with the employee's work performance, what he does on the job and whether he obeys the plant's rules and regulations. This and other information about employees is obtained through line supervisors. . . . For all the Company has done is to add a different method of supervision to the receiving room—an electronic eye (i.e., the television cameras) in addition to a human eye. Regardless of the type of supervision (a camera, a supervisor, or both) the employee works with the knowledge that supervision may be watching him at any time.[57]

Similarly, arbitrators have upheld the use of "spotters" or other investigative personnel for surveillance purposes.[58]

Although cases of wiretapping are rare, under certain circumstances arbitrators have credited such evidence. Thus, in *A. B. Chance Co.,*[59] Arbitrator Peter Florey credited evidence obtained as a result of a "pen register" (a mechanical device placed on a telephone line that registers where a call originates). While no actual monitoring or recording of a conversation took place, the arbitrator held that so long as the pen register is admissible in a criminal proceeding, it could not be ruled out in an arbitration case. In a decision involving the actual recording of a conversation, Arbitrator J. H. Marcus, in *Sun Drug Co.,*[60] found no infirmity in admitting a recorded conversation implicating the grievant in a bookmaking operation.

The West Coast Tripartite Committee has concluded that evidence acquired through the use of movie, television, or recording equipment is entitled to admission if relevant and reliable.[61] The only generalization as to the latter criterion, as noted by the committee, is that the evidence should be required to pass stringent examination to assure its reliability.

Failure of Grievant to Testify

As a totally voluntary method of settling disputes under a collective bargaining agreement, the grievance-arbitration mechanism accords the parties a free hand, not only in the selection of the arbitrator and his corresponding scope of authority but also in the manner of processing and presenting grievances before the arbitrator. Recognizing the voluntary nature of the grievance mechanism, arbitrators generally permit the parties great latitude in the selection, examination, and cross-examination of witnesses. Thus, it frequently happens that, for whatever reason, an advocate will not call the grievant to the stand. This strategy presents questions of the inferences that are to be drawn from a refusal by the grievant to testify.

Nondisciplinary Cases

Where the challenged action does not involve discipline or discharge, there is no particular problem arising from the failure of the grievant to testify. As noted by the West Coast Tripartite Committee, however, if evidence is omitted that only the grievant can supply, then an arbitrator is entitled (and indeed likely) to be skeptical of the merits of the grievance.[62]

Disciplinary Cases

The Fifth Amendment, in relevant part, provides that "[n]o person . . . shall be compelled in any criminal case to be a witness against himself." In the criminal law sector neither a prosecutor nor a judge can comment on the accused's failure to testify, nor, at least in theory, can the jury draw an inference from guilt from such failure. This principle was first expressed in *Griffin v. California*,[63] where a trial court, instructing the jury, stated that failure of a defendant to deny or explain the evidence of which the defendant had knowledge does not create a presumption of guilt nor by itself warrant an inference of guilt. While the trial court recognized that the accused had a constitutional right not to testify, it nevertheless instructed the jury that it could take into consideration (and indeed draw negative inferences from) any evidence or facts which the defendant can reasonably be expected to deny or explain because of facts within his knowledge.

Writing for the majority, Mr. Justice Douglas, reversing the trial court, stated:

> It is not every one who can safely venture on the witness stand, though entirely innocent of the charge against him. Excessive timidity, nervousness when facing others and attempting to explain transactions of a suspicious character, and offenses charged against him, will often confuse and embarrass him to such a degree as to increase rather than remove prejudices against him. It is not every one, however honest, who would therefore willingly be placed on the witness stand.[64]

Consistent with the comments of Justice Douglas, some arbitrators have refused to draw any inferences from a refusal to testify. Thus, Arbitrator John Sembower has stated:

> The Arbitrator disregards any adverse inferences which might be drawn from the Grievant's not being present at the hearing. While this is in no sense a criminal matter, there is an inescapable analogy between the absence from an arbitration hearing of the Grievant in a disciplinary case and the rule of law that a defendant in court may not be required to take the stand if he chooses not to do so, and it shall not be held against him if he does not.[65]

Similarly, Arbitrator James Altieri, in *Publisher's Ass'n of New York City*,[66] refused to find an adverse inference from the grievant's failure to testify where the employer failed to make out a prima facie case.

Another approach was taken by Arbitrator Peter Seitz in *U.S. Steel Corp.*[67] At issue was the propriety of discipline for an alleged participation in a strike in violation of a no-strike clause. The only aspect of the case in which the question of the failure to testify became relevant was the matter of excuses offered by individual grievants purporting to establish that they had not been absent by reason of participating in the strike but rather were absent for other legitimate reasons. One grievant failed to appear at the hearing but the union offered his prepared statement that he had telephoned the employer and told him that he was unable to report for work because of circumstances beyond his control (the grievant alleged that he had told the superintendent that he had to stay home to take care of a sick son). While the arbitrator held that the grievant's statement was insufficient proof of the facts set forth, the arbitrator nevertheless commented that the failure of the witness to testify in support of the alibi could be weighed against him.

Likewise, in *Southern Bell Telephone & Telegraph Co.*,[68] Arbitrator Whitley McCoy, stressing that the employer had made out a prima facie case against the grievant, examined the employee's refusal to testify only in relation to the weight to be given the employee's defense in rebuttal of the employer's case:

> While we have held that the burden of first proceeding, and the burden of proof, are upon the Company to prove reasonable cause for the discharge, the making of a prima facie case discharged the burden of first proceeding and cast upon the Union the burden of rebuttal of that prima facie case. An alibi proved

by two witnesses, when the evidence shows that there were other witnesses to the alibi whom the Union deliberately refrained from calling, does not in my opinion sufficiently rebut that prima facie case.[69]

Arbitrator McCoy, in a different decision, expanded on this concept:

I think that the inferences to be drawn from a refusal to testify are limited to evidentiary *facts*, and do not extend to the ultimate *conclusion* of guilt or innocence which must be drawn from evidentiary facts. Inferences may be resorted to in aid of evidentiary facts; they cannot supply facts of which there is no evidence. Findings of fact must be based on credible evidence. The failure to deny or refute incredible evidence does not change the character of that evidence from incredible to credible. Testimony that is merely weak can gain strength from failure to deny; but testimony that is utterly incredible can never become credible in that way.[70]

In the *NRM Corp.* decision,[71] Arbitrator Edwin Teple was faced with a discharge growing out of a collateral criminal proceeding. Apparently the grievant reported his car stolen and was subsequently arrested for filing a false report when it was discovered that he knew in advance that it was to be stripped. Before his discharge the grievant informed his employer that, upon advice of counsel, he was going to plead guilty to the charge, but denied that he was in fact guilty. After entering his guilty plea, the grievant was promptly discharged. The arbitrator found the discharge proper, based on the employer's concerns for staffing an honest work force. Commenting on the grievant's failure to testify, the arbitrator stated:

If the grievant had a logical explanation for his involvement in this incident, and could truthfully claim no knowledge of the activities which gave rise to the charges filed against him, he had the opportunity to appear at the oral hearing and testify in his own behalf. His failure to do so removes any basis he might have had for objecting to the implications naturally drawn from the information obtained by the police and the formal charge thereafter filed. He can not avoid the opportunity to appear and explain, and then question otherwise proper conclusions drawn from his plea of guilty to the charge.[72]

Willard Wirtz cites a decision by Saul Wallen[73] where the grievant had been indicted for allegedly stealing tires from his employer's plant. Claiming his Fifth Amendment right not to testify, the employee was acquitted of the theft charge. He was discharged for the same offense and at the arbitration hearing once again refused to testify. Arbitrator Wallen upheld the discharge on the ground that the grievant failed to satisfy his obligations to his employer to cooperate in stopping thievery from the plant. As noted by Wirtz, what is interesting in the case was that the grievant's decision not to testify about the incident—which was part of his due-process-of-law right in court and which arguably saved him from a larceny conviction—was itself an element in the finding of just cause for his discharge.

In *New York Times Co.*,[74] Arbitrator Peter Seitz sustained an employee's suspension for allegedly participating in gambling activities. The grievant was unwilling to testify at the hearing because of the pendency of a criminal proceeding. Since only a suspension was assessed, Arbitrator Seitz found it unnecessary to subscribe to the employer's theory that the grievant's presence at the hearing, coupled with his failure to take the stand to refute the employer's case, results in an adverse inference.

SUMMARY—Professor Fleming has correctly noted that the problems of self-incrimination and the failure to testify are almost certain to be different before an arbitrator than a court of law. The question of constitutional-type privileges usually arises in a collateral rather than a direct way in the arbitral forum. More important, since the arbitrator has neither the power of subpoena nor the power to hold a party in contempt, the issue is not whether to compel him to testify, but rather whether it is permissible to draw an inference against him because he has not testified.[75]

Arbitrator Russell Smith, in a recent address before the National Academy of Arbitrators, has analyzed the problem as follows:

> An arbitration proceeding is not a criminal proceeding; hence there is technically no basis for reliance upon the Fifth Amendment. But this is not dispositive of the issue. Some of the basic principles of our jurisprudence, notably the concept of due process, have been borrowed and applied in the negotiation of the grievance procedure and in its application, and the notion that an employee ought not to have to testify when a disciplinary penalty assessed against him is being reviewed has some appeal. The employee must, if called and if guilty of the act charged, either testify falsely or confess his guilt. Thus, if he is honest, he will convict himself out of his own mouth; if he is dishonest, he will have added to his dishonesty in testifying to

the fact of his guilt if otherwise established. His dilemma will be acute. If an arbitrator regards the Fifth Amendment privilege as one of the really important constitutional guarantees, he may be inclined to think a like privilege should exist in the arbitral review of managerial action; if, however, he has some skepticism about the basic validity of the privilege in general, or if he thinks the employer-employee relationship has unique characteristics, he will take a different view.[76]

An examination of arbitral opinion indicates that arbitrators do in fact draw inferences from the grievant's failure to testify, although it is sometimes unclear just how the inference may operate. Neutrals have recognized that there are many reasons why a grievant might not testify, including the fact that some persons make poor witnesses because of their demeanor, their inability to respond to direct questions, and their tendency to become rattled. As stated by the West Coast Tripartite Committee, advocates in both the judicial and arbitral forums will keep a witness off the stand, "not because he is dishonest, but because he is bumbling, inarticulate, unintelligent, or easily confused or confounded, one in whose mouth the truth may indeed lie, but never to be dislodged."[77] Accordingly, arbitrators have not assumed that the most logical inference to be drawn from a grievant's failure to testify is that he would only give testimony damaging to his cause. The more reasoned awards appear to mandate that before any negative inferences are to be drawn from a failure to testify, the employer must establish a prima facie case. Once that task is satisfied, however, an, arbitrator may well resolve an uncontested fact against the grievant. Although an arbitrator may not assert that he or she is finding for the employer on a specific issue because the grievant did not contest the facts as alleged by the employer, still it is not unexpected that the union's case is necessarily weakened when an important witness fails to challenge otherwise damaging evidence.

Considerations Concerning Admission of Evidence From an Adversary or Third Person[78]

Calling a Witness From the Other Side

In the arbitral forum it is generally permissible for a party to call witnesses from the opposite side. The New York Tripartite Committee has stated that in the absence of a privilege or some other bar, an adverse party should, if requested, be required to produce evidence or to testify.[79] The committee did note, however, that while it is permissible for a party to call witnesses from the opposing side, such witnesses may be treated as hostile and should be protected by the arbitrator against unfair tactics on direct examination.[80]

Except for an unusual case, such as the situation where the grievant knows best what occurred, the Chicago Tripartite Committee has declared that the arbitrator should rule that the grievant may not be called as a witness at the outset of the case in a discharge or disciplinary matter.[81] Although the committee has taken the position that it is unwise and undesirable to encourage calling a witness from the other side, it nevertheless concluded that no limitations should be placed by the arbitrator on the parties calling witnesses whose general interests identify them with the other party.

Where the issue concerns calling the grievant, the West Coast Committee split. The employer representatives opted for the capacity to call the grievant; the union representatives regarded it as an intrusion in the development of their cases. The committee concluded that while the judicial analogy supports the employer's position, arbitral procedure may, on occasion, be contrary.[82]

In *Tectum Corp.*,[83] at the conclusion of the union's case, the grievant, although present, had not been called as a witness. When the employer requested that the grievant take the stand, the union objected. Ruling that the grievant should testify, the arbitrator stated:

> It is true that this arbitrator, like arbitrators of most labor contract disputes, does not have legal authority to subpoena a witness or to compel a witness to testify. . . . Usually, as here, the parties proceed to the arbitration of a labor contract dispute voluntarily without the compulsion of a court order. In such voluntary cases, the rulings of the arbitrator on procedural matters such as the admission or exclusion of evidence and the requirement of a party to testify or to produce documents and papers are carried out by the parties on a voluntary basis. . . .
>
> Although the formalities of the courtroom and all of the fine points of the rules of evidence applicable to a trial before a jury are inappropriate in an arbitration hearing, a fair hearing cannot be had unless each party is allowed to present competent testimony and other evidence in support of its position. . . . In the instant case the Company requested that the grievant answer questions directly bearing upon the arbitration case.

This arbitrator's ruling that the grievant should submit to questioning by the Company subject to the right of the Union to object to specific questions was based upon the arbitrator's opinion that neither the Company nor the Union should be allowed to withhold relevant and material testimony or other evidence except possibly in special circumstances not here involved such as possible criminal incrimination, trade secrets, and classified Defense matters.[84]

Arbitrator Wirtz has taken the position that the tradition against calling a bargaining unit witness does more than any other single element to prevent reliable fact determination by the arbitrator. Wirtz asserts that there is no legitimate reason or justification for this tradition, and that arbitrators could meet this problem if they chose, since the view that the arbitrator does not have the power to call other employees as witnesses is dubious, at least as a practical matter.[85]

Notwithstanding this view, frequently an employer will not require a bargaining unit employee to testify against another unit employee because of possible disruptive effects at the work place. As noted by one arbitrator, there are problems with calling persons to testify whose general interests identify them with the other party, and it may not be good labor relations to do so. Moreover, there is the problem whether the witness should be considered a "hostile" witness at the outset of the examination:

> If a person is called, there is the question whether by calling him he is made the witness of the party calling him so that the party is bound by his testimony and must examine him as on direct examination even though he is a hostile witness. My own practice has been to regard him from the outset as an adversary witness and hence to permit him to be examined as if on cross-examination. But it may be that the better practice would be to regard him as the calling party's witness until his hostility develops, then to permit him to be questioned as if on cross.[86]

As an alternative to calling a bargaining unit employee and having him testify, an employer may attempt a compromise and obtain a written statement or affidavit from the employee and subsequently introduce it at the hearing. Such efforts have generally been unsuccessful since affidavits are subject to hearsay objections.[87] For example, in *Commercial Nat'l Bank*,[88] Arbitrator Martin Lubow did not credit an out-of-court statement by an employee that would have implicated the grievant in a theft. Recognizing the difficulty of producing one union member to offer testimony against another, the arbitrator stated that had there been an objection to this testimony by the union, he would have sustained it. Likewise, in *Bethlehem Steel Corp.*,[89] the employer refused to produce an employee who was allegedly assaulted by the grievant since both were bargaining unit employees. Instead the employer offered the results of a polygraph exam which, if credited, would have verified that the charge was meritorious. Arbitrator Ralph Seward refused to credit this evidence based, in part, on the hearsay nature of the exam.

Lending a different twist to the problem of compelling a bargaining unit employee to testify against a fellow union member is *United Parcel Services, Inc.*[90] In that decision Arbitrator Lubow found that where a bargaining unit employee refused to testify at the hearing, claiming he could not testify against a fellow union member, such testimony would have been damaging to the grievant. As such, the arbitrator effectively held that absence of testimony by a unit employee could operate against the grievant, at least under the facts of this case where both parties had agreed that the absent witness had a direct view of the incident at issue.

The fact that the parties have a general privilege to present evidence does not derogate from the power of the arbitrator to regulate the order of presentation. The usual procedure in labor arbitration involving the discharge of an employee is for the employer to proceed first with the presentation of its case, giving the reasons for and the factual basis upon which it based the discharge. In *Local 560, IBT v. Eazor Express*,[91] a New Jersey state court sustained an arbitrator's decision refusing to permit an employer in a discharge case to call the grievant as its first witness. The employer claimed it had an absolute right to present its case as it saw fit and to determine whom it would call as a witness and the sequence in which its witnesses would be called to testify. The court found no violation of procedural due process by the arbitrator's decision. In sustaining the arbitrator, the court stated that there was no showing that the employer was harmed by being deprived of the opportunity of calling the grievant as its *first* witness since the arbitrator had assured the company that the grievant would be called to testify, and that the cross-examination could go beyond the scope of the direct examination. Moreover, the arbitrator assured the employer that if the union did not call the grievant as a witness, he would see to it that the employer could call him directly. The court concluded that absent some abuse of discretion prejudicial to one of the parties, the arbitrator's control of the order of proofs will not be disturbed. As noted by the court:

> To take away this power from the arbitrator would permit the case to be developed in any illogical, disjointed or uncoordinated manner either or both parties chose to adopt. Procedural due process does not go that far. It is enough that a party is given an opportunity to be heard and a fair hearing.[92]

Duty of an Adversary to Produce Evidence

While it is agreed that it is desirable that all facts should be elicited at the hearing which are relevant and material to the issues in question, not infrequently cases will arise where one party refuses to disclose information. As discussed in a subsequent section,[93] the deliberate withholding of evidence until the hearing may, in certain circumstances, provide sufficient grounds for an arbitrator to exclude the evidence. An arbitrator may likewise resolve an issue against a party that refuses a request for relevant information. For example, in *American Telephone & Telegraph Co.*,[94] Arbitrator Saul Wallen, in commenting on the power of an arbitrator to compel production of evidence, stated:

> An arbitrator has no right to compel the production of documents (it might be otherwise if the arbitration is carried out under an arbitration statute) by either side. He may, however, give such weight as he deems appropriate to the failure of a party to produce documents on demand. The degree of weight to be attached to such failure will depend upon the relevancy of the documents requested to the issues at hand. If the information would appear to be strongly pertinent, the withholding of it may be vital in the making of a decision. If it is of doubtful relevancy and merely represents an attempt by one party to probe through the files of another on the mere chance that its position may be generally strengthened thereby, then the failure to produce such records should be disregarded.[95]

Similarly, in *C&P Telephone Co. of West Virginia*,[96] the union, prior to the date the arbitration board convened for the formal hearing, filed a request captioned "Motion for Discovery and Inspection of Records." The motion was for an order permitting the union to inspect the personnel records of the grievant. Specifically, the union requested (a) the employee's application for employment; (b) work records, including absence records; (c) supervisory records covering the employee's duties, qualifications, and competence; and (d) medical records for the period prior to the employee's accident. In support of its position the union asserted that the records were necessary for a proper presentation of its case.

After ruling that the board of arbitration had authority to compel the employer to produce the documents in question,[97] Arbitrator Harry Dworkin stated:

> Apart from specific rules, it is a salutary principle of arbitration procedure that both parties to the dispute be accorded a full and complete hearing and an opportunity to present such evidence, documentary or otherwise, as it is germane to the issues, without regard to whether one or another party has possession or custody of such evidence. The object and purpose of arbitration is to arrive at a fair and just decision, and to this end parties should be assisted in obtaining competent and material evidence where such production may reasonably be had. The laudatory air and purpose of arbitration would be defeated and impaired were a party to be denied his just rights solely because the other party to the dispute refused to disclose material evidence which it has under its control. . . .
>
> . . .
>
> Although the arbitration board is of the opinion that the union's request in the instant case should be granted, it should extend only to such documents and writings which appear to be relevant and pertinent to the issues presented for ultimate determination. The exercise of the arbitrator's authority should be reasonable, and a party is entitled to be protected against "fishing expeditions" and the examination of files and records which may not be considered as being pertinent.[98]

In *Murray Corp.,*[99] Arbitrator David Wolff refused an employer's offer to present certain evidence to him on condition that he not reveal it to the union. Where the employer refused to disclose the identity of the employee who accused the grievant of ordering a slowdown but instead offered the arbitrator a statement from the employee, the arbitrator ruled that such nondisclosure would result in a denial to the grievant of her right to a full and complete appraisal of the facts.

It should also be recognized that where a search for requested information will involve substantial time and expense on the part of the employer, arbitrators have ordered the union to reimburse the employer for expenses.[100]

Aside from the general policy of not undermining the grievance procedure by withholding relevant information, there is an additional reason the parties should be concerned with full and complete disclosure. In *Teamsters v. ABAD*,[101] a state court vacated an arbitrator's award sustaining a discharge where it was found that the employer, through a supervisor, had apparently submitted incomplete production records of the grievant, while representing that the documents were accurate and complete. Citing a New Jersey statute that allows vacating an award for corruption, the court held that the employer's conscious withholding of a portion of the records constituted corruption per se.[102]

Authority of the Arbitrator to Order Disclosure of Evidence

Collective Bargaining Agreements—Some collective bargaining agreements contain provisions requiring complete and full disclosure of relevant information necessary to negotiate and administer the agreement. In such cases an arbitrator can be expected to mandate that the parties honor the agreement and, absent a compelling reason,[103] disclose relevant information. The parties should take care, however, that the agreement clearly requires disclosure, for an arbitrator may not order disclosure unless the contract clearly authorizes such an order. For example, in *Hoover Chemical*,[104] Arbitrator David Keefe considered a claim by the union that the company produce certain records and witnesses at the hearing pursuant to the following contractual provision:

> Either party to the Agreement is permitted to call witnesses, and upon request shall submit evidence at any step of the grievance procedure, including the hearing before the arbitrator, for the purpose of substantiating their respective contentions or claims.

The arbitrator held that "the provision plainly provides that the sole purpose which can activate the demand for evidence is substantiation of the contention or claim of the side submitting such evidence and not to prove the case for the other side."[105]

Rules of the American Arbitration Association—In granting a discovery-type motion for medical evidence, Arbitrator Harry Dworkin, in *C&P Telephone Co.*,[106] cited Rule 28 of the American Arbitration Association. That rule, in relevant part, provides:

> The parties may offer such evidence as they desire and shall produce such additional evidence as the Arbitrator may deem

necessary to an understanding and determination of the dispute. When the Arbitrator is authorized by law to subpoena witnesses and documents he may do so upon his own initiative or upon the request of any party.[107]

It was also noteworthy that the arbitrator found Rule 46 applicable.

The Arbitrator shall interpret and apply these Rules insofar as they relate to his powers and duties.[108]

Subpoenas—In *Hirst Enterprises, Inc.,*[109] Arbitrator Justin discussed the arbitral process as a means of obtaining information in the possession of the other party. The arbitrator stated that if the union believes that facts exist that could support its claim, and if those facts are in possession of the employer, the union could secure it in the arbitral proceeding by requesting the arbitrator to direct the company to produce them. Upon a proper showing that such facts were material to the issues in the dispute, the arbitrator noted that a *subpoena duces tecum* would issue.[110]

As stated by one authority,[111] if an arbitrator's request is ignored, enforcement is then available through the courts, not as an enforcement of subpoena powers created by a state statute or by the U.S. Arbitration Act,[112] but as an enforcement of the arbitrator's power to compel production of material evidence under Section 301 of the Labor-Management Relations Act.[113] In *Great Scott Supermarkets v. Local 337,*[114] a federal district court enforced an arbitrator's award notwithstanding a claim that the arbitrator exceeded his authority when he issued a subpoena requiring a union attorney to furnish documents relating to a grievance hearing. The union did not challenge the power of an arbitrator to issue a subpoena; however, the union argued that under the Federal Rules of Civil Procedure the arbitrator exceeded his authority by demanding the production of documents which fell into the category of the work product of an attorney. In sustaining the arbitrator the court reasoned that an arbitrator derives his jurisdiction and authority through the collective bargaining agreement. If the parties intended that the discovery rules were to be applied in the grievance procedure, such a provision should have been included. Absent such a reference, the court concluded that the discovery rules do not apply to an arbitration proceeding.

What is interesting in the *Great Scott* decision is that the court cited the Arbitration Act as authority for the arbitrator to issue the subpoena. Likewise, in *Local Lodge 1746* v. *United Aircraft Corp.*,[115] a federal court held that under Section 7 of the Arbitration Act,[116] it possessed the authority to enforce an arbitrator's subpoena of a witness and the delivery of records that was issued pursuant to a Connecticut statute. Although the federal court allowed discovery, it did not uphold a carte blanche discovery privilege. Rather, the employer was ordered to produce its investigative records for an *in camera* inspection by the arbitrator. Focusing on the discretion of the arbitrator, the court reasoned:

> It must be assumed that the presiding arbitrator is an experienced person well versed in evaluating the alleged claims of the employer, that some files contain classified security information involving national defense or plant security, personal health records and other confidential data. All of this should be screened from the file, except where the arbitrator determines it to be relevant evidence in the dispute. Even in the latter instances, proper safeguards should be ordered, so that no unnecessary harm or prejudice or unnecessary embarrassment may be caused to anyone.[117]

Obligation to Supply Information Under Section 8(a)(5) of the National Labor Relations Act[118]

An incumbent bargaining agent is, under Section 8(a)(5) of the National Labor Relations Act,[119] entitled to requested information relevant and necessary to the performance of its bargaining function. But, as noted by the Supreme Court in *Detroit Edison Co.* v. *NLRB*,[120] a union's bare assertion that it needs information to process a grievance does not automatically oblige the employer to supply all the information in the manner requested."[121] Citing *NLRB* v. *Truitt Mfg. Co.*,[122] the Court stated that the duty to supply information turns upon the circumstances of a particular case.

In *NLRB* v. *Acme Industrial Co.*,[123] the Supreme Court upheld an order of the NLRB requiring an employer to disclose facts surrounding the removal of machinery. The Board found, and the Court affirmed, that the information requested was "necessary in order to enable the Union to evaluate intelligently the grievances filed."[124] In addition, the Court ruled that the Board need not await an arbitrator's determination of the relevancy of the requested information before it can enforce the union's statutory rights under Section 8(a)(5). Accordingly, under the statute the Board may make a "threshold determination concerning the potential relevance of . . . requested information."[125]

The test of "relevance" for purposes of the duty to disclose is a liberal "discovery-type standard."[126] Thus, in *Transport of New Jersey*,[127] the NLRB ordered an employer to furnish to the union the names and addresses of passenger witnesses to a bus accident involving a bargaining unit member. The Board stated that under the standard of relevancy as applied by both the Board and the courts, it is sufficient that the union's request for information be supported by a showing of "probable" or "potential" relevancy.[128] However, in *Anheuser-Busch, Inc.*,[129] the Board held that the statements of prospective employee-witnesses, prepared by the witnesses themselves and thereafter given to the employer, need not be disclosed to the union. Unlike the situation in *Transport of New Jersey*, the Board reasoned that witnesses' statements are fundamentally different from the types of information contemplated by the Supreme Court in *Acme*. Requiring pre-arbitration disclosure of witnesses' statements would, argued the Board, not advance the grievance and arbitration process. Relying in part on the Supreme Court's decision in *NLRB v. Robbins Tire & Rubber Co.*,[130] the Board cited the potential dangers of premature release, including the risk that employers, or in some cases unions, will coerce or intimidate employees in an effort to make them change their testimony or not testify at all.[131] The Board also noted that witnesses may be reluctant to give statements, absent assurances that their statements will not be disclosed at least until after the investigation and adjudication are complete.[132]

Although courts have rarely found circumstances that permit a party to summarily withhold information,[133] there are exceptions. Where the interests against disclosure are legitimate and substantial, both the Board and the courts have held that a party need not disclose, even though the requested information may be relevant. Thus, in the *Detroit Edison* decision,[134] the Supreme Court upheld an employer's claim of privilege against disclosure of psychological testing information and reversed a Board order to make available, directly to the union, the aptitude tests, answer sheets, and employee-linked scores that had been used in making disputed promotion decisions. The Court rejected the proposition that the union interests in arguably relevant information must always predominate over all other interests, however legitimate.[135] Stressing the sensitive nature of testing information, the Court found no evidence that the employer had fabricated concern for employee confidentiality only to frustrate the union in the discharge of its responsibilities.

In another "confidentiality" decision, the Board held that an employer was not obligated to furnish the union with the names of undercover operatives employed during an investigation of an alleged theft, whose reports were relied on by the employer in its decision to discharge employees. Although the case did not involve employee-witnesses, the incident in question did involve allegations of crimes believed to have been carried out by a gang of 10 employees with suspected connections with organized crime. Thus, a real possibility of intimidation and harassment of the undercover operatives was found to require a dismissal of a Section 8(a)(5) complaint.[136]

SUMMARY—The employer's duty to supply information to the union can arise with respect to either (1) the negotiation of a mandatory subject of bargaining or (2) the processing of a grievance under a collective bargaining agreement. In both cases it is clear that the Board and the courts have, with few exceptions, required disclosure, although not always in the form requested by the union. Using Taft-Hartley as a means of discovery when processing grievances does, however, have the disadvantage of being a relatively expensive and time-consuming process.

As an alternative, the advocate may request the arbitrator to issue a subpoena pursuant to state law or the federal arbitration statute. Whether the federal arbitration act applies to collective bargaining agreements is still a question that lacks a definitive answer at the federal level; nevertheless, some courts have cited the statute in upholding the arbitrator's authority to issue a subpoena.

Even if the arbitrator has no enforceable power to issue a subpoena under state or federal law, once relevant information is requested, an arbitrator can be expected to give such weight as he deems appropriate to the failure of a party to produce such evidence. In this respect Professor Fleming has proposed the following guidelines which should be useful to the advocate when dealing with problems of access to information.

In the absence of any showing of prejudice, relevant information in the hands of one party should be made available to the other party in an arbitration proceeding at the request of the arbitrator.

In the event the party to whom such a request is made refuses to honor it, and in the absence of a subpoena power in the hands of the arbitrator, an inference may be drawn against the party refusing to produce the evidence.

. . .

The arbitrator should, on request of a party, excise irrelevant portions of a document after privately inspecting it.[137]

Finally, as a caution to the public sector advocate, it is not uncommon that a state may preclude a party from disclosing certain information without first obtaining consent from the employee involved.[138] Moreover, at the federal level, the Fourth Circuit has affirmed a lower court decision holding that the Privacy Act of 1974[139] operates as a valid defense to a union's request, pursuant to a collective bargaining agreement, of employee personnel data.[140] Accordingly, the public sector practitioner is cautioned that a state or federal statute may operate as a bar to a legitimate claim to relevant information.

9

Evidence and the Credibility of Testimony

Introduction

Perhaps the best characterization of problems of evidence and credibility issues has been stated by the West Coast Area Tripartite Committee: "There is only one reliable guide to credibility, and that is there are no reliable guides to credibility."[1] The committee, nevertheless, lists a number of factors that the advocate should be cognizant of in assessing the credibility of witnesses:

1. His demeanor while testifying and the manner in which he testifies;
2. The character of his testimony;
3. The extent of his capacity to perceive, to recollect, or to communicate any matter about which he testifies;
4. The extent of his opportunity to perceive any matter about which he testifies;
5. His character for honesty or veracity or their opposites;
6. The existence or nonexistence of a bias, interest, or other motive;
7. A statement previously made by him that is consistent with his statement at the hearing;
8. A statement made by him that is inconsistent with any part of his testimony at the hearing;
9. The existence or nonexistence of any fact testified to by him;
10. His attitude toward the action in which he testifies or toward the giving of the testimony;
11. His admission of untruthfulness.[2]

Demeanor

The demeanor of a witness is generally considered the manner in which a person testifies.[3] Important considerations include his appearance, gestures, voice, and attitude. All have been documented by the arbitral community in resolving disputed facts:

> [G]rievant . . . took the instinctive protective reaction of denying everything. In addition, his testimony was highly evasive when required to account for his actions.[4]

> Grievant['s] demeanor was not that of a man intent on giving a truthful account of the events here involved. Some of his statements were highly improbable, and some were inconsistent to a degree which went far beyond the normal variation which often appears in repeated accounts of events as given by a credible witness.[5]

Not all arbitrators, however, are convinced that the attitude and demeanor of a witness is a reliable criterion in resolving credibility issues. Arbitrator Jaffee is on record as treating a witness's demeanor as suspect:

> I have long been of the opinion that the "attitude and demeanor" of witnesses is almost always a shaky foundation on which to rest conclusions. I have seen witnesses whose nervousness or other "physical manifestations" while testifying (or listening to testimony) seemed more conducive to lying, and others who spoke "forthrightly" and made "eyeball" contact with their opponents, and yet the former told the truth while the latter did not. I may note in passing that I have difficulty in understanding that the fact that [L] sat "cross-armed and cross-legged" indicates anything either way on this aspect.[6]

Similarly, Arbitrator Mittenthal has declared that very few conclusions can be drawn from witness-stand behavior:

> I must confess I can rarely determine anything from a witness's demeanor. Is he perspiring heavily because of general nervousness or because of discomfort with the statements he is making? Is his facial tic, a twitching lip, or a flaring nostril a personal characteristic or a symptom of disbelief in his own words? There is no way the arbitrator can answer this type of question with any confidence. I have seen men with beatific expressions invoke God and tell a forceful and sensible story which later turns out to be a string of lies. I have seen confused men stumble through their testimony without a shred of confidence and tell a doubtful story which later turns out to be gospel truth. For me, a sterling appearance and directness are no more proof of truth than a motley look and meekness are proof of falsity.[7]

Although consideration of witness demeanor is a subjective inquiry that is also laced with procedural difficulties,[8] it can be expected that an arbitrator will apply this criterion when confronted with conflicting testimony. Moreover, a reviewing court can be expected to defer to the arbitrator when challenges are made in this regard. Thus, in *Sharpe v. Carolina Freight*,[9] a federal court upheld the arbitrator against a challenge that in his award he improperly considered the grievant's personal attitude and behavior at the hearing.

Character of Testimony

Testimony that is specific and detailed is likely to carry more weight than testimony that is evasive and conclusionary.[10] As noted by one arbitrator,

> His identification of her as the person who punched him on the side four times was forthright and unequivocal. His testimony had, as the saying goes, a ring of truth to it. It tipped the scales of credibility in his favor.[11]

Perception, Memory, and Communication

> The common law system of proof is exacting in its insistence upon the most reliable sources of information. . . . One of the earliest and most pervasive manifestations of this attitude is the rule requiring that a witness who testifies to a fact which can be perceived by the senses must have had an opportunity to observe, and must have actually observed the fact.[11a]

1. *Perception.* A demonstration that a witness was not in position to observe an event because of certain sensory deficiencies (poor eyesight, hearing, position, etc.) will have the effect of impeaching the testimony concerning that event. In addition, frequently an initial observation is faulty because the observer has no prior knowledge that a dispute will develop concerning what he has seen or heard and his casual sensory impression is not sharp or keen.[12] An advocate may be expected to develop such factors on cross-examination of the witness, or through extrinsic evidence (i.e., through the testimony of other witnesses).

2. *Memory.* Arbitrators have recognized that precise details may elude a witness over an extended period of time and thus a witness may be confused as to facts which initially he correctly perceived.[13] As such, a witness may be attacked by

showing that his memory is now sufficiently clouded so that any account of the facts at issue is, at best, speculative. As an alternative, a witness's credibility may be attacked by demonstrating that he lacks the capacity to recollect a matter about which he testified. For example, if a witness cannot recollect important facts surrounding an incident, it is not unreasonable to assume that his capacity to remember a related event is suspect.

3. *Communication.* As noted by one arbitrator,

> The manner in which a witness expresses what he saw and heard may fail to communicate exactly his initial perception of the occurrence, so that after listening to the testimony and the cross-examination of the witnesses, the factfinder may not have had transmitted to him a completely accurate impression of the facts, even though they were initially observed carefully and well remembered by the witness.[14]

Accordingly, a witness who fails to communicate clearly may appear confused, thus diminishing his credibility before the arbitrator.

Character for Honesty and Veracity

Among the factors considered by arbitrators in resolving credibility issues is the witness's character for honesty and veracity. If a witness has a reputation for honesty, his testimony can be expected to be more credible than a witness who has a reputation for dishonesty and lying. Indeed, arbitrators have cited specific instances of the conduct of a witness for the purpose of attacking or supporting credibility.[15] Thus, Arbitrator Duff, in *International Nickel Co.*,[16] concluded that the grievant's veracity was not reliable where it was shown that on his original employment application the grievant falsified the nature of his discharge from the Navy. Likewise, Arbitrator Ogilvie, in *Lockheed Propulsion Co.*,[17] considered the grievant's falsification of an application not as a reason for a discharge, but as a basis for ascertaining credibility. Noting this fact, the arbitrator concluded that greater weight must be given to the testimony of other witnesses.

In sustaining a discharge, Arbitrator Miller, in *Cadillac Gage Co.*,[18] focused on the grievant's overall attitude toward his employer in assessing his general character. Specific instances of conduct cited include: refusing to accept authority;

insubordination; profane language toward management; and a generally belligerent and hostile attitude.

Bias, Interest, or Motive

Arbitrators have frequently cited the existence or nonexistence of bias, interest, or other motive in resolving issues of credibility:

> In the instant case, all parties concede that the [S's] are hostile to the grievant. It is admitted that there is trouble between [J] and [S] and the grievant and his wife. [S] has been convicted of murder and is incarcerated. There is evidence tending to show that the probable motive of the [S's] in coming forward to reveal this alleged crime of the grievant arose out of the action of the County Welfare Department to take [J's] son into custody, and that [S] and [J] believed that the grievant and his wife were responsible for having their son taken away.[19]

> Here, most of the testimony was produced by witnesses who are members of the bargaining unit and the same Union. A clear division existed between those who favored the grievant and those who were "against" him. Few witnesses will deliberately falsify but there is a common tendency to "put your best foot forward." This tendency, either consciously or subconsciously, leads many witnesses to remember and express testimony in a way favorable to the result which they hope the Hearing will produce.[20]

Merely because a witness lacks an interest in the outcome does not imply that he is telling the truth. Moreover, having an interest or stake in the outcome does not disqualify a witness; rather, the arbitrator can be expected to subject that testimony to a greater degree of scrutiny than would otherwise be the case if the witness had no interest or bias.[21]

Where an employer's witness and the grievant give testimony which is in conflict, absent a showing of personal bias by management's witness, the grievant's testimony is often considered to be less credible since, it is argued, he has a personal interest in the outcome.

> Obviously the grievant and his wife have a strong and direct interest in denying the charge against him. The testimony of two company officials must be accorded significantly more weight than the opposing testimony unless the credibility of the officials can be successfully attacked.[22]

> In addition, the Grievant was the only witness who had any substantial stake in the outcome of the proceedings.[23]

The foreman appears to be a strict supervisor, but the union did not produce any evidence to indicate that he was unfair in his general dealings with employees or prone to carry on a vendetta against any individual. No reason was shown why the foreman in this case would testify untruthfully or have any animus against the grievant.[24]

Finally, the Arbitrator takes note that other arbitrators have consistently recognized in arbitrations involving disciplinary action that, in resolving credibility resolutions between an employee accused of employment misconduct and the employee's accusers, weight may be given to the fact that the accused employee has an incentive for denying the charges against her, in that she stands immediately to lose or gain in the case. . . . This recognition is especially cogent when the accusers have nothing to gain by their adverse testimony or when there is no demonstration of ill will toward the accused.[24a]

While this reasoning is not invalid, some arbitrators have held that no hard and fast rule should control. As noted by Arbitrator Mittenthal:

First, the employee who denies wrongdoing has a clear interest in avoiding punishment. This interest, by itself, is no basis for discrediting his testimony. But it does serve to weaken his credibility just as the foreman's lack of interest serves to strengthen his credibility. Only if the foreman's credibility is substantially greater than the employee's should management win. Interest alone may tilt the scales in some cases but not in others.[25]

Consistency or Inconsistency

Other considerations being equal, a consistent story will strengthen the credibility of a witness; an inconsistent story will weaken credibility.

I cannot in good conscience accept the testimony of the two Union witnesses. I say this not from any technical definition of credibility—but from attending the hearing and seeing the witnesses, their conduct, their demeanor and their conflicting testimony.[26]

[D]espite the frequent repetition of his testimony in the course of direct examination, cross-examination, re-direct examination, recross-examination, and yet more examination, abrupt and frequent interruptions by both Counsel, etc.—[the witness's] testimony remained remarkably consistent and coherent. His testimony . . . was specific and detailed and was factual rather than merely conclusionary.[27]

[The grievant] gave evasive testimony concerning several matters about which he was examined. He first denied certain minor law violations, but on cross-examination he was finally forced to admit them.[28]

Merely because a witness's testimony is not contradicted during cross-examination, however, does not render that witness credible. One must take into consideration other factors, such as the education of the grievant,[29] the nature of the contradiction, and the inherent probability of the facts asserted[30] in assessing the credibility of a witness's testimony.

The Existence or Nonexistence of any Fact Testified to by the Witness (Specific Contradiction)

The existence of some fact different from that reported by a witness will have the effect of diminishing the witness's credibility. Facts incompatible or in conflict with a fact reported by an opponent's witness can be established through the testimony of other witnesses or through the introduction of exhibits. In either case the goal of the impeaching party will be to establish some fact different from that reported by the witness being impeached.[30a]

Admission of Untruthfulness or Dishonesty

A witness's admission of untruthfulness or dishonesty will be damaging to his credibility, and an arbitrator can be expected to resolve any conflicts in testimony against such a witness.

> The grievant who had admitted effecting the falsification, now denies it. He would have the arbitrator believe that his Committeeman performed the surgery which changed the card. This brings the issue on that point to one of credibility. The grievant caught in the web of his changing stories, is a self-convicted liar.[31]

Conclusion

It is useful to distinguish evidence offered for impeachment purposes from the principal evidence offered in any given case. This distinction centers on whether the evidence is offered to lessen the personal credibility of a witness. The advocate who desires to support or impeach the credibility of a witness has two primary means at his disposal. The witness may be cross-examined for the purpose of uncovering any sensory or character deficiencies that would bias his testimony. This mode may often reveal that the witness made a prior statement that is inconsistent with his present testimony. In addition, "extrinsic" evidence (exhibits or testimony of other witnesses) may be introduced to attack or support a witness's testimony.

Because the arbitration mechanism is often viewed as an adversary process, the parties are allowed great latitude in the examination and cross-examination of witnesses when an issue of credibility is presented.[32] The factors that are noted above are general guides that the arbitral community has cited when resolving conflicts in testimony. In the last analysis, however, the ultimate decision may often rest on a common-sense "gut" reaction by the arbitrator. As such, an arbitrator who cites a specific criterion in resolving a credibility issue may merely be attempting to rationalize a decision based upon considerations unknown to the parties.[33]

10

New Evidence and the Arbitral Process

Introduction

A problem frequently encountered by arbitrators concerns evidence offered for the first time at the arbitration hearing. Common situations include cases where (1) the nature of the grievance or the charge against the employee is changed at the arbitration hearing; (2) evidence is available but nevertheless is not disclosed during the early stages of the grievance procedure; (3) new evidence is discovered after commencement of the grievance process and introduced for the first time at arbitration; (4) evidence is submitted after the close of the hearing; and (5) new evidence is discovered after the arbitrator has issued the award.

In general, an arbitrator's decision to accept or reject new evidence involves balancing the need to ascertain all facts relevant to the case with the overall policy concerns of conducting a fair hearing.

Changing the Nature of the Grievance

The Supreme Court, in *NLRB* v. *Acme Industrial Co.*,[1] stated that "arbitration can function properly only if the grievance procedures leading to it can sift out unmeritorious claims."[2] This machinery generally consists of a series of steps which must be followed prior to arbitration. Failure to submit a claim through the early stages of grievance machinery prior to arbitration denies the parties the opportunity to negotiate a resolution of their complaint. Accordingly, arbitrators will generally refuse to consider a claim which has not been alleged in the lower steps of the grievance procedure, although there are recognized exceptions, such as when exhaustion would be futile, or where compliance has been implicity or explicitly waived.[3] Thus Professor Fleming has noted:

> Since surprise is by hypothesis something new at least to one of the parties to the bargaining relationship, many arbitrators felt that it is a mistake to proceed with arbitration until it is clear that the parties cannot resolve the matter through negotiation. They [argue] that to proceed would undermine the collective bargaining process. ... There was a feeling that within the framework of a permanent umpireship the normal procedure is to refer the issue back to the parties for consideration of the new charge, or the new evidence.[4]

Consistent with this policy, arbitrators generally hold that an employer may not present evidence of alleged offenses which were not specified as reasons for the discharge when notice was given.[5] For example, in *Sealtest Dairy Products*,[6] Arbitrator Morvant ruled that once a grievant has been informed of the reasons for the disciplinary action, the employer is irrevocably committed to that reason. In the cited case the employer had initially notified the grievant that he was discharged because of insubordination. At the hearing the employer, apparently for the first time, argued that the grievant had a poor employment record, and this fact, coupled with his short tenure of employment, did not qualify him for consideration as to a lighter penalty. Stressing the function of the grievance procedure and the nature of the "surprise" evidence, the arbitrator declared:

> Once the Company is committed to specific charges initially made, any deviation therefrom at the arbitration hearing is generally considered irrelevant. For an arbiter to permit at the hearing significant changes in position over the initial dispute, he runs the risk of circumventing the grievance procedure, in that advance knowledge could have produced effective rebuttal resulting in a compromise or settlement between the parties rather than arbitration.
>
> ...
>
> ... [A]ny attempt to introduce a "new charge" for consideration at the hearing must be ruled against; because any serious change during the arbitration hearing in the charge initially made in discharge action tends to surprise the other party, and places them at a disadvantage in that they were deprived of discussing the charge in the grievance procedure, and that they cannot effectively rebut that which they did not anticipate. Con-

sequently, any allegations by the Company of a poor past conduct record of the grievant must be ruled a "new charge" and
irrelevant as to the reason for his discharge which was insubordination.[7]

However, in *Lyon, Inc.*[8] Arbitrator Gabriel Alexander admitted evidence that an employee had falsified his employment application as an additional ground supporting his discharge. The arbitrator noted that although this evidence was
discovered subsequent to the notice of discharge, the employer notified the union of its intention to rely on this fact as soon
as it was discovered.

**Evidence Available but Not Disclosed During the Grievance
Procedure**

It is generally agreed that development of sound labor-
management relations mandates full disclosure of all relevant
facts during the grievance procedure.[9] Thus, it has been stated:

> Arbitration is merely a method for determining a pre-exist-
> ing dispute which the parties have been unable to settle in the
> prior steps of the grievance machinery. The arbitration hearing
> is not the place for the presentation of new claims, although the
> more thorough investigation which precedes arbitration often
> results in the discovery of evidence not theretofore known and
> of arguments not theretofore conceived. The essential facts sup-
> porting the claim of the Union should be revealed in the earlier
> steps of the grievance machinery if such facts are known to the
> Union. In the absence of such revelation, the entire purpose of
> the grievance machinery remains unfulfilled, and the possi-
> bilities of settlement are lost. The same, of course, is true with
> regard to the Company's claim and existing evidence in its fa-
> vor. If such evidence is not made known by one side to the other
> it may not be accepted for the first time in arbitration. This is
> particularly so where the evidence which has been withheld is
> the principal evidence in support of the Union's case.[10]

Likewise, in *Loma Corp.*,[11] Arbitrator Sisk refused to credit "surprise" evidence produced by the grievant at the hearing.
The arbitrator declared:

> There is general agreement concerning the admission of "sur-
> prise evidence." Obviously if evidence is not available during
> the grievance procedure or comes into possession of either par-
> ty only after the grievance procedure it should be admitted if it
> sheds light on the issue before the arbitrator. However, if the
> evidence is available at the time of the grievance procedure and
> if it is deliberately withheld or suppressed by either party dur-

ing the grievance procedure then it should not be submitted to the arbitration procedure.[12]

In those cases where a party has been permitted to present evidence at the hearing that was available but nevertheless not disclosed in the lower steps of the grievance procedure, arbitrators have concluded that the evidence is not "new," but merely a more detailed presentation of an earlier position. Alternatively, arbitrators have cited that no undue hardship would result if the evidence was credited. For example, in *Zinsco Electrical Products,*[13] the employer argued that testimony of a union witness should be excluded because it had been withheld in violation of a contractual provision stating that "all parties agree not to withhold any of the facts pertaining to the grievance in order to try and reach a settlement." Crediting the testimony, Arbitrator Caraway in part based his decision on the fact that the agreement did not penalize either party for withholding facts pertaining to the grievance. While the arbitrator recognized that the exchange of facts should be freely made by both parties in the interest of settling grievances, no contractual authority was found to exclude from the hearing any withheld facts, witnesses, or documents.

Likewise, in *Southern Iron & Equipment Co.,*[14] the union objected to the introduction of the grievant's prior inconsistent statements involving a fight with a supervisor on the theory that such statements were not referred to in the grievance procedure prior to the arbitration. In ruling against the union, Arbitrator Rutherford reasoned:

> Arbitration authorities generally agree that it is advisable to present as much evidence as possible prior to the arbitration hearing; however, it does not follow that evidence must be rejected by the Arbitrator simply because it has not been previously revealed in the grievance procedure. If such new evidence is a "surprise" to the other party, the Arbitrator might possibly exclude it or grant a continuance to allow the surprised party to examine the evidence and prepare a reply. In this case there can be no claim of "surprise" such as to justify even a continuance. The grievant himself is the person who allegedly made the remark.[15]

Arbitrator Bernard Marcus, in *Inland Steel Container Co.,*[16] summarized the policy for not requiring the revelation of all evidence prior to arbitration:

> The union's position, that evidence not disclosed during grievance meetings may not be introduced in the arbitration hearing, is insupportable. In fact, were the union's contention to be sustained, the whole purpose of arbitration would be defeated, and

formalism substituted thereunder. It was a desire to escape formalism which was largely responsible for the now almost universal acceptance of arbitration as the best solution to labor contract disputes.[17]

Similarly, in *Hospital Service Plan of New Jersey*,[17a] Arbitrator David Kaplan ruled that a theory or defense not asserted in the lower stages of the grievance procedure could be argued for the first time at an arbitration hearing:

> Arbitrators have long recognized that during the grievance steps the parties do not prepare for such meetings as exhaustively and as completely as they do when they are preparing a case for arbitration. However, arbitrators are often harsh with parties who engage, what has been commonly referred to as "ace in the hole" type of presentation of evidence. Where a party deliberately and intentionally holds evidence until the arbitration, arbitrators had admitted such evidence but on condition that the "surprised" party be given a reasonable adjournment in order to be afforded the opportunity to rebut such "surprise" material. In addition, arbitrators are inclined to grant adjournments for good cause in the interest of getting all of the facts and allowing each party to bring to the arbitrator's attention all rebuttal evidence. Under such a procedure, the arbitrator is completely informed of all the issues that the parties may wish to bring to his attention and [the parties] are permitted to support their allegations with whatever evidence is in their possession. . . . I do not favor procedural rigidity or technicalities in arbitration, unless there is a specific requirement in a contract such as time limitations.[17b]

However, in *Foster Wheeler Corp*,[17c] Arbitrator Shister held that where an employer did not raise the issue of arbitrability in the lower grievance steps, it may not raise the issue for the first time at the hearing.[17d]

New Evidence Discovered After Commencement of the Grievance Procedure

The analysis in the above section should be distinguished from a situation where evidence comes to light after the grievance has been processed but before the hearing. In this case the evidence may be admitted even if the evidence was available earlier, subject to protecting the other party from surprise.[18] Thus the arbitrator, at the request of the surprised party, may grant an adjournment to consider the new evidence. As stated by the New York Tripartite Committee:

> In some situations . . . it is the practice of the parties not to present all the evidence during the grievance procedure. In other situations the parties may recognize from the outset that a

particular grievance must be arbitrated and pass quickly through the steps of the grievance procedure. In cases like these, evidence not disclosed prior to the hearing should be admitted. The arbitrator, however, should grant adjournments or take other measures to insure a fair hearing and to protect a party taken by surprise as to evidence concerning a material issue.[19]

In *Pittsburgh Steel Co.*,[20] Arbitrator Valtin received the new material into evidence and accorded the surprised party an election to have the case suspended or to proceed with the hearing.

Finally, as summarized by Elkouri & Elkouri:

[W]hatever element of unfairness may be involved in the use of new evidence, it is largely mitigated or eliminated by the fact that arbitrators who accept newly submitted evidence will take any reasonable steps necessary to insure the opposite party adequate opportunity to respond thereto, regardless of whether the evidence has been withheld in good or bad faith.[21]

Evidence Submitted After the Close of the Hearing

Reopening the Record Based on New Evidence

In a case where a hearing has been held in which all the parties have participated, arbitrators generally consider the matter offically closed for the taking of evidence. As cited by Arbitrator Gentile in *Food Employers Council*,[22] when evaluating requests for reopening the record, the arbitrator must balance the reasons for the request so as neither to abuse his discretionary authority nor to deprive one of the parties of a right to a full and complete hearing. Finding that the evidence sought to be introduced addressed only credibility issues and that this evidence was available prior to the hearing, the arbitrator denied the union's request to reopen the record.

In *Borden Co.*,[23] Arbitrator Morvant elaborated on this principle:

Generally new evidence submitted by one of the parties after the hearing has been closed should be ignored, or stricken from the record, because the other party is unable to refute it, or have his day in court. Still, even in courts of law, new trials are ordered when it is discovered that new evidence has been uncovered which has a bearing on the case and which might result in a different result or decision. This same privilege exists for arbitration cases as well. Perhaps even more leniency should be shown in arbitration cases than in courts of law, because the parties are not always vested in the law nor are they always astute in case preparation. To close the door of justice on such individuals would not serve the purpose for which the arbitration procedure was established and intended. Consequently, allowances should be made which would protect the less astute and permit him to present his case to the best of his ability and leave him with the feeling that he has had his full day in court.[24]

In *Madison Institute,*[25] Arbitrator Levy upheld the union's request for a reopening of the hearing where it was demonstrated that the evidence was unavailable and went to the critical issue in the case (seniority). In crediting the evidence the arbitrator declared:

> [W]here certain evidence is evidentiary and of material import and the admission thereof will probably affect the outcome of a cause, is unavailable at the time of the hearing, and if the same is produced subsequently without seriously affecting any substantial right, and it is shown that reasonable grounds existed for its non-production at the time of the hearing, the arbitrator may, in his discretion, reopen the arbitration for the introduction of such evidence only. The reason for this rule is to afford to each of the parties full opportunity to present such material evidence as will assist the arbitrator in ascertaining the truth of all matters in controversy.[26]

Similarly, Arbitrator Marshall, in *Gateway Products Corp.,*[27] recognized that the arbitral mechanism is a different forum from a court proceeding, and thus the considerations for reopening the record in order to receive additional evidence are different. In granting a motion for a rehearing, the arbitrator stated:

> While it is true that in an ordinary case at law it is exceedingly dubious as to whether the Company would be granted a motion to reopen the trial of a law suit on the basis of newly discovered evidence within the framework of the fact situation here involved, the arbitrator nevertheless rules that the affidavit together with the accompanying documentary evidence are admissible and allows them as part of the record in this proceedings. The Arbitrator is not bound by technical rules of evidence and the sole object of an arbitration proceeding is to secure a fair and equitable resolution of the differences which arise in the administration of the collective bargaining agreement. While rules of evidence are suggestive of what constitutes a fair hearing and a fair appraisal of the evidence, to follow them slavishly could only result in a distortion of the collective bargaining relationship.[28]

Submission of Evidence in Briefs

Arbitrators uniformly agree that an *ex parte* submission of evidence after the close of the hearing will not be credited. In addition, it is an accepted principle in labor arbitration that while parties have the right to file posthearing briefs, the contents therein should be limited to argument and should refer only to testimony and evidence adduced at the hearing itself.[29] A classic case is the decision of Arbitrator Dworkin in *Ohio Steel Foundry*.[30] When the union filed its brief it attached a supplementary statement alleging that during the interim between the close of the hearing and the filing of the brief, the employer had allegedly communicated with the discharged grievant's new employer, resulting in the discharge of the grievant from his new job. In disregarding the evidence, the arbitrator reasoned:

> The union has acknowledged its awareness that a post-hearing brief should be confined to the evidence introduced at the hearing. . . . It is essential that the arbitrator hear testimony from the witnesses themselves, whenever possible. The opposing side is entitled to the opportunity of cross-examining the witnesses and to submit responsive evidence. Arbitrators consistently adhere to the principle that no new evidence may be offered or considered after the close of the hearing. It is therefore improper to inject evidentiary matter in a post-hearing brief. Where such evidence appears in the brief, inadvertently or otherwise, the arbitrator is required to disregard such, and this must necessarily be the course which the arbitrator will follow in the instant case.[31]

Likewise, in *Royal Industries*,[32] Arbitrator Davey refused to consider posthearing citations of two arbitration opinions not previously disclosed to the union. Arbitrator Mulhall, in *H. H. Meyer Packing Co.*,[33] credited a motion to strike specific pages of manufacturers' catalogs intended to cite literature touching on the issues presented in the arbitration. The arbitrator rejected the employer's argument that the citations from its journals are no different from those in law review articles, or other popular magazines such as *Time* or *The New York Times*. The arbitrator further declared:

> [S]hould the Company have been "surprised" by new evidence or a new argument that objection should have been made to at the hearing and not in a post-hearing brief.[34]

In *North American Aviation, Inc.*,[35] the union made a motion (apparently at the close of the hearing) that the arbitrator not consider any of the facts presented by the employer in its reply brief if those facts were not advanced by the company during the processing of the grievance procedure. Examining the collective bargaining agreement, Arbitrator Komaroff determined that it was the intention of the parties that they present their respective positions to the other party as completely as possible. The arbitrator nevertheless found that, although this was the intention of the parties, it had not been their practice to advance every argument and set forth every fact on the grievance forms. In ruling on the union's motion, the arbitrator stated:

> Many collective bargaining agreements specifically state that no facts may be presented in arbitration which were not first presented in the grievance procedure. This is not true of the collective bargaining agreement between the parties in this case. . . . [T]he contract does not prevent the parties from elaborating upon their basic positions by the introduction of facts and arguments which may not have been introduced during the grievance procedure. . . . This interpretation of the agreement is further supported by the numerous briefs submitted by both parties in arbitration cases. Such briefs have consistently presented facts and advanced arguments which were not set forth in the appeal or disposition of the grievance.[36]

Evidence and Postaward Considerations

Under the rules of the American Arbitration Association,[37] an arbitrator has the power to reopen a hearing on his own motion or at the request of either party *before* the award is made. However, if the reopening of the hearing would prevent the making of the award within the specific time agreed upon by the parties, the matter may not be reopened unless both parties agree upon the extension of the time limit.

It is clear that once the award is made the jurisdiction of the arbitrator is at an end and no power exists for reopening the hearing based on new evidence. The only option available would be a suit to set aside the award because of gross error or mistake,[38] or an independent action to enforce the terms of the agreement.[39] This alternative, however, may prove to be of little value in light of the policy adopted by the courts of refusing to review the merits of an arbitrator's award.[40] For example, in *Hines v. Anchor Motor Freight, Inc.*,[41] the Supreme Court held that, absent a showing of breach of fair representation by the union, individuals were not entitled to relitigate a discharge merely because they offered newly discovered evidence that the charges against them were false and that in fact they were discharged without cause. The grievance procedure, noted the Court, cannot be expected to be error free and the finality provision of arbitration has sufficient force to surmount occasional instances of mistake.

In *Pressmen, Local 28* v. *Newspaper Agency Corp.*,[41a] a federal district court considered the validity of an amended award based on evidence submitted to the arbitrator after a first award had issued. In his first award, the arbitrator ruled that the employer could unilaterally discontinue overtime payments to night shift employees who were required to report to work early, and that the arbitrator had no power to change management's decision. Subsequently, counsel for the union moved the arbitrator to reconsider and reverse his decision because his findings were "significantly in error with regard to material facts" (the arbitrator had incorrectly held that a "zone" shift began at 4:00 p.m. and ended at 11:30 p.m.; the shift actually began at 6:00 p.m. and ended at 1:45 a.m.). The arbitrator agreed to reconsider his original decision and requested the parties to submit evidence regarding hours worked. While the employer did not agree that the arbitrator still had jurisdiction to consider the matter, it nevertheless made available the information requested.

As a result of the new information, the arbitrator issued a second award, which reversed his earlier decision. In that award he stated that he did not consider the additional information as new evidence but a clarification of the actual work and pay practice central to the issue before the arbitrator.[41b] When the employer refused to abide by the second decision, the union filed an action for enforcement. In granting summary judgment for the employer, the federal district court declared that when the arbitrator renders his final award, his power under the agreement is exhausted. A review of the transcript indicates that all parties had ample opportunity to present all evidence they deemed relevant. The court reasoned that the fact that the arbitrator's findings were in error, standing alone, cannot constitute sufficient grounds for reconsideration and a subsequent decision and, thus, the second award was void.[41c]

SUMMARY—It is a general principle that new evidence or argument will not be admitted at the arbitration proceeding unless some special reason exists for not disclosing it prior to the hearing. As noted by Arbitrator Willard Wirtz:

> There are obvious interests, from the standpoint of the parties' continuing relationship, in keeping [evidence that has been withheld] out. It is important to the efficient functioning of the grievance procedure that the company and the union representatives do their job below. ... The grievance procedure will work better, furthermore, if any practice of saving the best ammunition for the hearing before the arbitrator is discouraged.[42]

The advocate who discovers material evidence that was previously unavailable is advised to disclose it prior to the hearing. While it is neither practicable nor common to disclose every minute detail and argument that will ultimately be made at the hearing, any "surprise" evidence that goes to the essence of the case is subject to exclusion by an arbitrator.

It is especially noteworthy that the courts have accorded great deference to arbitrators when deciding what evidence to credit and specifically whether to credit evidence not presented at the lower stages of the grievance procedure. For example, in *Instrument Workers* v. *Minneapolis-Honeywell Regulator Co.*,[43] a federal court refused to set aside an award sustaining the discharge of an employee that was in part based on evidence not disclosed at the lower steps of the grievance procedure. The court ruled that an arbitrator does have power to base his award on such evidence and that a rule to the contrary would "convert an arbitrator's hearing into a technical and very restricted review and would be contrary to the spirit and purpose of arbitration."

Moreover, in *City of Manitowoc* v. *Police Department*,[44] a decision involving a public sector interest dispute, the Wisconsin Supreme Court refused to vacate an arbitrator's award where the arbitrator refused to consider new evidence submitted by the city as part of its posthearing brief. Even though the Wisconsin statute provided that the arbitrator shall give weight to changes in circumstances during the pendency of arbitration, the court stressed that the evidence was submitted in an "ex parte" fashion without notice to the union and without affording the union the opportunity for cross-examination.

Likewise, in *Shopping Cart, Inc.* v. *Food Employees*,[45] an arbitrator refused to hear additional evidence of a handwriting expert after the hearing had been closed but before the award was issued. In refusing to vacate the award, the court held that the refusal to hear testimony did not deny the employer a fair hearing. Although the court did not hold that an arbitrator may always decline to hear testimony offered after the close of the hearing,[46] the court sustained the arbitrator where the employer had a full opportunity to present evidence at the hearing, it knew or should have known that testimony of this type would be relevant, and it sought no continuance of the hearing for the purpose of producing such testimony.

Again, arbitrators have great discretion in determining what evidence to credit. Evidence deliberately withheld at the lower stages of the grievance procedure is the most suspect. Evidence that is in fact newly discovered will have a greater chance of being credited if it was disclosed within a reasonable time after its discovery. Once the hearing is closed, however, arbitrators are reluctant to reopen the record based on claims of newly discovered evidence, although some arbitrators have recognized that leniency should be shown in the arbitral forum (as opposed to a court of law) where the parties are generally less conversant with adversary proceedings and there is no indication of bad faith.[47]

11

Conclusion

I think there are a lot of things that a typical lawyer has to un-
learn before he becomes an arbitrator. I would like to outline
two or three of those things: In the first place, I don't think he
has much use for his training as to rules of evidence. We don't
have any rules of evidence in arbitration, by and large, and I
think it is a good thing.[1]

When legal principles are invoked in arbitration proceedings it is well not to brush them aside impatiently but to
recall that behind them lies the weight of thought tested by experience. . . . If the policy is unimportant, the legal rule may
safely be disregarded.[2]

It is generally recognized that the rules of evidence had
their origin in the perceived duty of courts to shield unso-
phisticated laymen jurors from irrelevant and prejudicial testimony or exhibits offered at trial. As it exists today, the arbitration process is a democratic, simple, expeditious method of
settling industrial disputes. With good reason the technical
and procedural restrictions characteristic of the judicial system are absent in the arbitral forum. As such, a working knowledge and application of the rules of evidence in an arbitral
setting is important only to the extent that the search for truth
is facilitated. The arbitrator, who functions as a judge sitting
without a jury, should acquire a knowledge of the rules of evidence and particularly the reasons behind the rules, not as an
end in itself, but rather as a means of ascertaining the truth
consistent with the mandates of conducting a due process
hearing. Given this focus, evidentiary objections of advocates,
as noted by the West Coast Tripartite Committee, would then
appear helpful, not as demands for exclusion, but as mere re-
minders to the arbitrator of possible unreliability of proffered
testimony or exhibits.

121

Appendix A

Voluntary Labor Arbitration Rules of the American Arbitration Association*

1. *Agreement of Parties*—The parties shall be deemed to have made these Rules a part of their arbitration agreement whenever, in a collective bargaining agreement or Submission, they have provided for arbitration by the American Arbitration Association (hereinafter AAA) or under its Rules. These Rules shall apply in the form obtaining at the time the arbitration is initiated.

2. *Name of Tribunal*—Any Tribunal constituted by the parties under these Rules shall be called the Voluntary Labor Arbitration Tribunal.

3. *Administrator*—When parties agree to arbitrate under these Rules and an arbitration is instituted thereunder, they thereby authorize the AAA to administer the arbitration. The authority and obligations of the Administrator are as provided in the agreement of the parties and in these Rules.

4. *Delegation of Duties*—The duties of the AAA may be carried out through such representatives or committees as the AAA may direct.

5. *National Panel of Labor Arbitrators*—The AAA shall establish and maintain a National Panel of Labor Arbitrators and shall appoint arbitrators therefrom, as hereinafter provided.

6. *Office of Tribunal*—The general office of the Labor Arbitration Tribunal is the headquarters of the AAA, which may, however, assign the administration of an arbitration to any of its Regional Offices.

7. *Initiation Under an Arbitration Clause in a Collective Bargaining Agreement*—Arbitration under an arbitration clause in a collective bargaining agreement may, under these Rules, be initiated by either party in the following manner:

---

*As amended and in effect January 1, 1979. Reprinted with the permission of the American Arbitration Association.

(a) By giving written notice to the other party of intention to arbitrate (Demand), which notice shall contain a statement setting forth the nature of the dispute and the remedy sought, and

(b) By filing at any Regional Office of the AAA three copies of said notice, together with a copy of the collective bargaining agreement, or such parts thereof as relate to the dispute, including the arbitration provisions. After the Arbitrator is appointed, no new or different claim may be submitted, except with the consent of the Arbitrator and all other parties.

8. *Answer*—The party upon whom the Demand for Arbitration is made may file an answering statement with the AAA within seven days after notice from the AAA, in which event he shall simultaneously send a copy of his answer to the other party. If no answer is filed within the stated time, it will be assumed that the claim is denied. Failure to file an answer shall not operate to delay the arbitration.

9. *Initiation Under a Submission*—Parties to any collective bargaining agreement may initiate an arbitration under these Rules by filing at any Regional Office of the AAA two copies of a written agreement to arbitrate under these Rules (Submission), signed by the parties and setting forth the nature of the dispute and the remedy sought.

10. *Fixing of Locale*—The parties may mutually agree upon the locale where the arbitration is to be held. If the locale is not designated in the collective bargaining agreement or Submission, and if there is a dispute as to the appropriate locale, the AAA shall have the power to determine the locale and its decision shall be binding.

11. *Qualifications of Arbitrator*—No person shall serve as a neutral Arbitrator in any arbitration in which that person has any financial or personal interest in the result of the arbitration, unless the parties, in writing, waive such disqualification.

12. *Appointment from Panel*—If the parties have not appointed an Arbitrator and have not provided any other method of appointment, the Arbitrator shall be appointed in the following manner: Immediately after the filing of the Demand or Submission, the AAA shall submit simultaneously to each party an identical list of names of persons chosen from the Labor Panel. Each party shall have seven days from the mailing date in which to cross off any names objected to, number the remaining names indicating the order of preference, and return the list to the AAA. If a party does not return the list within the time specified, all persons named therein shall be deemed acceptable. From among the persons who have been approved on both lists, and in accordance with the designated order of mutual

preference, the AAA shall invite the acceptance of an Arbitrator to serve. If the parties fail to agree upon any of the persons named or if those named decline or are unable to act, or if for any other reason the appointment cannot be made from the submitted lists, the Administrator shall have the power to make the appointment from other members of the Panel without the submission of any additional lists.

13. *Direct Appointment by Parties*—If the agreement of the parties names an Arbitrator or specifies a method of appointing an Arbitrator, that designation or method shall be followed. The notice of appointment, with the name and address of such Arbitrator, shall be filled with the AAA by the appointing party.

If the agreement specifies a period of time within which an Arbitrator shall be appointed, and any party fails to make such appointment within that period, the AAA may make the appointment.

If no period of time is specified in the agreement, the AAA shall notify the parties to make the appointment and if within seven days thereafter such Arbitrator has not been so appointed, the AAA shall make the appointment.

14. *Appointment of Neutral Arbitrator by Party-Appointed Arbitrators*—If the parties have appointed their Arbitrators, or if either or both of them have been appointed as provided in Section 13, and have authorized such Arbitrators to appoint a neutral Arbitrator within a specified time and no appointment is made within such time or any agreed extension thereof, the AAA may appoint a neutral Arbitrator, who shall act as Chairman.

If no period of time is specified for appointment of the neutral Arbitrator and the parties do not make the appointment within seven days from the date of the appointment of the last party-appointed Arbitrator, the AAA shall appoint such neutral Arbitrator, who shall act as Chairman.

If the parties have agreed that the Arbitrators shall appoint the neutral Arbitrator from the Panel, the AAA shall furnish to the party-appointed Arbitrators, in the manner prescribed in Section 12, a list selected from the Panel, and the appointment of the neutral Arbitrator shall be made as prescribed in such Section.

15. *Number of Arbitrators*—If the arbitration agreement does not specify the number of Arbitrators, the dispute shall be heard and determined by one Arbitrator, unless the parties otherwise agree.

16. *Notice to Arbitrator of Appointment*—Notice of the appointment of the neutral Arbitrator shall be mailed to the Arbitrator by the AAA and the signed acceptance of the Arbitrator shall be filed with the AAA prior to the opening of the first hearing.

17. *Disclosure by Arbitrator of Disqualification*—Prior to accepting appointment, the prospective neutral Arbitrator shall disclose any circumstances likely to create a presumption of bias or which he believes might disqualify him as an impartial Arbitrator. Upon receipt of such information, the AAA shall immediately disclose it to the parties. If either party declines to waive the presumptive disqualification, the vacancy thus created shall be filled in accordance with the applicable provisions of these Rules.

18. *Vacancies*—If any Arbitrator should resign, die, withdraw, refuse or be unable or disqualified to perform the duties of the office, the AAA shall, on proof satisfactory to it, declare the office vacant. Vacancies shall be filled in the same manner as that governing the making of the original appointment, and the matter shall be reheard by the new Arbitrator.

19. *Time and Place of Hearing*—The Arbitrator shall fix the time and place for each hearing. At least five days prior thereto the AAA shall mail notice of the time and place of hearing to each party, unless the parties otherwise agree.

20. *Representation by Counsel*—Any party may be represented at the hearing by counsel or by other authorized representative.

21. *Stenographic Record*—Any party may request a stenographic record by making arrangements for same through the AAA. If such transcript is agreed by the parties to be, or in appropriate cases determined by the Arbitrator to be, the official record of the proceeding, it must be made available to the Arbitrator, and to the other party for inspection, at a time and place determined by the Arbitrator. The total cost of such a record shall be shared equally by those parties that order copies.

22. *Attendance at Hearings*—Persons having a direct interest in the arbitration are entitled to attend hearings. The Arbitrator shall have the power to require the retirement of any witness or witnesses during the testimony of other witnesses. It shall be discretionary with the Arbitrator to determine the propriety of the attendance of any other persons.

23. *Adjournments*—The Arbitrator for good cause shown may adjourn the hearing upon the request of a party or upon his own initiative, and shall adjourn when all the parties agree thereto.

24. *Oaths*—Before proceeding with the first hearing, each Arbitrator may take an Oath of Office, and if required by law, shall do so. The Arbitrator has discretion to require witnesses to testify under oath administered by any duly qualified person, and if required by law or requested by either party, shall do so.

25. *Majority Decision*—Whenever there is more than one Arbitrator, all decisions of the Arbitrators shall be by majority vote. The award shall also be made by majority vote unless the concurrence of all is expressly required.

26. *Order of Proceedings*—A hearing shall be opened by the filing of the Oath of the Arbitrator, where required, and by the recording of the place, time and date of hearing, the presence of the Arbitrator and parties, and counsel if any, and the receipt by the Arbitrator of the Demand and answer, if any, or the Submission.

Exhibits, when offered by either party, may be received in evidence by the Arbitrator. The names and addresses of all witnesses and exhibits in order received shall be made a part of the record.

The Arbitrator has discretion to vary the normal procedure under which the initiating party first presents its claim, but in any case shall afford full and equal opportunity to all parties for presentation of relevant proofs.

27. *Arbitration in the Absence of a Party*—Unless the law provides to the contrary, the arbitration may proceed in the absence of any party, who, after due notice, fails to be present or fails to obtain an adjournment. An award shall not be made solely on the default of a party. The Arbitrator shall require the other party to submit such evidence as he may require for the making of an award.

28. *Evidence*—The parties may offer such evidence as they desire and shall produce such additional evidence as the Arbitrator may deem necessary to an understanding and determination of the dispute. When the Arbitrator is authorized by law to subpoena witnesses and documents, he may do so upon his own initiative or upon the request of any party. The Arbitrator shall be the judge of the relevancy and materiality of the evidence offered and conformity to legal rules of evidence shall not be necessary. All evidence shall be taken in the presence of all of the Arbitrators and all of the parties except where any of the parties is absent in default or has waived his right to be present.

29. *Evidence by Affidavit and Filing of Documents*—The Arbitrator may receive and consider the evidence of witnesses by affidavit, but shall give it only such weight as he deems proper after consideration of any objections made to its admission.

All documents not filed with the Arbitrator at the hearing but which are arranged at the hearing or subsequently by agreement of the parties to be submitted, shall be filed with the AAA for transmission to the Arbitrator. All parties shall be afforded opportunity to examine such documents.

30. *Inspection*—Whenever the Arbitrator deems it necessary, he may make an inspection in connection with the subject matter of the dispute after written notice to the parties who may, if they so desire, be present at such inspection.

31. *Closing of Hearings*—The Arbitrator shall inquire of all parties whether they have any further proofs to offer or witnesses to be heard. Upon receiving negative replies, the Arbitrator shall declare the hearings closed and a minute thereof shall be recorded. If briefs or other documents are to be filed, the hearings shall be declared closed as of the final date set by the Arbitrator for filing with the AAA. The time limit within which the Arbitrator is required to make the award shall commence to run, in the absence of other agreement by the parties, upon the closing of the hearings.

32. *Reopening of Hearings*—The hearings may be reopened by the Arbitrator on his own motion, or on the motion of either party, for good cause shown, at any time before the award is made, but if the reopening of the hearings would prevent the making of the award within the specific time agreed upon by the parties in the contract out of which the controversy has arisen, the matter may not be reopened, unless both parties agree upon the extension of such time limit. When no specific date is fixed in the contract, the Arbitrator may reopen the hearings, and the Arbitrator shall have 30 days from the closing of the reopened hearings within which to make an award.

33. *Waiver of Rules*—Any party who proceeds with the arbitration after knowledge that any provision or requirement of these Rules has not been complied with and who fails to state objection thereto in writing, shall be deemed to have waived the right to object.

34. *Waiver of Oral Hearings*—The parties may provide, by written agreement, for the waiver of oral hearings. If the parties are unable to agree as to the procedure, the AAA shall specify a fair and equitable procedure.

35. *Extensions of Time*—The parties may modify any period of time by mutual agreement. The AAA for good cause may extend any period of time established by these Rules, except the time for making the award. The AAA shall notify the parties of any such extension of time and its reason therefor.

36. *Serving of Notices*—Each party to a Submission or other agreement which provides for arbitration under these Rules shall be deemed to have consented and shall consent that any papers, notices or process necessary or proper for the initiation or continuation of an arbitration under these Rules and for any court action in connection therewith or the entry of judgment on an award made thereunder, may be served upon such party (a) by mail addressed to such party or

its attorney at its last known address, or (b) personal service, within or without the state wherein the arbitration is to be held.

37. *Time of Award*—The award shall be rendered promptly by the Arbitrator and, unless otherwise agreed by the parties, or specified by the law, not later than 30 days from the date of closing the hearings, or if oral hearings have been waived, then from the date of transmitting the final statements and proofs to the Arbitrator.

38. *Form of Award*—The award shall be in writing and shall be signed either by the neutral Arbitrator or by a concurring majority if there be more than one Arbitrator. The parties shall advise the AAA whenever they do not require the Arbitrator to accompany the award with an opinion.

39. *Award Upon Settlement*—If the parties settle their dispute during the course of the arbitration, the Arbitrator, upon their request, may set forth the terms of the agreed settlement in an award.

40. *Delivery of Award to Parties*—Parties shall accept as legal delivery of the award the placing of the award or a true copy thereof in the mail by the AAA, addressed to such party at its last known address or to its attorney, or personal service of the award, or the filing of the award in any manner which may be prescribed by law.

41. *Release of Documents for Judicial Proceedings*—The AAA shall, upon the written request of a party, furnish to such party at its expense certified facsimiles of any papers in the AAA's possession that may be required in judicial proceedings relating to the arbitration.

42. *Judicial Proceedings*—The AAA is not a necessary party in judicial proceedings relating to the arbitration.

43. *Administrative Fee*—As a nonprofit organization, the AAA shall prescribe an administrative fee schedule to compensate it for the cost of providing administrative services. The schedule in effect at the time of filing shall be applicable.

44. *Expenses*—The expense of witnesses for either side shall be paid by the party producing such witnesses.

Expenses of the arbitration, other than the cost of the stenographic record, including required traveling and other expenses of the Arbitrator and of AAA representatives, and the expenses of any witnesses or the cost of any proofs produced at the direct request of the Arbitrator, shall be borne equally by the parties unless they agree otherwise, or unless the Arbitrator in the award assesses such expenses or any part thereof against any specified party or parties.

45. *Communication with Arbitrator*—There shall be no communication between the parties and a neutral Arbitrator other than at

oral hearings. Any other oral or written communications from the parties to the Arbitrator shall be directed to the AAA for transmittal to the Arbitrator.

46. *Interpretation and Application of Rules*—The Arbitrator shall interpret and apply these Rules insofar as they relate to the Arbitrator's powers and duties. When there is more than one Arbitrator and a difference arises among them concerning the meaning or application of any such Rules, it shall be decided by majority vote. If that is unobtainable, either Arbitrator or party may refer the question to the AAA for final decision. All other Rules shall be interpreted and applied by the AAA.

Appendix B

Code of Professional Responsibility for Arbitrators of Labor-Management Disputes*

Foreword

This "Code of Professional Responsibility for Arbitrators of Labor-Management Disputes" supersedes the "Code of Ethics and Procedural Standards for Labor-Management Arbitration," approved in 1951 by a Committee of the American Arbitration Association, by the National Academy of Arbitrators, and by representatives of the Federal Mediation and Conciliation Service.

Revision of the 1951 Code was initiated officially by the same three groups in October, 1972. The Joint Steering Committee named below was designated to draft a proposal.

Reasons for Code revision should be noted briefly. Ethical considerations and procedural standards are sufficiently intertwined to warrant combining the subject matter of Parts I and II of the 1951 Code under the caption of "Professional Responsibility." It has seemed advisable to eliminate admonitions to the parties (Part III of the 1951 Code) except as they appear incidentally in connection with matters primarily involving responsibilities of arbitrators. Substantial growth of third party participation in dispute resolution in the public sector requires consideration. It appears that arbitration of new contract terms may become more significant. Finally, during the interval of more than two decades, new problems have emerged as private sector grievance arbitration has matured and has become more diversified.

JOINT STEERING COMMITTEE

. . .

November 30, 1974

---

*Adopted by the National Academy of Arbitrators, the American Arbitration Association, and the Federal Mediation and Conciliation Service.

Preamble

Background

Voluntary arbitration rests upon the mutual desire of management and labor in each collective bargaining relationship to develop procedures for dispute settlement which meet their own particular needs and obligations. No two voluntary systems, therefore, are likely to be identical in practice. Words used to describe arbitrators (Arbitrator, Umpire, Impartial Chairman, Chairman of Arbitration Board, etc.) may suggest typical approaches but actual differences within any general type of arrangement may be as great as distinctions often made among the several types.

Some arbitration and related procedures, however, are not the product of voluntary agreement. These procedures, primarily but not exclusively applicable in the public sector, sometimes utilize other third party titles (Fact Finder, Impasse Panel, Board of Inquiry, etc.). These procedures range all the way from arbitration prescribed by statute to arrangements substantially indistinguishable from voluntary procedures.

The standards of professional responsibility set forth in this Code are designed to guide the impartial third party serving in these diverse labor-management relationships.

Scope of Code

This Code is a privately developed set of standards of professional behavior. It applies to voluntary arbitration of labor-management grievance disputes and of disputes concerning new or revised contract terms. Both "ad hoc" and "permanent" varieties of voluntary arbitration, private and public sector, are included. To the extent relevant in any specific case, it also applies to advisory arbitration, impasse resolution panels, arbitration prescribed by statutes, fact-finding, and other special procedures.

The word "arbitrator," as used hereinafter in the Code, is intended to apply to any impartial person, irrespective of specific title, who serves in a labor-management dispute procedure in which there is conferred authority to decide issues or to make formal recommendations.

The Code is not designed to apply to mediation or conciliation, as distinguished from arbitration, nor to other procedures in which the third party is not authorized in advance to make decisions or recommendations. It does not apply to partisan representatives on tripartite boards. It does not apply to commercial arbitration or to other uses of arbitration outside the labor-management dispute area.

Format of Code

Bold Face type, sometimes including explanatory material, is used to set forth general principles. *Italics* are used for amplification of general principles. Ordinary type is used primarily for illustrative or explanatory comment.

Application of Code

Faithful adherence by an arbitrator to this Code is basic to professional responsibility.

The National Academy of Arbitrators will expect its members to be governed in their professional conduct by this Code and stands ready, through its Committee on Ethics and Grievances, to advise its members as to the Code's interpretation. The American Arbitration Association and the Federal Mediation and Conciliation Service will apply the Code to the arbitrators on their rosters in cases handled under their respective appointment or referral procedures. Other arbitrators and administrative agencies may, of course, voluntarily adopt the Code and be governed by it.

In interpreting the Code and applying it to charges of professional misconduct, under existing or revised procedures of the National Academy of Arbitrators and of the administrative agencies, it should be recognized that while some of its standards express ethical principles basic to the arbitration profession, others rest less on ethics than on considerations of good practice. Experience has shown the difficulty of drawing rigid lines of distinction between ethics and good practice and this Code does not attempt to do so. Rather, it leaves the gravity of alleged misconduct and the extent to which ethical standards have been violated to be assessed in the light of the facts and circumstances of each particular case.

I. Arbitrators' Qualifications and Responsibilities to the Profession

A. General Qualifications

1. Essential personal qualifications of an arbitrator include honesty, integrity, impartiality, and general competence in labor relations matters.

An arbitrator must demonstrate ability to exercise these personal qualities faithfully and with good judgment, both in procedural matters and in substantive decisions.

a. Selection by mutual agreement of the parties or direct designation by an administrative agency are the effective methods of appraisal of this combination of an individual's potential and performance, rather than the fact of placement on a roster of an administrative agency or membership in a professional association of arbitrators.

2. An arbitrator must be as ready to rule for one party as for the other on each issue, either in a single case or in a group of cases. Compromise by an arbitrator for the sake of attempting to achieve personal acceptability is unprofessional.

B. Qualifications for Special Cases

1. An arbitrator must decline appointment, withdraw, or request technical assistance when he or she decides that a case is beyond his or her competence.

a. An arbitrator may be qualified generally but not for specialized assignments. Some types of incentive, work standard, job evaluation, welfare program, pension, or insurance cases may require specialized knowledge, experience, or competence. Arbitration of contract terms also may require distinctive background and experience.

b. Effective appraisal by an administrative agency or by an arbitrator of the need for special qualifications requires that both parties make known the special nature of the case prior to appointment of the arbitrator.

C. Responsibilities to the Profession

1. An arbitrator must uphold the dignity and integrity of the office and endeavor to provide effective service to the parties.

a. To this end, an arbitrator should keep current with principles, practices, and developments that are relevant to his or her own field of arbitration practice.

2. An experienced arbitrator should cooperate in the training of new arbitrators.

3. An arbitrator must not advertise or solicit arbitration assignments.

a. It is a matter of personal preference whether an arbitrator includes "Labor Arbitrator" or similar notation on letterheads, cards, or announcements. *It is inappropriate, however, to include memberships or offices held in professional societies or listings on rosters of administrative agencies.*

b. *Information provided for published biographical sketches, as well as that supplied to administrative agencies, must be accurate.* Such information may include membership in professional organizations (including reference to significant offices held), and listings on rosters of administrative agencies.

II. Responsibilities to the Parties

A. *Recognition of Diversity in Arbitration Arrangements*

1. An arbitrator should conscientiously endeavor to understand and observe, to the extent consistent with professional responsibility, the significant principles governing each arbitration system in which he or she serves.

a. Recognition of special features of a particular arbitration arrangement can be essential with respect to procedural matters and may influence other aspects of the arbitration process.

2. Such understanding does not relieve an arbitrator from a corollary responsibility to seek to discern and refuse to lend approval or consent to any collusive attempt by the parties to use arbitration for an improper purpose.

B. *Required Disclosures*

1. Before accepting an appointment, an arbitrator must disclose directly or through the administrative agency involved, any current or past managerial, representational, or consultative relationship with any company or union involved in a proceeding in which he or she is being considered for appointment or has been tentatively designated to serve. Disclosure must also be made of any pertinent pecuniary interest.

a. The duty to disclose includes membership on a Board of Directors, full-time or part-time service as a representative or advocate, consultation work for a fee, current stock or bond ownership (other than mutual fund shares or appropriate trust arrangements), or any other pertinent form of managerial, financial, or immediate family interest in the company or union involved.

2. When an arbitrator is serving concurrently as an advocate for or representative of other companies or unions in labor relations matters, or has done so in recent years, he or she must disclose such activities before accepting appointment as an arbitrator.

An arbitrator must disclose such activities to an administrative agency if he or she is on that agency's active roster or seeks placement on a roster. Such disclosure then satisfies this requirement for cases handled under that agency's referral.

a. It is not necessary to disclose names of clients or other specific details. It is necessary to indicate the general nature of the labor relations advocacy or representational work involved, whether for companies or unions or both, and a reasonable approximation of the extent of such activity.

b. *An arbitrator on an administrative agency's roster has a continuing obligation to notify the agency of any significant changes pertinent to this requirement.*

c. When an administrative agency is not involved, an arbitrator must make such disclosure directly unless he or she is certain that both parties to the case are fully aware of such activities.

3. An arbitrator must not permit personal relationships to affect decision-making.

Prior to acceptance of an appointment, an arbitrator must disclose to the parties or to the administrative agency involved any close personal relationship or other circumstance, in addition to those specifically mentioned earlier in this section, which might reasonably raise a question as to the arbitrator's impartiality.

a. Arbitrators establish personal relationships with many company and union representatives, with fellow arbitrators, and with fellow members of various professional associations. There should be no attempt to be secretive about such friendships or acquaintances, but disclosure is not necessary unless some feature of a particular relationship might reasonably appear to impair impartiality.

4. If the circumstances requiring disclosure are not known to the arbitrator prior to acceptance of appointment, disclosure must be made when such circumstances become known to the arbitrator.

5. The burden of disclosure rests on the arbitrator. After appropriate disclosure, the arbitrator may serve if both parties so desire. If the arbitrator believes or perceives that there is a clear conflict of interest, he or she should withdraw, irrespective of the expressed desires of the parties.

C. *Privacy of Arbitration*

1. All significant aspects of an arbitration proceeding must be treated by the arbitrator as confidential unless this requirement is waived by both parties or disclosure is required or permitted by law.

a. Attendance at hearings by persons not representing the parties or invited by either or both of them should be permitted only when the parties agree or when an applicable law requires or permits. Occasionally, special circumstances may require that an arbitrator rule on such matters as attendance and degree of participation of counsel selected by a grievant.

b. *Discussion of a case at any time by an arbitrator with persons not involved directly should be limited to situations where advance approval or consent of both parties is obtained or where the identity of the parties and details of the case are sufficiently obscured to eliminate any realistic probability of identification.*

A commonly recognized exception is discussion of a problem in a case with a fellow arbitrator. *Any such discussion does not relieve the arbitrator who is acting in the case from sole responsibility for the decision, and the discussion must be considered as confidential.*

Discussion of aspects of a case in a classroom without prior specific approval of the parties is not a violation provided the arbitrator is satisfied that there is no breach of essential confidentiality.

c. *It is a violation of professional responsibility for an arbitrator to make public an award without the consent of the parties.*

An arbitrator may request but must not press the parties for consent to publish an opinion. Such a request should normally not be made until after the award has been issued to the parties.

d. It is not improper for an arbitrator to donate arbitration files to a library of a college, university, or similar institution without prior consent of all the parties involved. When the circumstances permit, there should be deleted from such donations any cases concerning which one or both of the parties have expressed a desire for privacy. As an additional safeguard, an arbitrator may also decide to withhold recent cases or indicate to the donee a time interval before such cases can be made generally available.

e. *Applicable laws, regulations, or practices of the parties may permit or even require exceptions to the above noted principles of privacy.*

D. *Personal Relationships With the Parties*

1. An arbitrator must make every reasonable effort to conform to arrangements required by an administrative agency or mutually desired by the parties regarding communications and personal relationships with the parties.

a. *Only an "arm's length" relationship may be acceptable to the parties in some arbitration arrangements or may be required by the rules of an administrative agency. The arbitrator should then have no contact of consequence with representatives of either party while handling a case without the other party's presence or consent.*

b. *In other situations, both parties may want communications and personal relationships to be less formal. It is then appropriate for the arbitrator to respond accordingly.*

E. Jurisdiction

1. An arbitrator must observe faithfully both the limitations and inclusions of the jurisdiction conferred by an agreement or other submission under which he or she serves.

2. A direct settlement by the parties of some or all issues in a case, at any stage of the proceedings, must be accepted by the arbitrator as relieving him or her of further jurisdiction over such issues.

F. Mediation by an Arbitrator

1. When the parties wish at the outset to give an arbitrator authority both to mediate and to decide or submit recommendations regarding residual issues, if any, they should so advise the arbitrator prior to appointment. If the appointment is accepted, the arbitrator must perform a mediation role consistent with the circumstances of the case.

a. *Direct appointment, also, may require a dual role as mediator and arbitrator of residual issues. This is most likely to occur in some public sector cases.*

2. When a request to mediate if first made after appointment, the arbitrator may either accept or decline a mediation role.

a. *Once arbitration has been invoked, either party normally has a right to insist that the process be continued to decision.*

b. *If one party requests that the arbitrator mediate and the other party objects, the arbitrator should decline the request.*

c. *An arbitrator is not precluded from making a suggestion that he or she mediate. To avoid the possibility of improper pressure, the arbitrator should not so suggest unless it can be discerned that both parties are likely to be receptive. In any event, the arbitrator's suggestion should not be pursued unless both parties readily agree.*

G. Reliance by an Arbitrator on Other Arbitration Awards or on Independent Research

1. An arbitrator must assume full personal responsibility for the decision in each case decided.

a. *The extent, if any, to which an arbitrator properly may rely on precedent, on guidance of other awards, or on independent research is dependent primarily on the policies of the parties on these matters, as expressed in the contract, or other agreement, or at the hearing.*

b. **When the mutual desires of the parties are not known or when the parties express differing opinions or policies, the arbitrator may exercise discretion as to these matters consistent with acceptance of full personal responsibility for the award.

H. *Use of Assistants*

1. An arbitrator must not delegate any decision-making function to another person without consent of the parties.

a. *Without prior consent of the parties, an arbitrator may use the services of an assistant for research, clerical duties, or preliminary drafting under the direction of the arbitrator which does not involve the delegation of any decision-making function.*

b. *If an arbitrator is unable, because of time limitations or other reasons, to handle all decision-making aspects of a case, it is not a violation of professional responsibility to suggest to the parties an allocation of responsibility between the arbitrator and an assistant or associate. The arbitrator must not exert pressure on the parties to accept such a suggestion.*

I. *Consent Awards*

1. Prior to issuance of an award, the parties may jointly request the arbitrator to include in the award certain agreements between them, concerning some or all of the issues. If the arbitrator believes that a suggested award is proper, fair, sound, and lawful, it is consistent with professional responsibility to adopt it.

a. *Before complying with such a request, an arbitrator must be certain that he or she understands the suggested settlement adequately in order to be able to appraise its terms. If it appears that pertinent facts or circumstances may not have been disclosed, the arbitrator should take the initiative to assure that all significant aspects of the case are fully understood. To this end, the arbitrator may request additional specific information and may question witnesses at a hearing.*

J. *Avoidance of Delay*

1. It is a basic professional responsibility of an arbitrator to plan his or her work schedule so that present and future commitments will be fulfilled in a timely manner.

a. *When planning is upset for reasons beyond the control of the arbitrator, he or she, nevertheless, should exert every reasonable effort to fulfill all commitments. If this is not possible, prompt notice at the arbitrator's initiative should be given to all parties affected. Such notices should include reasonably accurate estimates of any additional time required. To the extent pos-*

sible, priority should be given to cases in process so that other parties may make alternative arbitration arrangements.

2. An arbitrator must cooperate with the parties and with any administrative agency involved in avoiding delays.

a. *An arbitrator on the active roster of an administrative agency must take the initiative in advising the agency of any scheduling difficulties that he or she can foresee.*

b. *Requests for services, whether received directly or through an administrative agency, should be declined if the arbitrator is unable to schedule a hearing as soon as the parties wish. If the parties, nevertheless, jointly desire to obtain the services of the arbitrator and the arbitrator agrees, arrangements should be made by agreement that the arbitrator confidently expects to fulfill.*

c. *An arbitrator may properly seek to persuade the parties to alter or eliminate arbitration procedures or tactics that cause unnecessary delay.*

3. Once the case record has been closed, an arbitrator must adhere to the time limits for an award, as stipulated in the labor agreement or as provided by regulation of an administrative agency or as otherwise agreed.

a. *If an appropriate award cannot be rendered within the required time, it is incumbent on the arbitrator to seek an extension of time from the parties.*

b. If the parties have agreed upon abnormally short time limits for an award after a case is closed, the arbitrator should be so advised by the parties or by the administrative agency involved, prior to acceptance of appointment.

K. *Fees and Expenses*

1. An arbitrator occupies a position of trust in respect to the parties and the administrative agencies. In charging for services and expenses, the arbitrator must be governed by the same high standards of honor and integrity that apply to all other phases of his or her work.

An arbitrator must endeavor to keep total charges for services and expenses reasonable and consistent with the nature of the case or cases decided.

Prior to appointment, the parties should be aware of or be able readily to determine all significant aspects of an arbitrator's bases for charges for fees and expenses.

a. *Services Not Primarily Chargeable on a Per Diem Basis*

By agreement with the parties, the financial aspects of many "permanent" arbitration assignments, of some interest disputes, and of some "ad hoc" grievance assignments do not include a per diem fee for services as a primary part of the total understanding. *In such situations, the arbitrator must adhere faithfully to all agreed upon arrangements governing fees and expenses.*

b. *Per Diem Basis for Charges for Services*

(1) *When an arbitrator's charges for services are determined primarily by a stipulated per diem fee, the arbitrator should establish in advance his or her bases for application of such per diem fee and for determination of reimbursable expenses.*

Practices established by an arbitrator should include the basis for charges, if any, for:

(a) hearing time, including the application of the stipulated basic per diem hearing fee to hearing days of varying lengths;

(b) study time;

(c) necessary travel time when not included in charges for hearing time;

(d) postponement or cancellation of hearings by the parties and the circumstances in which such charges will normally be assessed or waived;

(e) office overhead expenses (secretarial, telephone, postage, etc.);

(f) the work of paid assistants or associates.

(2) *Each arbitrator should be guided by the following general principles:*

(a) *Per diem charges for a hearing should not be in excess of actual time spent or allocated for the hearing.*

(b) *Per diem charges for study time should not be in excess of actual time spent.*

(c) *Any fixed ratio of study days to hearing days, not agreed to specifically by the parties, is inconsistent with the per diem method of charges for services.*

(d) *Charges for expenses must not be in excess of actual expenses normally reimbursable and incurred in connection with the case or cases involved.*

(e) *When time or expense are involved for two or more sets of parties on the same day or trip, such time or expense charges should be appropriately prorated.*

(f) *An arbitrator may stipulate in advance a minimum charge for a hearing without violation of (a) or (e) above.*

(3) *An arbitrator on the active roster of an administrative agency must file with the agency his or her individual bases for*

determination of fees and expenses if the agency so requires. Thereafter, it is the responsibility of each such arbitrator to advise the agency promptly of any change in any basis for charges.

Such filing may be in the form of answers to a questionnaire devised by an agency or by any other method adopted by or approved by an agency.

Having supplied an administrative agency with the information noted above, an arbitrator's professional responsibility of disclosure under this Code with respect to fees and expenses has been satisfied for cases referred by that agency.

(4) If an administrative agency promulgates specific standards with respect to any of these matters which are in addition to or more restrictive than an individual arbitrator's standards, an arbitrator on its active roster must observe the agency standards for cases handled under the auspices of that agency or decline to serve.

(5) When an arbitrator is contacted directly by the parties for a case or cases, the arbitrator has a professional responsibility to respond to questions by submitting his or her bases for charges for fees and expenses.

(6) When it is known to the arbitrator that one or both of the parties cannot afford normal charges, it is consistent with professional responsibility to charge lesser amounts to both parties or to one of the parties if the other party is made aware of the difference and agrees.

(7) If an arbitrator concludes that the total of charges derived from his or her normal basis of calculation is not compatible with the case decided, it is consistent with professional responsibility to charge lesser amounts to both parties.

2. An arbitrator must maintain adequate records to support charges for services and expenses and must make an accounting to the parties or to an involved administrative agency on request.

III. Responsibilities to Administrative Agencies

A. General Responsibilities

1. An arbitrator must be candid, accurate, and fully responsive to an administrative agency concerning his or her qualifications, availability, and all other pertinent matters.

2. An arbitrator must observe policies and rules of an administrative agency in cases referred by that agency.

3. An arbitrator must not seek to influence an administrative agency by any improper means, including gifts or other inducements to agency personnel.

a. It is not improper for a person seeking placement on a roster to request references from individuals having knowledge of the applicant's experience and qualifications.

b. Arbitrators should recognize that the primary responsibility of an administrative agency is to serve the parties.

IV. Prehearing Conduct

1. All prehearing matters must be handled in a manner that fosters complete impartiality by the arbitrator.

a. The primary purpose of prehearing discussions involving the arbitrator is to obtain agreement on procedural matters so that the hearing can proceed without unnecessary obstacles. If differences of opinion should arise during such discussions and, particularly, if such differences appear to impinge on substantive matters, the circumstances will suggest whether the matter can be resolved informally or may require a prehearing conference or, more rarely, a formal preliminary hearing. When an administrative agency handles some or all aspects of the arrangements prior to a hearing, the arbitrator will become involved only if differences of some substance arise.

b. *Copies of any prehearing correspondence between the arbitrator and either party must be made available to both parties.*

V. Hearing Conduct

A. General Principles

1. An arbitrator must provide a fair and adequate hearing which assures that both parties have sufficient opportunity to present their respective evidence and argument.

a. *Within the limits of this responsibility, an arbitrator should conform to the various types of hearing procedures desired by the parties.*

b. An arbitrator may: encourage stipulations of fact; restate the substance of issues or arguments to promote or verify understanding; question the parties' representatives or witnesses, when necessary or advisable, to obtain additional pertinent information; and request that the parties submit additional evidence, either at the hearing or by subsequent filing.

c. *An arbitrator should not intrude into a party's presentation so as to prevent that party from putting forward its case fairly and adequately.*

B. *Transcripts or Recordings*

1. Mutual agreement of the parties as to use or nonuse of a transcript must be respected by the arbitrator.

a. *A transcript is the official record of a hearing only when both parties agree to a transcript or an applicable law or regulation so provides.*

b. An arbitrator may seek to persuade the parties to avoid use of a transcript, or to use a transcript if the nature of the case appears to require one. *However, if an arbitrator intends to make his or her appointment to a case contingent on mutual agreement to a transcript, that requirement must be made known to both parties prior to appointment.*

c. If the parties do not agree to a transcript, an arbitrator may permit one party to make a transcript at its own cost. The arbitrator may also make appropriate arrangements under which the other party may have access to a copy, if a copy is provided to the arbitrator.

d. Without prior approval, an arbitrator may seek to use his or her own tape recorder to supplement note taking. The arbitrator should not insist on such a tape recording if either or both parties object.

C. *Ex Parte Hearings*

1. In determining whether to conduct an ex parte hearing, an arbitrator must consider relevant legal, contractual, and other pertinent circumstances.

2. An arbitrator must be certain, before proceeding ex parte, that the party refusing or failing to attend the hearing has been given adequate notice of the time, place, and purposes of the hearing.

D. *Plant Visits*

1. An arbitrator should comply with a request of any party that he or she visit a work area pertinent to the dispute prior to, during, or after a hearing. An arbitrator may also initiate such a request.

a. *Procedures for such visits should be agreed to by the parties in consultation with the arbitrator.*

E. *Bench Decisions or Expedited Awards*

1. When an arbitrator understands, prior to acceptance of appointment, that a bench decision is expected at the conclusion of the hearing, the arbitrator must comply with the understanding unless both parties agree otherwise.

a. *If notice of the parties' desire for a bench decision is not given prior to the arbitrator's acceptance of the case, issuance of such a bench decision is discretionary.*

b. *When only one party makes the request and the other objects, the arbitrator should not render a bench decision except under most unusual circumstances.*

2. When an arbitrator understands, prior to acceptance of appointment, that a concise written award is expected within a stated time period after the hearing, the arbitrator must comply with the understanding unless both parties agree otherwise.

VI. Post Hearing Conduct

A. Post Hearing Briefs and Submissions

1. An arbitrator must comply with mutual agreements in respect to the filing or nonfiling of post hearing briefs or submissions.

a. An arbitrator, in his or her discretion, may either suggest the filing of post hearing briefs or other submissions or suggest that none be filed.

b. When the parties disagree as to the need for briefs, an arbitrator may permit filing but may determine a reasonable time limitation.

2. An arbitrator must not consider a post hearing brief or submission that has not been provided to the other party.

B. Disclosure of Terms of Award

1. An arbitrator must not disclose a prospective award to either party prior to its simultaneous issuance to both parties or explore possible alternative awards unilaterally with one party, unless both parties so agree.

a. Partisan members of tripartite boards may know prospective terms of an award in advance of its issuance. Similar situations may exist in other less formal arrangements mutually agreed to by the parties. In any such situation, the arbitrator should determine and observe the mutually desired degree of confidentiality.

C. Awards and Opinions

1. The award should be definite, certain, and as concise as possible.

a. When an opinion is required, factors to be considered by an arbitrator include: desirability of brevity, consistent with the nature of the case and any expressed desires of the parties; need to use a style and form that is understandable to responsible representatives of the parties, to the grievant and supervisors, and to others in the collective bargaining relationship; necessity of meeting the significant issues; forthrightness to an extent not harmful to the relationship of the parties; and avoidance of gratuitous advice or discourse not essential to disposition of the issues.

D. *Clarification or Interpretation of Awards*

1. No clarification or interpretation of an award is permissible without the consent of both parties.

2. Under agreements which permit or require clarification or interpretation of an award, an arbitrator must afford both parties an opportunity to be heard.

E. *Enforcement of Award*

1. The arbitrator's responsibility does not extend to the enforcement of an award.

2. In view of the professional and confidential nature of the arbitration relationship, an arbitrator should not voluntarily participate in legal enforcement proceedings.

Appendix C

The United States Arbitration Act*

Chapter 1.—General Provisions

Section 1. "Maritime Transactions" and "Commerce" Defined; Exceptions to Operation of Title

"Maritime transactions," as herein defined, means charter parties, bills of lading of water carriers, agreements relating to wharfage, supplies furnished vessels or repairs of vessels, collisions, or any other matters in foreign commerce which, if the subject of controversy, would be embraced within admiralty jurisdiction; "commerce," as herein defined, means commerce among the several States or with foreign nations, or in any Territory of the United States or in the District of Columbia, or between any such Territory and another, or between any such Territory and any State or foreign nation, or between the District of Columbia and any State or Territory or foreign nation, but nothing herein contained shall apply to contracts of employment of seamen, railroad employees, or any other class of workers engaged in foreign or interstate commerce.

Section 2. Validity, Irrevocability, and Enforcement of Agreements to Arbitrate

A written provision in any maritime transaction or a contract evidencing a transaction involving commerce to settle by arbitration a controversy thereafter arising out of such contract or transaction, or the refusal to perform the whole or any part thereof, or an agreement in writing to submit to arbitration an existing controversy arising out of such a contract, transaction, or refusal, shall be valid, irrevocable, and enforceable, save upon such grounds as exist at law or in equity for the revocation of any contract.

---

*9 U.S.C.§§1–14.

Section 3. Stay of Proceedings Where Issue Therein Referable to Arbitration

If any suit or proceeding be brought in any of the courts of the United States upon any issue referable to arbitration under an agreement in writing for such arbitration, the court in which such suit is pending, upon being satisfied that the issue involved in such suit or proceeding is referable to arbitration under such an agreement, shall on application of one of the parties stay the trial of the action until such arbitration has been had in accordance with the terms of the agreement, providing the applicant for the stay is not in default in proceeding with such arbitration.

Section 4. Failure to Arbitrate Under Agreement; Petition to United States Court Having Jurisdiction for Order to Compel Arbitration; Notice and Service Thereof; Hearing and Determination

A party aggrieved by the alleged failure, neglect, or refusal of another to arbitrate under a written agreement for arbitration may petition any United States district court which, save for such agreement, would have jurisdiction under Title 28, in a civil action or in admiralty of the subject matter of a suit arising out of the controversy between the parties, for an order directing that such arbitration proceed in the manner provided for in such agreement. Five days' notice in writing of such application shall be served upon the party in default. Service thereof shall be made in the manner provided by the Federal Rules of Civil Procedure. The court shall hear the parties, and upon being satisfied that the making of the agreement for arbitration or the failure to comply therewith is not in issue, the court shall make an order directing the parties to proceed to arbitration in accordance with the terms of the agreement. The hearing and proceedings, under such agreement, shall be within the district in which the petition for an order directing such arbitration is filed. If the making of the arbitration agreement or the failure, neglect, or refusal to perform the same be in issue, the court shall proceed summarily to the trial thereof. If no jury trial be demanded by the party alleged to be in default, or if the matter in dispute is within admiralty jurisdiction, the court shall hear and determine such issue. Where such an issue is raised, the party alleged to be in default may, except in cases of admiralty, on or before the return day of the notice of application, demand a jury trial of such issue, and upon such demand the court shall make an order referring the issue or issues to a jury in the manner provided by the Federal Rules of Civil Procedure, or may specially call a jury for that purpose. If the jury find that no agreement in writing for arbitration was made or that there is no default in proceeding thereunder, the proceeding shall be dismissed. If the jury find that an agreement for arbitration was made in writing and that there is a default in proceeding thereunder, the court shall make an order summarily directing the parties to proceed with the arbitration in accordance with the terms thereof.

Section 5. *Appointment of Arbitrators or Umpire*

If in the agreement provision be made for a method of naming or appointing an arbitrator or arbitrators or an umpire, such method shall be followed; but if no method be provided therein, or if a method be provided and any party thereto shall fail to avail himself of such method, or if for any other reason there shall be a lapse in the naming of an arbitrator or arbitrators or umpire, or in filling a vacancy, then upon the application of either party to the controversy the court shall designate and appoint an arbitrator or arbitrators or umpire, as the case may require, who shall act under the said agreement with the same force and effect as if he or they had been specifically named therein; and unless otherwise provided in the agreement the arbitration shall be by a single arbitrator.

Section 6. *Application Heard as Motion*

Any application to the court hereunder shall be made and heard in the manner provided by law for the making and hearing of motions, except as otherwise herein expressly provided.

Section 7. *Witnesses Before Arbitrators; Fees; Compelling Attendance*

The arbitrators selected either as prescribed in this title or otherwise, or a majority of them, may summon in writing any person to attend before them or any of them as a witness and in a proper case to bring with him or them any book, record, document, or paper which may be deemed material as evidence in the case. The fees for such attendance shall be the same as the fees of witnesses before masters of the United States courts. Said summons shall issue in the name of the arbitrator or arbitrators, or a majority of them, and shall be signed by the arbitrators, or a majority of them, and shall be directed to the said person and shall be served in the same manner as subpoenas to appear and testify before the court; if any person or persons so summoned to testify shall refuse or neglect to obey said summons, upon petition the United States court in and for the district in which such arbitrators, or a majority of them, are sitting may compel the attendance of such person or persons before said arbitrator or arbitrators, or punish said person or persons for contempt in the same manner provided on February 12, 1925, for securing the attendance of witnesses or their punishment for neglect or refusal to attend in the courts of the United States.

Section 8. Proceedings Begun by Libel in Admiralty and Seizure of Vessel or Property

If the basis of jurisdiction be a cause of action otherwise justiciable in admiralty, then, notwithstanding anything herein to the contrary the party claiming to be aggrieved may begin his proceeding hereunder by libel and seizure of the vessel or other property of the other party according to the usual course of admiralty proceedings, and the court shall then have jurisdiction to direct the parties to proceed with the arbitration and shall retain jurisdiction to enter its decree upon the award.

Section 9. Award of Arbitrators; Confirmation; Jurisdiction; Procedure

If the parties in their agreement have agreed that a judgment of the court shall be entered upon the award made pursuant to the arbitration, and shall specify the court, then at any time within one year after the award is made any party to the arbitration may apply to the court so specified for an order confirming the award, and thereupon the court must grant such an order unless the award is vacated, modified, or corrected as prescribed in sections 10 and 11 of this title. If no court is specified in the agreement of the parties, then such application may be made to the United States court in and for the district within which such award was made. Notice of the application shall be served upon the adverse party, and thereupon the court shall have jurisdiction of such party as though he had appeared generally in the proceeding. If the adverse party is a resident of the district within which the award was made, such service shall be made upon the adverse party or his attorney as prescribed by law for service of notice of motion in an action in the same court. If the adverse party shall be a nonresident, then the notice of the application shall be served by the marshal of any district within which the adverse party may be found in like manner as other process of the court.

Section 10. Same; Vacation; Grounds; Rehearing

In either of the following cases the United States court in and for the district wherein the award was made may make an order vacating the award upon the application of any party to the arbitration—

(a) Where the award was procured by corruption, fraud, or undue means.

(b) Where there was evident partiality or corruption in the arbitrators, or either of them.

(c) Where the arbitrators were guilty of misconduct in refusing to postpone the hearing, upon sufficient cause shown, or in refusing to hear evidence pertinent and material to the controversy; or of any other misbehavior by which the rights of any party have been prejudiced.

(d) Where the arbitrators exceeded their powers, or so imperfectly executed them that a mutual, final, and definite award upon the subject matter submitted was not made.

(e) Where an award is vacated and the time within which the agreement required the award to be made has not expired the court may, in its discretion, direct a rehearing by the arbitrators.

Section 11. Same; Modification or Correction; Grounds; Order

In either of the following cases the United States court in and for the district wherein the award was made may make an order modifying or correcting the award upon the application of any party to the arbitration—

(a) Where there was an evident material miscalculation of figures or an evident material mistake in the description of any person, thing, or property referred to in the award.

(b) Where the arbitrators have awarded upon a matter not submitted to them, unless it is a matter not affecting the merits of the decision upon the matter submitted.

(c) Where the award is imperfect in matter of form not affecting the merits of the controversy.

The order may modify and correct the award, so as to effect the intent thereof and promote justice between the parties.

Section 12. Notice of Motions to Vacate or Modify; Service; Stay of Proceedings

Notice of a motion to vacate, modify, or correct an award must be served upon the adverse party or his attorney within three months after the award is filed or delivered. If the adverse party is a resident of the district within which the award was made, such service shall be made upon the adverse party or his attorney as prescribed by law for service of notice of motion in an action in the same court. If the adverse party shall be a nonresident then the notice of the application shall be served by the marshal of any district within which the adverse party may be found in like manner as other process of the court. For the purposes of the motion any judge who might make an order to stay the proceedings in an action brought in the same court may make an order, to be served with the notice of motion, staying the proceedings of the adverse party to enforce the award.

Section 13. Papers Filed with Order on Motions; Judgment; Docketing; Force and Effect; Enforcement

The party moving for an order confirming, modifying, or correcting an award shall, at the time such order is filed with the clerk for the entry of judgment thereon, also file the following papers with the clerk:

(a) The agreement; the selection or appointment, if any, of an additional arbitrator or umpire; and each written extension of the time, if any, within which to make the award.

(b) The award.

(c) Each notice, affidavit, or other paper used upon an application to confirm, modify, or correct the award, and a copy of each order of the court upon such an application.

The judgment shall be docketed as if it was rendered in an action.

The judgment so entered shall have the same force and effect, in all respects, as, and be subject to all the provisions of law relating to, a judgment in an action; and it may be enforced as if it had been rendered in an action in the court in which it is entered.

Section 14. Contracts Not Affected

This title shall not apply to contracts made prior to January 1, 1926.

Appendix D

Uniform Arbitration Act*

Act Relating to Arbitration and to Make Uniform The Law With Reference Thereto

Section 1. (Validity of Arbitration Agreement.)

A written agreement to submit any existing controversy to arbitration or a provision in a written contract to submit to arbitration any controversy thereafter arising between the parties is valid, enforceable and irrevocable, save upon such grounds as exist at law or in equity for the revocation of any contract. This act also applies to arbitration agreements between employers and employees or between their respective representatives (unless otherwise provided in the agreement.)

Section 2. (Proceedings to Compel or Stay Arbitration.)

(a) On application of a party showing an agreement described in Section 1, and the opposing party's refusal to arbitrate, the Court shall order the parties to proceed with arbitration, but if the opposing party denies the existence of the agreement to arbitrate, the Court shall proceed summarily to the determination of the issue so raised and shall order arbitration if found for the moving party, otherwise, the application shall be denied.

(b) On application, the courts may stay an arbitration proceeding commenced or threatened on a showing that there is no agreement to arbitrate. Such an issue, when in substantial and bona fide dispute, shall be forthwith and summarily tried and the stay ordered if found for the moving party. If found for the opposing party, the court shall order the parties to proceed to arbitration.

---

*Adopted by the National Conference of the Commissioners on Uniform State Laws, August 20, 1955, as amended August 24, 1956. Approved by the House of Delegates of the American Bar Association, August 26, 1955, and August 30, 1956.

(c) If an issue referable to arbitration under the alleged agreement is involved in action or proceeding pending in a court having jurisdiction to hear applications under subdivision (a) of this Section, the application shall be made therein. Otherwise and subject to Section 18, the application may be made in any court of competent jurisdiction.

(d) Any action or proceeding involving an issue subject to arbitration shall be stayed if an order for arbitration or an application therefore has been made under this section or, if the issue is severable, the stay may be with respect thereto only. When the application is made in such action or proceeding, the order for arbitration shall include such stay.

(e) An order for arbitration shall not be refused on the ground that the claim in issue lacks merit or bona fides or because any fault or grounds for the claim sought to be arbitrated have not been shown.

Section 3. (Appointment of Arbitrators by Courts.)

If the arbitration agreement provides a method of appointment of arbitrators, this method shall be followed. In the absence thereof, or if the agreed method fails or for any reason cannot be followed, or when an arbitrator appointed fails or is unable to act and his successor has not been duly appointed, the court on application of a party shall appoint one or more arbitrators. An arbitrator so appointed has all the powers of one specifically named in the agreement.

Section 4. (Majority Action by Arbitrators.)

The powers of the arbitrators may be exercised by a majority unless otherwise provided by the agreement or by this act.

Section 5. (Hearing.)

Unless otherwise provided by the agreement:

(a) The arbitrators shall appoint a time and place for the hearing and cause notification to the parties to be served personally or by registered mail not less than five days before the hearing. Appearance at the hearing waives such notice. The arbitrators may adjourn the hearing from time to time as necessary and, on request of a party and for good cause, or upon their own motion may postpone the hearing to a time not later than the date fixed by the agreement for making the award unless the parties consent to a later date. The arbitrators may hear and determine the controversy upon the evidence produced notwithstanding the failure of a party duly notified to appear. The court on application may direct the arbitrators to proceed promptly with the hearing and determination of the controversy.

(b) The parties are entitled to be heard, to present evidence material to the controversy and to cross-examine witnesses appearing at the hearing.

(c) The hearing shall be conducted by all the arbitrators but a majority may determine any question and render a final award. If, during the course of the hearing, an arbitrator for any reason ceases to act, the remaining arbitrator or arbitrators appointed to act as neutrals may continue with the hearing and determination of the controversy.

Section 6. (Representation by Attorney.)

A party has the right to be represented by an attorney at any proceeding or hearing under this act. A wavier thereof prior to the proceeding or hearing is ineffective.

Section 7. (Witnesses, Subpoenas, Depositions.)

(a) The arbitrators may issue (cause to be issued) subpoenas for the attendance of witnesses and for the production of books, records, documents and other evidence, and shall have the power to administer oaths. Subpoenas so issued shall be served, and upon application to the Court by a party or the arbitrators, enforced, in the manner provided by law for the service and enforcement of subpoenas in a civil action.

(b) On application of a party and for use as evidence, the arbitrators may permit a deposition to be taken, in the manner and upon the terms designated by the arbitrators, of a witness who cannot be subpoenaed or is unable to attend the hearing.

(c) All provisions of law compelling a person under subpoena to testify are applicable.

(d) Fees for attendance as a witness shall be the same as for a witness in the _____ Court.

Section 8. (Award.)

(a) The award shall be in writing and signed by the arbitrators joining in the award. The arbitrators shall deliver a copy to each party personally or by registered mail, or as provided in the agreement.

(b) An award shall be made within the time fixed therefore by the agreement or, if not so fixed, within such time as the court orders on application of a party. The parties may extend the time in writing either before or after the expiration thereof. A party waives the objection that an award was not made within the time required unless he notifies the arbitrators of his objection prior to the delivery of the award to him.

Section 9. (Change of Award by Arbitrators.)

On application of a party or, if an application to the court is pending under Sections 11, 12, or 13, on submission to the arbitrators by the court under such conditions as the court may order, the arbitrators may modify or correct the award upon the grounds stated in paragraphs (1) and (3) of subdivision (a) of Section 13, or for the purpose of clarifying the award. The application shall be made within twenty days after delivery of the award to the applicant. Written notice thereof shall be given forthwith to the opposing party, stating he must serve his objection thereto if any, within ten days from the notice. The award so modified or corrected is subject to the provisions of Sections 11, 12 and 13.

Section 10. (Fees and Expenses of Arbitration.)

Unless otherwise provided in the agreement to arbitrate, the arbitrators' expenses and fees, together with other expenses, not including counsel fees, incurred in the conduct of the arbitration, shall be paid as provided in the award.

Section 11. (Confirmation of an Award.)

Upon application of a party, the court shall confirm an award, unless within the time limits hereinafter imposed grounds are urged for vacating or modifying or correcting the award, in which case the court shall proceed as provided in Sections 12 and 13.

Section 12. (Vacating an Award.)

(a) Upon application of a party, the court shall vacate an award where:

(1) The award was procured by corruption, fraud or other undue means:

(2) There was evident partiality by an arbitrator appointed as a neutral or corruption in any of the arbitrators or misconduct prejudicing the rights of any party;

(3) The arbitrators exceeded their powers;

(4) The arbitrators refused to postpone the hearing upon sufficient cause being shown therefore or refused to hear evidence material to the controversy or otherwise so conducted the hearing, contrary to the provisions of Section 5, as to prejudice substantially the rights of a party; or

(5) There was no arbitration agreement and the issue was not adversely determined in proceedings under Section 2 and the party did not participate in the arbitration hearing without raising the objection;

But the fact that the relief was such that it could not or would not be granted by a court of law or equity is not ground for vacating or refusing to confirm the award.

(b) An application under this Section shall be made within ninety days after delivery of a copy of the award to the applicant, except that, if predicated upon corruption, fraud or other undue means, it shall be made within ninety days after such grounds are known or should have been known.

(c) In vacating the award on grounds other than stated in clause (5) of Subsection (a) the court may order a rehearing before new arbitrators chosen as provided in the agreement, or in the absence thereof, by the court in accordance with Section 3, or, if the award is vacated on grounds set forth in clauses (3), and (4) of Subsection (a) the court may order a rehearing before the arbitrators who made the award or their successors appointed in accordance with Section 3. The time within which the agreement requires the award to be made is applicable to the rehearing and commences from the date of the order.

(d) If the application to vacate is denied and no motion to modify or correct the award is pending, the court shall confirm the award.

Section 13. *(Modification or Correction of Award.)*

(a) Upon application made within ninety days after delivery of a copy of the award to the applicant, the court shall modify or correct the award where:

(1) There was an evident miscalculation of figures or an evident mistake in the description of any person, thing or property referred to in the award;

(2) The arbitrators have awarded upon a matter not submitted to them and the award may be corrected without affecting the merits of the decision upon the issues submitted; or

(3) The award is imperfect in a matter of form, not affecting the merits of the controversy.

(b) If the application is granted, the court shall modify and correct the award so as to effect its intent and shall confirm the award as so modified and corrected. Otherwise, the court shall confirm the award as made.

(c) An application to modify or correct an award may be joined in the alternative with an application to vacate the award.

Section 14. *(Judgment or Decree on Award.)*

Upon the granting of an order confirming, modifying or correcting an award, judgment or decree shall be entered in conformity therewith and be enforced as any other judgment or decree. Costs of the application and of the proceedings subsequent thereto, and disbursements may be awarded by the court.

[*Section 15. (Judgment Roll, Docketing.)*

(a) On entry of judgment or decree, the clerk shall prepare the judgment roll consisting, to the extent filled, of the following:

(1) The agreement and each written extension of the time within which to make the award;

(2) The award;

(3) A copy of the order confirming, modifying or correcting the award; and

(4) A copy of the judgment or decree.

(b) The judgment or decree may be docketed as if rendered in an action.]

Section 16. (Applications to Court.)

Except as otherwise provided, an application to the court under this act shall be by motion and shall be heard in the manner and upon the notice provided by law or rule of court for the making and hearing of motions. Unless the parties have agreed otherwise, notice of an initial application for an order shall be served in the manner provided by law for the service of a summons in an action.

Section 17. (Court, Jurisdiction.)

The term "court" means any court of competent jurisdiction of this State. The making of an agreement described in Section 1 providing for arbitration in this State confers jurisdiction on the court to enforce the agreement under this Act and to enter judgment on an award thereunder.

Section 18. (Venue.)

An initial application shall be made to the court of the (county) in which the agreement provides the arbitration hearing shall be held or, if the hearing has been held, in the county in which it was held. Otherwise the application shall be made in the (county) where the adverse party resides or has a place of business or, if he has no residence or place of business in this State, to the court of any (county). All subsequent applications shall be made to the court hearing the initial application unless the court otherwise directs.

Brackets and parenthesis enclose language which the Commissioners suggest may be used by those States desiring to do so.

Section 19. (Appeals.)

(a) An appeal may be taken from:

(1) An order denying an application to compel arbitration made under Section 2;

(2) An order granting an application to stay arbitration made under Section 2(b);

(3) An order confirming or denying confirmation of an award;

(4) An order modifying or correcting an award;

(5) An order vacating an award without directing a rehearing; or

(6) A judgment or decree entered pursuant to the provisions of this act.

(b) The appeal shall be taken in the manner and to the same extent as from orders or judgments in a civil action.

Section 20. (Act Not Retroactive.)

This act applies only to agreements made subsequent to the taking effect of this act.

Section 21. (Uniformity of Interpretation.)

This act shall be so construed as to effectuate its general purpose to make uniform the law of those states which enact it.

Section 22. (Constitutionality.)

If any provision of this act or the application thereof to any person or circumstance is held invalid, the invalidity shall not affect other provisions or applications of the act which can be given without the invalid provision or application, and to this end the provisions of this act are severable.

Section 23. (Short Title.)

This act may be cited as the Uniform Arbitration Act.

Section 24. (Repeal.)

All acts or parts of acts which are inconsistent with the provisions of this act are hereby repealed.

Section 25. (Time of Taking Effect.)

This act shall take effect _____

Notes

Chapter 1

[1]Conference on Training of Law Students in Labor Relations, Vol. III, Transcript of Proceedings (1947), 636–37, as cited in Elkouri & Elkouri, *How Arbitration Works* (BNA Books, 1973), 254.

[2]The Chicago, West Coast, and Pittsburgh Tripartite Committees have all agreed that the traditional rules of evidence applicable in the judicial system should not *per se* be applied in an arbitral setting. See, *Problems of Proof in Arbitration*, Proceedings of the Nineteenth Annual Meeting, National Academy of Arbitrators (BNA Books, 1967).

[3]*Id.* at 89.

[4]*Id.* at 246.

Chapter 2

[1]See, for example, *A. P. Green Refractories Co.*, 67-1 ARB ¶ 8338 (Krimsley, 1967); *Caterpillar Tractor Co.*, 77-2 ARB ¶ 8515 (Dolnick, 1977); *Chrysler Corp.*, 67-1 ARB ¶ 8135 (Kabaker, 1967); *American Airlines, Inc.*, 67-1 ARB ¶ 8028 (Sembower); *Ingersoll Products Div.*, 66-3 ARB ¶ 9065 (Larkin, 1966) (discharge sustained for theft of co-worker's lunch where grievant one of only 25 percent who did not carry lunch and where observed in washroom where lunches were kept "chewing something"); *Mead Corp.*, 66-2 ARB ¶ 8511 (Keefe, 1966) (discharge sustained for sabotage of company machine notwithstanding absence of "direct evidence" where grievant observed at place where damage took place as well as rapid departure from area immediately prior to time it occurred). But see *New York Shipbuilding Corp.*, 66-1 ARB ¶ 8299 (Crawford, 1966) (circumstantial evidence insufficient, without more, to establish guilt of horseplay and malicious mischief); *New Haven Trap Rock Co.*, 66-1 ARB ¶ 8082 (Summers, C. 1965).

[2]*A. P. Green Refractories, Co.*, supra note 1, at 4207.

[3]48 LA 949, 950–51 (Jenkins, 1967).

[4]*Perry's Adm'x v. Inter-Southern Life Ins. Co.*, 248 Ky. 491, 58 S.W.2d 906 (1933).

[5]Issues relating to credibility of witnesses will be discussed in Chapter 9. Questions of relevancy are discussed in the next chapter.

Chapter 3

[1]See R. Smith, "The Search for Truth," in *Truth, Lie Detectors, and Other Problems in Labor Arbitration*, Proceedings of the Thirty-First Annual Meeting, National Academy of Arbitrators (BNA Books, 1979), 49.

[2]See Fed. R. Evid. 401, effective July 1, 1975, as amended to April 1, 1979.

[3]Shulman, "Reason, Contract and Law in Labor Relations," 68 Harv. L. Rev. 999, 1017 (1955).

[4]Report of the West Coast Tripartite Committee, in Problems of Proof in Arbitration, Proceedings of the Nineteenth Annual Meeting, National Academy of Arbitrators (BNA Books, 1967), 164.

[5]Fed. R. Evid. 610 provides: "Evidence of the beliefs or opinions of a witness on matters of religion is not admissible for the purpose of showing that by reason of their nature his credibility is impaired or enhanced." As stated by the Advisory Committee's note, however, an inquiry for the purpose of showing interest or bias because of religious beliefs is not within this prohibition.

Chapter 4

[1]Report of the West Coast Tripartite Committee, in Problems of Proof in Arbitration, Proceedings of the Nineteenth Annual Meeting, National Academy of Arbitrators (BNA Books, 1967), 195.

[2]Dockside Machine & Boilerworks, Inc., 55 LA 1221, 1226 (Block, 1970). In Hospital Service Plan of N.J., 62 LA 616 (1974). Arbitrator Kaplan considered the initial problem of classifying conduct as "criminal" for the proper application of a quantum standard: "A threshold question often arises as to whether the offense for which an employee is discharged is in the nature of a criminal violation, and therefore an issue as to which quantum of proof standard shall be applicable. Such issues are dealt with by referring to the penal laws of the state wherein the offense was committed. The burden of proof to show that an offense falls within the criminal statute of the state is upon the party asserting it." Id. at 619 n.2.

[3]Great Atlantic & Pacific Tea Co., 63-1 ARB ¶ 8027 (Turkus, 1962).

[4]Aaron, "Some Procedural Problems in Arbitration," 10 Vand. L. Rev. 733, 741–42 (1957).

[5]Gorske, "Burden of Proof in Grievance Arbitration," 43 Marq. L. Rev. 135, 156 (1959).

[6]Kroger Co., 25 LA 906, 908 (Smith, 1955). See also Donaldson Company Inc., 60 LA 1240 (McKenna, 1973); New England Tel. Co., 59 LA 799 (Schmertz, 1972); Whirlpool Corp., 58 LA 421 (Daugherty, 1972); Koenig Trucking Co., 60 LA 899 (Howlett, 1973); Borg-Warner Corp., 27 LA 148 (Dworkin, 1956). For examples of the use of the "preponderance" test even though the grievant's act was also a crime, see Sylvester Garrett's discussion in United States Steel Corp., III Basic Steel Arb. 1467, and Hugo Black, Jr., sustaining a discharge for theft in Southern Greyhound Lines, 43 LA 113 (1964).

[7]Day and Zimmermann, Inc., 63 LA 1289, 1292 (Stratton, 1974).

[8]Aaron, supra note 4, at 649, 743.

[9]See Elkouri & Elkouri, How Arbitration Works (BNA Books, 1973), 277–78; see, e.g., Spartek, Inc., 77-1 ARB ¶ 8230 (Gibson, 1977); St. Joseph Lead Co., 29 LA 781 (Bothwell, 1957); Jones & Laughlin Steel, 29 LA 525 (Cahn), 1957); Ingersoll Prods. Div., Borg-Warner Corp., 49 LA 882 (Larkin, 1967).

[10]See Gorske, supra note 5; Report of the Pittsburgh Tripartite Committee, in Problems of Proof in Arbitration, supra note 1, at 257.

As noted by Arbitrators Updegraff and McCoy, the party who bears the burden of proof is obliged to present his case first: "The right to put one's evidence first is generally considered an advantage, and is given to the party who carries the burden of proof partly to offset the disadvantages inherent in that burden but partly also because the logical method of proceeding is for the one who has advanced a grievance to state and prove it." R. Smith, L. Merrifield, and D. Rothschild, *Collective Bargaining and Labor Arbitration* (Bobbs-Merrill Co., 1970), 228.

[11]Gorske, *supra* note 5, at 153.

[12]*Sealtest Dairy Products Co.,* 35 LA 205, 208–209 (Morvant, 1960).

[13]*Id.*

[14]See O. Fairweather, *Practice and Procedure in Labor Arbitration* (BNA Books, 1973), 201.

[15]*McCall Printing Co.,* 64 LA 584 (Lubic, 1975) (employer's failure to apply discharge penalty in similar cases warrants reinstatement of employee); *Naval Air Rework Facility,* 72 LA 1266 (Mire, 1979) (suspension proper for tardiness where employee, claiming breakdown of auto, failed to produce any evidence in support of defense); *Babcock & Wilcox Co.,* 72 LA 1073 (Mullin, 1979) (discharge overturned where grievant produced medical evidence of psychoneurosis); *General Electric Co.,* 69 LA 721 (King, 1977) (mitigating circumstances demonstrated by grievant—suicide of brother).

[16]48 LA 319 (Frey, 1966).

[17]*Id.* at 319–20.

[18]71 LA 222 (Spritzer, 1978) (employer does not bear burden of proving just cause for termination after it has demonstrated that legitimate company rule containing discharge penalty was violated subject to union's right to demonstrate that rule was improperly applied or that penalty was unreasonable).

[19]See Labor Management Relations Act, Sec. 203(d).

[20]83 LRRM 2652 (5th Cir. 1973).

[21]Jones, "An Effort to Describe One Person's Decisional Thinking," in *Decisional Thinking of Labor Arbitrators and Federal Judges as Triers of Fact: Selected Discussion Materials and Problems* (Unpublished report delivered at the Thirty-Third Annual Meeting, National Academy of Arbitrators, Los Angeles, Cal., June 10–13, 1980), 164–65.

Chapter 5

[1]American Arbitration Association, *Voluntary Labor Arbitration Rules* (1979) [hereinafter cited as *1979 AAA Rules*], Rule 24. See Appendix A for a full text of the Rules.

[2]See, e.g., *Seaview Industries, Inc.,* 39 LA 125 (Duncan, 1962) (handwriting expert); *National Union of Hospital & Health Care Employees,* 77-2 ARP ¶ 8554 (Handsaker, 1977) (handwriting expert); *Westinghouse Elec. Corp.* 43 LA 450 (Singletary, 1964) (polygraph examiner); *Daystrom Furniture Co.,* 65 LA 1157 (Laughlin) (polygraph); *Thompson Grinder Co.,* 70-2 ARB ¶ 8821 (Belshaw, 1970) (medical findings); *General Mills, Inc.,* 69 LA 254 (Traynor, 1977) (medical evidence); see also Sears, "Observations on Psychiatric Testimony in Arbitration," in *Arbitration and Social Change,* Proceedings of the Twenty-Second Annual Meeting, National Academy of Arbitrators (BNA Books, 1970), 151.

[3]Fed. R. Evid. 611(c) provides: "Leading questions should not be used on the direct examination of a witness except as may be necessary to develop his testimony. Ordinarily leading questions should be permitted on cross-examination. When a party calls a hostile witness, an adverse party, or a witness identified with an adverse party, interrogation may be by leading questions." As noted by the Advisory Committee, Rule 611(c) continues the traditional view that the suggestive powers of the leading question are as a general proposition undesirable.

[4]See Report of the Chicago Area Tripartite Committee, in Problems of Proof in Arbitration, Proceedings of the Nineteenth Annual Meeting, National Academy of Arbitrators (BNA Books, 1967), 101–102.

[5]E. Cleary, McCormick on Evidence (Hornbook Series) (West Publishing Co., 1972), 43.

[6]See, e.g., Twin City Rapid Transit Co., 62-1 ARB ¶ 8128 (Levinson, 1961) ("in view of the fact that the checkers' evidence was wholly written and not subjected to the closer scrutiny of oral examination, as opposed to the grievant's oral testimony under oath, the benefit of the doubt should be resolved in favor of the grievant . . ."); Tower Iron Works, 62-2 ARB ¶ 8663 (Teele, 1961) (written evidence prepared by absent parties of limited value since parties could not be cross-examined; Pick-N-Pay Supermarkets, Inc., 52 LA 832 (Haughton, 1969) (employer's case defective where reliance placed on paid spotters who prepared reports and spotters not available for cross-examination).

[7]See Rule 611(c), supra note 3.

[8]Report of the Chicago Area Tripartite Committee, supra note 4, at 102.

[9]M. Trotta, Arbitration of Labor-Management Disputes (AMACOM, 1974), 100.

[10]Fed. R. Evid. 611(b) provides: "Cross-examination should be limited to the subject matter of the direct examination and matters affecting the credibility of the witness. The court may, in the exercise of its discretion, permit inquiry into additional matters as if on direct examination."

[11]1979 AAA Rules, Rule 26.

[12]See "Quantum and Burden of Proof," supra, p. 10.

[13]In Local 560, IBT v. Eazor Express, Inc., 65 LRRM 2647 (N.J. Super. 1967), a New Jersey court refused to vacate an arbitrator's award against a challenge that procedural due process was denied when the arbitrator refused to permit the employer to call the grievant as its first witness in a discharge case.

[14]263 F. Supp. 488, 64 LRRM 2580 (C.D. Calif. 1967).

[15]The court further stated: "This does not mean that the Arbitrator may not insist on orderly proceeding but it does not appear that legalistic technicalities are to prevail or control particularly where no statement of ground rules for the hearing is made by the Arbitrator in the initial stages." Id. at 2585.

[16]Fed. R. Evid. 612, in relevant part, provides:
"Except as otherwise provided in criminal proceedings . . . , if a witness uses a writing to refresh his memory for the purpose of testifying, either—
"(1) while testifying, or
"(2) before testifying, if the court in its discretion determines it is necessary in the interests of justice, an adverse party is entitled to have the writing produced at the hearing, to inspect it, to cross-examine the witness thereon,

and to introduce in evidence those portions which relate to the testimony of the witness. . . ."

[17]*Fed. R. Evid.* 615. See O. Fairweather, *Practice and Procedure in Labor Arbitration* (BNA Books, 1973), 159. For an excellent discussion of the policies for excluding witnesses, see *Seattle-Post Intelligencer*, 66 LA 717 (Stephan, 1976).

[18]*1979 AAA Rules*, Rule 22.

[19]In this regard, Owen Fairweather states that "arbitrators are seldom willing to exclude the grievant, and for this reason, . . . he is often called as the employer's initial witness." Fairweather, *supra* note 17.

[20]*Code of Professional Responsibility for Arbitrators of Labor-Management Disputes*, Sec. 5(A)(1)(b). See Appendix B for a full text of the Code.

[20a]65 LA 987 (1975).

[20b]*Id.* at 991.

[21]*1979 AAA Rules*, Rule 28, in relevant part, provides: "The Arbitrator shall be judge of the relevancy and materiality of the evidence offered and conformity to the legal rules of evidence shall not be necessary." See generally Annot., 75 ALR 3d 132 (1977) (refusal of arbitrators to receive evidence, or to permit briefs or arguments, on particular issues as grounds for relief from award).

[22]90 LRRM 2767 (S.D.N.Y. 1975).

[23]86 LRRM 3086 (D.C.R.I. 1974).

[24]*Id.* at 3087, citing *Newark Stereotypers Union v. Newark Morning Ledger Co.*, 397 F.2d 594, 68 LRRM 2561 (3rd Cir. 1968).

[25]See, "New Evidence and the Arbitral Process," *infra*, p. 109.

[26]350 F. Supp. 1221, 82 LRRM 2107 (E.D. Pa. 1972). See also *Machinists, Local 701 v. Holiday Oldsmobile*, 356 F.Supp. 1325, 84 LRRM 2200 (N.D. Ill. 1972) (arbitrator properly refused to grant additional continuance); *Eckert v. Budd Co.*, __ F. Supp. __, 88 LRRM 2979 (E.D. Pa. 1975) (employee not improperly deprived of witnesses where record indicated that grievant did not raise claim before arbitrator or that arbitrator's aid was sought in same regard).

[27]The *Uniform Arbitration Act*, Sec. 12, in relevant part, provides: "Upon application of a party, the court shall vacate an award where:

. . .

"(4) The arbitrators refused to postpone the hearing upon sufficient cause being shown therefore or refused to hear evidence material to the controversy or otherwise so conducted the hearing . . . as to prejudice substantially the rights of a party." See Appendix D for a full text of the Act.

[28]*Green-Wood Cemetery v. Cemetery Workers*, 82 LRRM 2894 (N.Y.S.Ct. 1973).

[29]*1979 AAA Rules*, Rule 32.

[30]See Rule 27 of the *1979 AAA Rules*, Appendix A, p. 127. The *Uniform Arbitration Act*, Sec. 5(a), in relevant part, provides: "The arbitrators may hear and determine the controversy upon the evidence produced notwithstanding the failure of a party duly notified to appear." In *Sunshine Convalescent Hospital*, 62 LA 276 (1974), Arbitrator Melvin Lennard concluded that an *ex parte* award was permissible where (1) the employer did not appear at the hearing and (2) the company attorney had previously represented to the union that his client was willing to proceed to arbitration. The arbitrator ruled that having assured the union that it should not commence an

action to compel arbitration, the employer could not later claim that a valid award cannot issue without a court order compelling arbitration. Similary, in *U.S. Immigration & Naturalization Service*, 59 LA 119 (1972), Arbitrator Lennard again held that he had authority to proceed *ex parte* to determine the merits of a grievance where the Service withdrew from the hearing on the ground that the arbitrator lacked jurisdiction over the subject matter. The arbitrator reasoned that authority to proceed *ex parte* existed once the parties have appeared and participated in the hearing, even if thereafter one of them should depart. Such a result, noted Arbitrator Lennard, is contemplated by the parties when they adopted the following contractual language: "If for any reason either party refuses to participate in the selection of an arbitrator, the Federal Mediation and Conciliation Service will be empowered to make a direct designation of an arbitrator to hear the case." *Id.* at 123.

Chapter 6

[1]E. Cleary, *McCormick on Evidence* (Hornbook Series) (West Publishing, 1972), 802–803.

[2]Report of the West Coast Tripartite Committee, in *Problems of Proof in Arbitration*, Proceedings of the Nineteenth Annual Meeting, National Academy of Arbitrators (BNA Books, 1967), 192.

[3]69-1 ARB ¶ 8223 (1968).

[4]*Id.* at 3767.

[5]*Fed. R. Evid.* 301 provides: "In all civil actions . . . a presumption imposes on the party against whom it is directed the burden of going forward with evidence to rebut or meet the presumption, but does not shift to such party the burden of proof in the sense of the risk of nonpersuasion, which remains throughout the trial upon the party on whom it was originally cast." Thus, the Federal Rules reject the "bursting bubble" theory of presumptions under which a presumption would totally disappear once evidence was introduced that would tend to establish that the presumed fact does not exist.

[6]See Report of the New York Tripartite Committee, in *Problems of Proof in Arbitration, supra* note 2, at 297.

[7]*Id.*

[8]*Enterprise Wire Co.*, 46 LA 359 (Daugherty, 1966). Additional criteria cited by Arbitrator Daugherty are: (a) Was the employer's rule or managerial order reasonably related to the orderly, efficient, and safe operation of the employer's business? (b) Did the employer, before administrating discipline to an employee, make an effort to discover whether the employee did in fact violate or disobey a rule or an order of management? (c) Was the employer's investigation conducted fairly and objectively? (d) At the investigation did the employer obtain substantial evidence or proof that the employee was guilty as charged?

[9]*Valley Steel Casting Co.*, 22 LA 520, 527 (Howlett, 1954).

[10]For a comprehensive treatment of past practice, see R. Mittenthal, "Past Practice and the Administration of Collective Bargaining Agreements," in *Arbitration and Public Policy*, Proceedings of the Fourteenth Annual Meeting, National Academy of Arbitrators (BNA Books, 1961), 30.

[11]O. Fairweather, *Practice and Procedure in Labor Arbitration* (BNA Books, 1973), 220.

[12]Quoted in *Lectures on the Law and Labor Management Relations,* Michigan University Law School, Summer Institute for International and Comparative Law (1951), 216–17.

[13]Section 203(d) of the Taft-Hartley Act provides: "Final adjustment by a method agreed upon by the parties is declared to be the desirable method for settlement of grievance disputes arising over the application or interpretation of an existing collective-bargaining agreement." 29 U.S.C. § 173(d). See also *Steelworkers v. American Manufacturing Co.,* 363 U.S. 564 (1960); *Steelworkers v. Warrior & Gulf Navigation Co.,* 363 U.S. 574 (1960); *Steelworkers v. Enterprise Wheel & Car Corp.* 363 U.S. 593 (1960).

[14]363 U.S. 574 (1960).

[15]*Id.* at 582–83.

[16]Report of the New York Tripartite Committee, in *Problems of Proof in Arbitration, supra* note 2, at 297.

[17]*Fed. R. Evid.* 201; Cleary, *supra* note 1, at 757.

[18]Cleary, *supra* note 1, at 560.

[19]See Report of the Chicago Area Tripartite Committee, in *Problems of Proof in Arbitration, supra* note 2, at 92.

[20]*Supra* note 2, at 189.

[21]See, e.g., D. Sears, "Observations on Psychiatric Testimony in Arbitration," in *Arbitration and Social Change,* Proceedings of the Twenty-Second Annual Meeting, National Academy of Arbitrators (BNA Books, 1970), 151; Fairweather, *supra* note 11, at 221; Elkouri & Elkouri, *How Arbitration Works* (BNA Books, 1973), 291–95; D. Miller "The Use of Experts in Arbitration: Expert Medical Evidence," in *Arbitration and Social Change, supra* this note, at 135; M. Volz, "Medical and Health Issues in Arbitration," in *Truth, Lie Detectors, and Other Problems in Labor Arbitration,* Proceedings of the Thirty-First Annual Meeting, National Academy of Arbitrators (BNA Books, 1979), 156.

[22]See, e.g., *North Shore Gas Co.,* 40 LA 37 (Sembower, 1963); *Dunlop Tire & Rubber Co.,* 64 LA 1099 (Mills, 1975) (doctor's deposition not accorded great weight absent opportunity for cross-examination by grievant). In *Proctor & Gamble Co.* v. *Independent Oil & Chemical Workers,* 87 LRRM 3179 (D.C. Md, 1974), a federal court let stand an arbitrator's award based in part on a written statement of a nontestifying physician.

[23]Chicago Tripartite Committee, in *Problems of Proof in Arbitration, supra* note 2, at 107–108.

[24]Nicholas Unkovic, an attorney and management advocate and Member of the Pittsburgh Tripartite Comm., has stated: "I would say, ordinarily, if I were an arbitrator, I would not keep out doctors' statements. Yet I realize the danger—it only costs $5 or $10 to get a doctor's statement. Still you have to keep moving, and I think if you adjourned the hearing to bring a doctor in, too much time would be consumed. My reaction is unless the medical evidence is the very heart of the case—to prove whether or not a fellow was permanently disabled, for example—I don't think you need the doctor." See "Workshop on Pittsburgh Tripartite Committee Report," in *Problems of Proof in Arbitration, supra* note 2, at 277.

[25]*North Shore Gas Co.,* 40 LA 37, 44 (1963). See also, *Reynolds Metals-Sherwin Plant,* 65 LA 678 (Caraway, 1975) (employer not justified in discharge of grievant where medical board of physicians consisting of company-appointed physician, union-appointed physician, and third physician not properly convened); *Air Carrier Engine Service Inc.,* 65 LA 666 (Naehr-

ing, 1975) (employee who was precluded from returning to work because company-appointed physician and grievant's physician failed to agree as to grievant's recovery from drug addiction reinstated with one-half backpay under contract requiring employer and union to mutually agree upon third physician in event of inability to reach agreement concerning employee's capacity to resume work); *Pacific Tel. & Tel. Co.*, 66 LA 433 (Barrett, 1976).

[26]See *International Harvester Co.*, 22 LA 138 (Platt, 1954).

[27]14 LA 253, 255 (Wallen, 1950). Arbitrator Marlin Volz has similarly stated: "Where the only reliable evidence consists of the conflicting opinions of the company's medical adviser and the employee's physician, it is usually held by arbitrators that the company properly may rely upon the findings and recommendations of its own medical expert, especially where they evidence a thorough understanding of the employee's condition." See Volz, *supra* note 21, at 175–76. Contra: *Sears, Roebuck & Co.*, 72 LA 238 (Blackmar, 1979).

[28]49 LA 535 (Doyle, 1967).

[29]*Id.* at 539.

[30]61 LA 1113 (Meiners, 1973).

[31]22 LA 138 (1954).

[32]*Id.* at 139.

[33]See, *American Iron & Machine Works Co.*, 19 LA 417 (Merrill, 1952).

[34]Miller, "The Use of Experts in Arbitration: Expert Medical Evidence," in *Arbitration and Social Change, supra* note 21, at 137. The problems of determining when expert medical evidence is medical fact or mere medical opinion is illustrated in *Penn Manor School District*, 73 LA 1227 (1979). In that case Arbitrator Crawford was presented with the issue of determining what was an "illness" for purposes of the school code granting pay to employees who are prevented from working. The only evidence submitted by the grievant, who had absented herself from school for three days because of fear of a catastrophic accident due to the Three Mile Island incident, was a written statement from her personal physician which indicated that the grievant was absent from her job because of "environmental stress, emotional stress and anxiety." Noting that arbitrators are simply not in a position to determine how emotional stress and fear affects people, Arbitrator Crawford, in holding for the grievant, stated that "we can hardly substitute our opinion concerning the grievant's condition for that of her personal lifelong physician." *Id.* at 1229. Although the grievant's personal physician arguably rendered a mere opinion, the arbitrator observed that the Three Mile incident affected people in varying degrees and that its mental health impact is still being studied. Accordingly, the arbitrator deferred to the opinion of the grievant's doctor rather than form his own conclusion as to the effect upon the grievant.

[35]Miller, *supra* note 34, at 145.

[35a]See, e.g., *Rudin Management Co.*, 74 LA 189 (Talmadge, 1979) (employer may test veracity of employee's illness claim by calling him at home or by requesting physician's statement certifying to his claimed illness before granting sick leave benefits); *Babcock & Wilcox Co.*, 61 LA 1 (Sherman, 1973) (medical evidence not credited where dated just before arbitration hearing).

[36]See, e.g., *Ideal Cement Co.*, 20 LA 480 (Merrill, 1953) ("[i]n view of the direct conflict in the medical testimony, with nothing to swing the balance preponderantly on one side or the other, I think that the Company is entitled

to rely on the views of its own medical advisers, if it has given [the grievant] fair notice and opportunity to overcome these views before reaching a final decision."). See also *Southern Cotton Oil Co.*, 26 LA 353 (Kelliher, 1956) (employer that challenges report of grievant's doctor required to undertake own medical investigation). Arbitrator Samuel Kates, in *Lamson & Sessions Co.*, 43 LA 61 (1964), declares some guiding principles involving the efforts of employees to return to work after disabling illnesses or injuries:

"1. When there is a conflict in medical evidence as to an employee's physical or mental fitness to undertake particular work, the arbitrator generally should determine merely whether the disputed management decision has been based upon bona fide nondiscriminatory expert opinions and advice which appear to the arbitrator to have been fairly and reasonably reached and given in the light of the known facts.

"2. In the absence of important differences in the degree or expertness possessed by the respective medical witnesses, the personal testimony of a medical witness who is subject to cross-examination at the arbitration hearing is generally entitled to more weight than mere written reports by others.

"3. In the absence of contractual requirements otherwise, management is ordinarily entitled to rely upon the opinions and advice of its own medical consultants if such opinions and advice meet the standards set forth in paragraph "1" above; and the Company may not be compelled to submit the decision of physical or mental fitness to outside experts against its wishes." *Id.* at 64. See also, *Rohm & Haas Texas, Inc.*, 68 LA 498 (White, 1977).

[37]See generally Fleming, "Some Problems of Evidence Before the Labor Arbitrator," 60 *Mich. L. Rev.* 134 (1961), especially 134–35 ("The Uses of Past Misconduct").

[38]See, e.g., *Arcrods Plant*, 47 LA 994 (Bradley, 1966) (two-year disciplinary record admitted when referenced in collective-bargaining agreement; argument that arbitrator limited to considering only disciplinary action for like offenses rejected); *Champion Spark Plug*, 67 LA 254 (Kates, 1976) (prior disciplinary incident should have been removed from employee's personnel file as being more than 24 months old, notwithstanding contention that incident was not considered); *Ingersoll Products Division of Borg-Warner*, 66-3 ARB ¶ 9065 (Larkin, 1966) (total employment considered in assessing degree of punishment); *N.Y.S. Dept. of Correctional Services*, 69 LA 344 (Kornblum, 1977) (antecedent acts considered by employer only for purpose of supporting appropriateness of the penalty to be imposed).

[39]*Aluminum Co. of America*, 8 LA 234, 235 (Pollard, 1945).

[40]*Ingersoll Products Division of Borg-Warner, supra* note 38, at 6710.

[41]See, e.g., *Anaconda Co.*, 69 LA 879 (Allen, 1977) (proper to consider employee work record of seven and eight years in assessing penalty for recent infraction where infractions were "numerous" [33 disciplinary incidents] and were not "bunched" in early years); *Stokely-Van Camp, Inc.*, 59 LA 655 (Griffin, 1972) (personnel file of employee predating previous promotion to management position not admissible in arbitration involving propriety of discharge, since promotion to management position wipes slate clean of previous warnings).

[42]See, e.g., *Houdaille Industries, Inc.*, 65 LA 797 (Moorhead, undated) (past record of unrelated events considered as a "throw-in" in sustaining discharge); *Arcrods Plant*, 47 LA 994 (Bradley, 1966), *supra* note 38.

[43]R. Fleming, *The Labor Arbitration Process* (University of Ill. Press., 1967), 167–68.

[44]*Butler Manufacturing Co.*, 70 LA 426 (Welch, 1978).

[45]W. Wirtz, "Due Process of Arbitration," in *The Arbitrator and the Parties,* Proceedings of the Eleventh Annual Meeting, National Academy of Arbitrators (BNA Books, 1958), 20.

[46]*Id.* See also *Northern Indiana Public Services Co.*, 69 LA 201 (Sembower, 1977) ("principle is virtually uniform in arbitration that the past record of an employee may be considered only in connection with the *quantum* of the penalty, and that the alleged misdeed which precipitated the disciplinary action first must stand up"). (Emphasis in original.) *Id.* at 208.

[47]*Supra* note 45 n. 22.

[48]See, e.g., *Link-Belt Co.*, 4 LA 434 (Gilden, et. al., 1946); *Consolidated Vultee Aircraft Corp.*, 10 LA 907 (Dwyer, 1948).

[49]*Id.*

[50]See, *Harshaw Chemical Co.*, 32 LA 23 (1958), as cited in Smith, Merrifield, and Rothschild, *Collective Bargaining and Labor Arbitration* (Bobbs-Merrill, 1970), 215.

[51]70 LA 1028 (Keltner, 1978). See also *Wolverine World Wide, Inc.*, 66 LA 796 (Herman, 1976) ("once a penalty has been issued by a supervisor armed with the appropriate authority, it may not be enlarged or amplified by higher supervision in a determination based upon the identical evidence which supported the original penalty"), *id.* at 799; *Durham Hosiery Mills*, 24 LA 356 (Livengood, 1955) (principle of "double jeopardy" violated where employee exposed more than once to punishment for same offense; employer not allowed, once discipline assessed, to come back at later date and say "We have decided that the penalty was not severe enough; because of what we have now learned about your earlier conduct, you are discharged"), *id.* at 358; *Abex Corp.*, 67 LA 1313 (Smedley, 1977) ("The so-called double jeopardy rule preventing imposition by management of more than one penalty for a single offense is not seriously questioned in any arbitral authority. It is a salutory and necessary rule going to the very heart of due process and fundamental fairness. If a second penalty may be invoked for one offense, why not a third and where and when will it stop? The worker is entitled to know his case is determined and settled and that further discipline will aply only if he errs anew"), *id.* at 1314; *U.S. Plywood-Champion Papers, Inc.*, 60 LA 443 (Warns, 1973) (discharge improper where employee was previously discharged but subsequently reinstated).

[52]*Amoco Oil Co.*, 61 LA 10 (Cushman, 1973). See also *Northwest Air Lines, Inc.*, 69-1 ARB ¶ 8122 (Rohman, 1968) (subsequent conviction for morals charge after discharge held inadmissible to substantiate discharge); *New York Telephone Co.*, 66 LA 1037 (Markowitz, 1976) (great weight of authority holds that employer cannot *enlarge* the reasons for disciplinary action beyond those provided at time of determination to impose discipline, but employer may continue investigation of case to buttress allegations) (emphasis in original); *American Air Filter*, 64 LA 899 (Young, 1975) (employer justified in imposing discharge where postdischarge evidence establishes employee selling company property; suspicions aroused at time of discharge); *White Front Stores, Inc.*, 61 LA 536 (Killion, 1973) (postdischarge assault "so immediate to and contemporaneous with abortive discharge that it canot be deemed 'post-discharge conduct' in a time sense").

[53]See, e.g., *Texaco Inc.*, 42 LA 408 (Prasow, 1963); *Chrysler Corp.*, 40 LA 935 (Alexander, 1963); *Philco Corp.* 43 LA 568 (Davis, 1964).

[54]See Chap. 9, *infra*. See, e.g., *Commodity Warehousing Corp.*, 60 LA 1260 (Doppelt, 1973) ("In over 20 years of working for the employer or its predecessor, the grievant has never even been disciplined. Obviously, the allegations herein made cannot be used to cast doubt on his credibility until proven."). *Id.* at 1265.

[55]Miller, "Evidence and Proof in Arbitration," 5 *J. Collective Negotiations*, No. 4, at 313 (1976).

[56]*Id.*

[57]Fleming *supra* note 43, at 170.

[58]*Id.*

[59]See, e.g., Elkouri & Elkouri, *supra* note 21, at 373–77; Fairweather, *supra* note 11, at 335–46; Fleming, *supra* note 43, at 78–106; Rynecki & Hill, *Preparing & Presenting a Public Sector Grievance Arbitration Case*, PERL No. 58 (IPMA, 1979), 51–52. Section 2(G) of the *Code of Professional Responsibility for Arbitrators* provides:

"1. An arbitrator must assume full personal responsibility for the decision in each case decided.

"a. The extent, if any, to which an arbitrator properly may rely on precedent, on guidance of other awards, or on independent research is dependent primarily on the policies of the parties on these matters, as expressed in the contract, or other agreement, or at the hearing.

"b. When the mutual desires of the parties are not known or when the parties express differing opinions or policies, the arbitrator may exercise discretion as to these matters, consistent with acceptance of full personal responsibility for the award."

[60]Fairweather, *supra* note 11, at 338–39.

[61]See cases cited *supra*, note 13.

[62]Arbitrator John Sembower, in *North Shore Gas Co.*, 40 LA 37 (1963), has stated: "While arbitration awards are not precedential to the same degree as court decisions, it is generally recognized that in the interest of uniformity of procedure and to save the time and expense of repetitious presentation of issues, due respect should be accorded a well-reasoned award on like facts in the same plant and between the same parties, in the absence of intervening circumstances of a different nature or undue passage of time." *Id.* at 42. See also *Timken Roller Bearing Co.*, 32 LA 595 (Boehm, 1958); *Holland Suco Color Co.*, 43 LA 1022 (Geissinger, 1964); *Allegheny Ludlum Steel Corp.*, 43 LA 1041 (Wallen, 1964); *Carbon Fuel Co.*, 77-1 ARB ¶ 8002 (Cantor, 1976) (prior award not *res judicate* in present dispute where different grievant is complaining party). In *Machinists, Local 1617 v. Associated Transp. Inc.*, 92 LRRM 2342 (M.D.N.C. 1976), a federal district court held that an arbitrator was not bound by a previous arbitration award in which the allegedly identical issue was decided in favor of a different employee of the same employer. The court noted, however, that the doctrine of *res judicata*, even if extended to arbitration proceedings, did not bind the arbitrator, since that doctrine applies only where the same controversy between the same litigants, including the grievant, has been previously litigated.

[63]9 LA 731 (1948). See also *Pet Milk Co.*, 13 LA 551 (Hampton, 1949) (prior award deemed equivalent of warning notice).

[64]9 LA at 732 (1948).

[65]Merrill, "A Labor Arbitrator Views His Work," 10 *Vand. L. Rev.* 789, 797–98 (1957).

[66]Rynecki & Hill, *supra* note 59.

[67]See, e.g., *Warner and Swasey Co.*, 65 LA 709 (Walter, 1975) (suspension reversed where charge based on report of employee not present at hearing); *McCord Corp.*, 64-1 ARB ¶ 8335 (Witney, 1963) (refusal to credit testimony of employees not present at hearing); *Pipe Coupling Manufactures, Inc.*, 68-1 ARB ¶ 8088 (McDermott, 1967) (suspension of employee rescinded where no evidence other than hearsay advanced; vagueness and inconclusiveness of such evidence requires that it be supported by other evidence); *Chippewa Valley Board of Education*, 62 LA 409 (McCormick, 1974) (hearsay admitted where evidence corroborates other evidence in record); *United Parcel Service, Inc.*, 74-2 ARB ¶ 8541 (King, 1974) (hearsay normally admitted, though effect restricted); *Bamberger's*, 59 LA 879 (Glushien, 1972) ("some kinds of hearsay no doubt are more compelling than others and carry a certain degree of probability. But in all or substantially all cases which the arbitrator can envisage, there must be apart from the hearsay a core of competent, reliable and credible evidence which the hearsay corroborates"). *Id.* at 882.

[68]For an exhaustive review of the subject the practitioner is advised to consult either E. Cleary, *McCormick on Evidence* (Hornbook Series) (West Publishing Co., 1972) or Wigmore, *Evidence*, Sec. 1361 (Treatise Series) (3d ed. 1940).

[69]Cleary, *supra* note 68.

[70]*Id.* at 584.

[71]*Coleman v. Southwick*, 9 John. 50 (N.Y. 1812), in 5 Wigmore, *Evidence*, Sec. 1362 at 4, as cited in Cleary, *supra* note 68, at 583.

[72]See Fed. R. Evid. 801(d)(2).

[73]Suffice it to note that merely concluding the silence of the grievant is not hearsay should not be dispositive with respect to resolving the guilt or innocence of the grievant. See, e.g., *United Mine Works, District 29*, 77-2 ARB ¶ 8573 (Rimer, 1977) (refusal to deny guilt not tantamount to admission of guilt). This subject will be discussed in a subsequent chapter. See "Illegally Obtained Evidence," *infra* p. 77.

[74]See Fed. R. Evid. 803(6).

[75]The Federal Rules do not recognize a separate *res gestae* exception, rather they recognize selected individual exceptions which have traditionally been classified as *res geste* exceptions. See Fed. R. Evid. 803(1) (present sense impression); 803(2) (excited utterance); and 803(3) (existing mental, emotional, or physical condition). In *Faribault State Hospital*, 68 LA 713 (1977). Arbitrator Lipson credited, under the *res gestae* exception, statements made by a grievant to co-workers during an apparent emergency at a state mental health institution. The record indicated that the grievant was discharged for "intended maliciousness and cruelty" to a patient. In holding that the testimony of the grievant's co-workers was covered by the *res gestae* exception (the grievant was subsequently killed after his discharge), the arbitrator stated that the admissibility of such statements is permitted under the Federal Rules on the theory that statements made contemporaneously with a crucial event, or where the declarant is excited, are likely to be true. *Id.* at 719. The arbitrator accordingly ruled that the grievant's estate was not liable for unearned wages and, furthermore, the grievant's widow was entitled to any insurance proceeds she would have received had the grievant not been improperly discharged.

[76]See, e.g., Report of the Chicago Area Tripartite Committee, in *Problems of Proof in Arbitration, supra* note 2, at 90 (employee disciplined for breaking into fellow employee's locker may testify to a conversation with his fellow employee agreeing to give him access to the locker); Report of the Pittsburgh Area Tripartite Committee, in *Problems of Proof in Arbitration, supra* note 2, at 250 (words spoken during fight between two employees may be testified to by an observer who saw the fight).

[77]C. Updegraff, *Arbitration and Labor Relations* (BNA Books, 1970), 231.

[78]29 *Am. Jur.* 2d., 5497 at 555.

[79]See, e.g., *Apollo Merchandisers Corp.*, 70 LA 614 (Roumell, 1978) (arbitrator ruled that customer complaints, although hearsay, were nevertheless entitled to some consideration where they buttress testimony of witnesses who were present at the hearing); *Hercules, Inc.*, 62 LA 1170 (Taylor, 1974) (memos admitted although arguably not discussed in lower stages of grievance procedure); *Chippewa Valley Board of Educaton*, 62 LA 409 (McCormick, 1974) (testimony of teacher regarding representations of her doctor).

[80]*Bower Roller Bearing Co.*, 22 LA 320, 323 (Bowles, 1954).

[81]See, e.g., *Code of Professional Responsibility for Arbitrators of Labor-Management Disputes*, National Academy of Arbitrators, American Arbitration Association, and Federal Mediation and Conciliation Service, Part 5, Section A(1) at 19 ("An arbitrator must provide a fair and adequate hearing which assures that both parties have a sufficient opportunity to present their respective evidence and argument.").

[82]*Supra* note 2, at 189.

[83]54 LRRM 2660 (1963).

[84]*Id.* at 2661.

[85]*In re Gaines' Estate*, 15 Cal. 2d 255, 100 P. 2d 1055 (S. Ct. Cal., 1940), as cited in *Radioear Corp.*, 61 LA 709 (May, 1973) at 715.

[86]*Board of Education of Cook County*, 73 LA 310 (Hill, 1979).

[87]*A.B.C. Coach Lines, Inc.*, 239 NLRB No. 89, 99 LRRM 1724 (1978).

[88]*Oconomowoc Canning Co.*, 77-1 ARB ¶ 8194 (Mueller, 1977). In discussing the effect of "zipper" clause former NLRB General Counsel John S. Irving has argued that there is a clear distinction between a situation where a party to a contract wishes to preserve the *status quo* and one where a party wishes to change it. As noted by Irving,

"In those cases involving a unilateral change, the employer relies on the existence of a zipper clause in the collective bargaining agreement not to establish that the contract precludes bargaining over new subjects during the term of the contract, but rather to establish that the contract gives the employer unfettered power to change any term or condition not contained in the contract. The Board has clearly stated that a zipper clause will not ordinarily be construed to grant the employer such unfettered power." See Reports on Case-Handling Developments at NLRB, "Employer Duty to Bargain: Effect of 'Zipper' Clause on Employer's Duty to Bargain During Term of Collective Bargaining Agreement," *Labor Relations Yearbook—1979* (BNA Books, 1980), 262.

[89]*Board of Education of Cook County, supra* note 86.

[90]Nolan, *Labor Arbitration Law and Practice* (West Publishing Co., 1979), 163.

[91]Kennecott Copper Corp., 70-2 ARB ¶ 8849, at 5850–51 (Abernethy, 1970).

[92]"Proof of oral statements made at the bargaining table, however, usually generates a substantial amount of testimony and seldom is of value. Nevertheless, there is no basis upon which such evidence can be excluded, assuming the issue of ambiguity exists, so long as the statements were made in the presence of both parties." Report of the Chicago Area Tripartite Committee, in Problems of Proof in Arbitration, supra note 2, at 96. It is noteworthy that the Uniform Commercial Code rejects the idea that an ambiguity must first be found before parol evidence may be received to interpret the language of an agreement which otherwise would be considered a final, complete agreement. See, UCC §2-202. Various arbitrators have questioned whether the trend as evidenced in the UCC should be applicable in the arbitral forum. See, Jones, "Workshop on West Coast Tripartite Committee Report," in Problems of Proof in Arbitration, supra note 2, at 214.

[93]Supra note 2, at 185.

[94]61 LA 703 (1973).

[95]63 LA 169 (undated). See also, Levi Strauss & Co., 69 LA 1 (Goodstein, 1977) (recognizing that there are provisions that are part of contract but are not in writing); Kennecott Copper, 70-2 ARB ¶ 8849 (Abernethy, 1970) ("[T]he Arbitrator should not enforce the obvious intent of patently erroneous language which the record establishes is contrary to the reasonable expectations of the contracting parties. Here it is appropriate to consider the evidence introduced by the Company to ascertain whether it does unmistakably establish error in the contract language adopted.").

[96]Report of the Chicago Area Tripartite Committee, in Problems of Proof in Arbitration, supra note 2, at 95.

[97]70-2 ARB ¶ 8849 (1970).

[98]Id. at 5851.

[99]Supra note 96.

[100]Id.

[101]See, e.g., A.M. Castle & Co., 41 LA 391 (Sembower, 1963) (arrangement for doctor to examine grievant disregarded as part of settlement efforts by parties); Price-Pfister Brass Mfg. Co., 25 LA 398 (Prasow, 1955) (offers of compromise not admissible when party announces in advance that the offer must not be considered a waiver of any rights under agreement); E.I. du Pont de Nemours & Co., 14 LA 494 (Cornsweet, 1950) (determination of issues in arbitration cannot be influenced by offers of settlement during negotiation of grievance); Cleaners Hanger Co., AAA Case No. 51-8 (Klein, 1962); Koppers Co., 61-1 ARB ¶ 8041 (Duff, 1960). See also Fairweather, "Exclusion of Evidence of Settlement Offers," supra note 11, at 236; M. Trotta, Arbitration of Labor-Management Disputes (AMACON, 1974), 97.

[102]E.I. du Pont de Nemours & Co., 14 LA 494, 497 (Cornsweet, 1950).

[103]Report of Pittsburgh Tripartite Committee, in Problems of Proof in Arbitration, supra note 2, at 253.

[104]Chicago Tripartite Committee, Problems of Proof in Arbitration, supra note 2, at 87–88.

[105]Hillbro Newspaper Printing Co., 48 LA 1166 (Roberts, 1967) (correspondence between parties containing settlement offer admissible where union made claim that offer was accepted).

[106]Supra note 2, at 190.

[107]The Pittsburgh Committee has stated that admissions against interest made in the course of offers of compromise are not excluded generally. Pittsburgh Area Tripartite Committee, in *Problems of Proof in Arbitration, supra* note 2, at 253. Likewise, Professor Wirtz has stated: "As to the rejection in evidence of settlement discussion, no one will disagree that the acceptance of such evidence would facilitate the arbitrator's function. But it is equally recognized that its acceptance would tend to inhibit the parties in their future negotiations. There is, of course, nothing to prevent the parties from agreeing to do so, and this is sometimes done if the parties believe the circumstances to be appropriate for the arbitrator's consideration. . . ." Wirtz, *supra* note 45, at 42.

[108]Privileges involving self-incrimination, confessions, and improperly obtained evidence are covered in subsequent sections.

[109]See *Fed. R. Evid.* 501.

[110]Report of the New York Tripartite Committee, in *Problems of Proof in Arbitration, supra* note 2, at 298–99.

[111]See, e.g., *Air Reduction Chemical & Carbide Co.*, 41 LA 24 (Warns, 1963); *Management Services Inc.*, 58 LA 552 (Nicholas, 1972).

[112]87 LRRM 2337 (D.C. Conn. 1974).

[113]_____ U.S. _____, 100 LRRM 2728 (1978).

Chapter 7

[1]*Hoag* v. *New Jersey*, 356 U.S. 464, 479 (1958), quoting *Restatement, Judgments* § 68 (1).

[2]*The Evergreens* v. *Nunan*, 141 F.2d 927, 928 (2d Cir. 1944) cert. denied, 323 U.S. 720 (1944).

[3]*Commissioner of Internal Revenue* v. *Sunnen*, 333 U.S. 591, 597 (1948).

[4]68 LA 69 (1977).

[5]*Id.* at 71.

[6]70-2 ARB ¶ 8531 (1970).

[7]*Id.* at 4748.

[8]*Id.*

[9]69-1 ARB ¶ 8158 (1968).

[10]*Id.* at 3534, citing *Yellow Cab Co.*, 44 LA 445, 446 (Jones, 1965).

[11]63 LA 1307 (1974).

[12]*Id.* at 1310. See also, *Stecher-Traung-Schmidt Corp.*, 58 LA 261 (Koven, 1972) (payments awarded by compensation board only signify that employee unable to compete in open market and do not establish that employee unable to perform same work performed prior to injury); *Reynolds Metals Co.*, 59 LA 64 (Welch, 1972) (arbitrator not bound by decision of Alabama Board of Appeals that grievant did not voluntarily resign from his job within meaning of law and that grievant's mental condition was such that he was not responsible for his actions, where (1) issue not fully adjudicated and (2) even if fully adjudicated in courts, issue would not, as to present dispute, be *res judicata*; doctrine of *res judicata* requires identity in thing sued for as well as identity in cause of action and if parties had wanted any question or issue to be decided by State Industrial Relations Agency or courts, such mention would be so noted in agreement); *Kaiser Steel Corp.*, 68 LA 192 (Christopher, 1977) (employer not justified in placing employee who had heart attack on disability layoff based on rating of 69 percent permanent disability of

workers' compensation board; extent of disability determined by board made in accordance with state law regarding benefits and it does not necessarily follow that findings are indicative of employee's actual inability to meet job requirements); *Vermont Structural Steel Corp.*, 60 LA 842 (Hogan, 1973) (employees did not engage in "strike" within meaning of agreement notwithstanding determination by state department of employment security that employees conduct constituted "work stoppage"; department applies "its laws and reasoning" whereas arbitrator applies "law of collective bargaining agreement"); *Victor Metal Products Corp.*, 66 LA 333 (Ray, 1976) (union entitled to arbitrate issue notwithstanding employer's argument that union has waived issue by electing to pursue matter through state employment security agency that is now subject of court review, since (1) parties and issue different and (2) no rule mandating election of remedies); *E-Systems, Inc.*, 62 LA 862 (Garaway, 1974) (Board & court decisions made in effort to compromise and settle workman's compensation claim not conclusive proof of employee's physical status to perform job, citing *Page Dairy Co.*, 42 LA 1051 (Kiroff, 1964), *Goodyear Tire & Rubber Co.*, 52 LA 55 (Ray, 1968), and *Corhart Refractories Co., Inc.*, 39 LA 138 (Volz, 1962)).

[13]1975 ARB ¶ 8068 (Sisk, 1975).

[14]*Id.* at 3287.

[15]*Id.* See also *Stokely-Van Camp, Inc.*, 59 LA 655 (Griffin, 1972) (grievant's statement before employment security agency admissible for purposes of cross-examination in arbitration hearing, but is given no consideration in deciding merits of case where statements in report not sworn and no certification that statement of facts are correct).

[16]25 LA 68 (1955).

[17]96 LRRM 2208 (1st. Cir. 1977).

[18]72-2 ARB ¶ 8490 (1972).

[19]*Id.* at 4700.

[20]63-2 ARB ¶ 8843 (1963).

[21]*Id.* at 5726–27.

[22]*Id.*

[23]61 LA 663 (1973).

[24]*Id.* at 665. In *Babcock & Wilcox Co.*, 60 LA 778 (1972), Arbitrator Harry J. Dworkin held that evidence suppressed by a court could subsequently be used to justify a discharge in the arbitral forum:
"This arbitrator feels that an arbitration proceeding is in many respects a proceeding *de novo*; that the decision and award in each case must be made on the basis of the evidence submitted during the course of the arbitration hearing, and subject to the applicable standards. Accordingly, neither a conviction nor acquittal in a criminal proceeding is controlling upon the arbitrator in a grievance processed under the Agreement. In cases of criminal prosecution, the decision of the court, either of guilt, acquittal, or other form of disposition is necessarily arrived at on the basis of the evidence adduced during the course of the trial, the applicable laws and rules governing criminal procedure. The arbitrator's judgment, decision, and award are based on the evidence adduced before him, the governing provisions of the Agreement, and other relevant circumstances. The ruling of the trial court suppressing evidence on the ground of illegal search and seizure, and violation of the Fourth Amendment, is not controlling; such judicial ruling does not determine, or proscribe the arbitrator's jurisdiction or authority."
Arbitrator Dworkin further stated that there are exceptions:

"The only exception to the foregoing principles is in the area of state-ments, or admissions, made by a party during the course of a criminal pro-ceeding, such as a confession, or plea of 'guilty.' Although such statements are not controlling, they are admissible in an arbitration proceeding as ad-missions against interest."

Id. at 782-83. See also Olin Corp., 60 LA 135 (Chernick, 1973) (suspension of employee who broke window of car during strike did not amount to placing employee in "double jeopardy" where civil authorities resolved matter after employee made restitution for damages, since civil adjudication was for act of property destruction which violated right of private citizen; moreover, employer not party to proceeding).

[25]61 LA at 665–66.

[26]67 LA 861 (Lubow, 1976).

[27]Id. at 867.

[28]Report of the West Coast Tripartite Committee, in Problems of Proof in Arbitration, Proceedings of the Nineteenth Annual Meeting, National Acad-emy of Arbitrators (BNA Books, 1967), 206.

[29]Report of the Chicago Area Tripartite Committee, in Problems of Proof in Arbitration, id. at 109.

[30]1975 ARB ¶ 8201 (1975).

[31]42 LA 734 (1964).

[32]Id. at 737.

Chapter 8

[1]See, e.g., Jones, " 'Truth' When the Polygraph Operator Sits as Arbi-trator (or Judge): The Deception of 'Detection' in the Diagnosis of Truth and Deception," in Truth, Lie Detectors, and Other Problems in Labor Arbi-tration, Proceedings of the Thirty-First Annual Meeting, National Academy of Arbitrators (BNA Books, 1979), 75; Burkey, "Lie Detectors in Labor Rela-tions," 19 Arb. J. 193 (1964); Levin, "Lie Detectors Can Lie," 15 Lab L.J. 708 (1964); Levitt, "Scientific Evaluation of the 'Lie Detector,' " 40 Iowa L. Rev. 440 (1955); Carver, "The Inquisitorial Process in Private Employment," 63 Cornell L. Rev. 1 (1977): Menocal and Williams, "Lie Detectors in Private Employment: A Proposal for Balancing Interests," 33 Geo. Wash. L. Rev. 932 (1965); R. Fleming, The Labor Arbitration Process (University of Illllinois Press, 1967), 194–97. For an exhaustive treatment on the subject, see "Poly-graph Control and Civil Liberties Protection Act," Hearings on S. 1845 Be-fore the Subcommittee on the Constitution of the Committee on the Judicia-ry, 95th Cong., 1st & 2nd Sess. (1977–1978).

[2]See, e.g., Lag Drug Co., 39 LA 1121 (Kelliher, 1962) ("As a matter of the 'Common Law of Labor Relations,' it must be found that the great weight of both arbitration and legal authority is opposed to the use of lie detector re-sults as competent evidence."); B. F. Goodrich Tire, 36 LA 552 (Ryder, 1961) (evidence admissible when employees signed statements prior to taking tests permitting exam); Wilkof Steel & Supply, 39 LA 883 (Maxwell, 1962) (re-sults admissible, but weight to be given evidence within arbitrator's discre-tion); American Maize-Products Co., 56 LA 421 (Larkin, 1971) (evidence admissible but only one element to be considered; where supported by other corroborative evidence, test may be given some weight); Illinois Bell, 39 LA 470 (Ryder, 1962) (polygraph evidence admitted where grievant consented to

test); *Ramsey Steel Co.*, 66-1 ARB ¶ 8310 (Carmichael, 1966) (results of lie detector inadmissible where evidence that grievant would have been disciplined notwithstanding results of exam); *Kwik Kafeteria, Inc.*, 66-1 ARB ¶ 8359 (Eiger, 1966) (results held not admissible as test results have "no probative power"); *Louis Zahn Drug Co.*, 40 LA 352 (Sembower, 1963) ("great weight of legal authority against use of lie detector results as evidence in criminal and civil cases."); *Saveway Inwood Service Station*, 44 LA 709 (Kornblum, 1965) (discharge motivated in part by results of polygraph not sustained due to polygraph's unreliability as proof of guilt); *Brink's Inc.*, 70 LA 909 (Pinkus, 1978) (evidence admissible but results "play little if any part in the conclusions of the arbitrator" where test not used to verify truthfulness).

[3]See *Illinois Bell Telephone Co.*, 39 LA 470 (Ryder, 1962).

[4]*Ramsey Steel Co.*, 66-1 ARB ¶ 8310, at 4062 (Carmichael, 1966).

[5]See e.g., *Lag Drug Co.*, 39 LA 1121 (Kelliher, 1962) (discharge not sustained of employee who refused to submit to exam where evidence of test results alone would not support discharge); *National Electric Coil*, 46 LA 756 (Gross, 1966) (no conclusion of guilt drawn from failure of employee to submit to lie detector); *American Maize-Products Co.*, 45 LA 1155 (Epstein, 1965) (conflict among scientific authority and legal and arbitrative precedents to warrant serious doubt about the probative value of the polygraph test); *Chapman Harbor*, 64 LA 27 (Neblett, 1975) (no adverse inference drawn from refusal to submit to exam); *B. F. Goodrich Tire Co.*, 36 LA 552 (Ryder, 1961) (discharge set aside); *Pearl Beer Distributing Co.*, 59 LA 820 (Britton, 1972) (employer improperly refused to reinstate employee who refused to take polygraph exam, absent published policy requiring employees to take test as condition of continued employment); Nolan, *Labor Arbitration Law and Practice* (West Publishing Co., 1979) ("With very few exceptions, arbitrators have held that employers may not punish for refusal to take a lie detector test. The exceptions to this general rule have occurred chiefly (a) where other evidence of some offense points to a small number of employees and it is difficult if not impossible to determine which in the small group are the true offenders, or (b) where the collective bargaining contract requires guards to cooperate fully in the investigation of thefts.") *Id.* at 153.

[6]See, e.g., *Warwick Electronics, Inc.*, 46 LA 95 (Daugherty, 1966) (employer properly issued written warnings to guards for refusing to submit to polygraph exams in connection with theft where collective bargaining agreement provided that guards would cooperate fully with employer in investigation of theft); *Bowman Transportation*, 61 LA 549 (Laughlin, 1973) (suspension sustained for refusal to submit to exam where employer had good cause to suspect employees of dishonest acts); *Allen Industries*, 26 LA 363 (Klamon, 1956).

[7]*Lag Drug Co.*, 39 LA 1121, 1122 (Ryder, 1962), citing *Town & Country Food Co.*, 39 LA 332 (Lewis, 1962).

[8]39 LA 70 (Ryder, 1962).

[9]481 F.2d 817, 83 LRRM 2652 (5th Cir. 1973).

[10]*Id.* at 2654.

[11]See, e.g., *Daystrom Furniture Co.*, 65 LA 1157 (Laughlin); but see *Owens-Corning Fiberglas Corp.*, 48 LA 1089 (Doyle, 1967) (although test results corroborate grievant, not crucial factor in decision).

¹²70 LA 909 (Pinkus, 1978).

¹³*Id.* at 912, citing 65 LA at 1162.

¹⁴*Bethlehem Steel Corp.*, 68 LA 581, 583 (Seward, 1977). See also, *Illinois Bell Telephone Co.*, 39 LA 470 (Ryder, 1962); *Marathon Electric Manufacturing Co.*, 31 LA 1040 (Duff, 1959) ("Voluntary stipulations would undoubtedly make such tests admissible in Arbitration proceedings."); *Bethlehem Steel Corp.*, 68 LA 583 (Seward, 1977) ("[t]hough arbitration proceedings are not controlled by the strict rules of evidence, wisdom suggests that [the arbitrator] should follow this judicial approach and admit polygraphic evidence only if both the Company and Union agree"); *Nettle Creek Industries*, 70 LA 100 (High, 1978) ("I am very much bothered by the fact that Grievant was asked to consent to the test without Union representation, but in view of the fact that the results of the polygraph test are not the primary evidence relied upon in this case, it is my finding that the absence of such representation is not sufficient to cause a reversal of the Company's action."); *Golden Pride, Inc.*, 68 LA 1232 (Jaffee, 1977) (discharge sustained notwithstanding grievant passed exam since parties did not agree on operator). See O. Fairweather, *Practice and Procedure in Labor Arbitration* (BNA Books, 1973), 263.

¹⁵*B. F. Goodrich Tire Co.*, 36 LA 552, 558 (Ryder, 1961). See also *Pearl Beer Distributing Co.*, 59 LA 820 (Britton, 1972) (employee consent to only one exam).

¹⁶Jones, *supra* note 1, at 101–102.

¹⁷Carver, "The Inquisitorial Process in Private Employment," 63 *Cornell L. Rev.* 1 (1977).

¹⁸*Bethlehem Steel Corp.*, 68 LA 581 (1977).

¹⁹"Privacy, Polygraphs, and Employment," Staff Report, Subcommittee on Constitutional Rights, Senate Committee on the Judiciary, 93rd Cong. 2d Sess. (1974), at 9.

²⁰Fairweather, *supra* note 14, at 263.

²¹A comprehensive ban against the use of lie detectors is mandated in a New Jersey statute providing: "Any person who is an employer who shall influence, request or require an employee to take or submit to a lie detector test as a condition of employment or continued employment is a disorderly person." N.J. Rev. Stat. § 2A: 170-90.1 (1966). The validity of this statute was upheld in *State* v. *Community Distributors, Inc.*, 64 N.J. 479, 317 A.2d 697 (1974). Other states that have enacted statutes regulating the polygraph include: Alaska [Alaska Stat. § 23.10.037 (1964)]; California [Cal. Lab. Code § 431.2 (West 1953)]; Connecticut [Conn. Pub. Act 488 (1966)]; Delaware [Del. Code tit. 19, § 1705 (1966)]; Hawaii [Hawaii Rev. Stat. § 378-21 & 22 (1965)]; Idaho [Idaho Code §§ 44-903, 44-904 (1973)]; Maryland [Md. Ann. Code art. 100, § 378-21 (1966)]; Massachusetts [Mass. Gen. Laws Ann. ch. 149, § 19 (1963)]; Michigan [Mich. Pub. Act 295, § 26 (1975)]; Minnesota [Minn. Stat. Ann. § 181.75(1) (1973)]; Oregon [Ore. Rev. Stat. §§ 659.225, 659.990 (1963)]; Pennsylvania [Pa. Stat. Ann. tit. 18, § 4666.1 (1969)]; Rhode Island [R.I. Gen. Laws §§ 28-6.1-1-2 (1964)]; Washington [Wash. Rev. Code §§ 49.44.120 (1965, amended, 152.1). In addition, some 23 states have enacted statutes licensing polygraph examiners. See "Polygraph Control and Civil Liberties Protection Act," Hearings on S. 1845, *supra* note 1.

²²Absent evidence that the polygraph is used to harass employees because of union-related activities, the NLRB has found no violation of the LMRA where employers have conditioned employment on taking a poly-

graph exam. See, e.g., *American Oil Co.*, 189 NLRB No. 2, 76 LRRM 1506 (1971) (employer did not violate LMRA when it terminated employees for refusal to take polygraph test where circumstances surrounding burglary suggested "inside job"); *Medicenter, Mid-South Hospital*, 221 NLRB No. 105, 90 LRRM 1576 (1975) (requirement that employees submit to polygraph examination as condition of continued employment mandatory subject of bargaining, even though employer resorted to it solely as effort to combat vandalism); *Mariano's Restaurant*, 230 NLRB No. 172, 95 LRRM 1620 (1977) (LRMA not violated where employer required two employees to submit to polygraph where requirement had been part of personnel policies prior to any concerted activities on employees' part and where no evidence that requirement was enforced to harass any employee); *Bosco Services*, 232 NLRB No. 124, 97 LRRM 1331 (1977) (no violation of LMRA where employee discharged after failing polygraph exam absent evidence that employer required test to mask discrimination).

[22a]*Miranda v. Arizona*, 384 U.S. 436, 467 (1966).

[23]387 U.S. 1, 47–48 (1966), citing *Murphy v. Waterfront Comm.*, 378 U.S. 52, 94 (1964) (White, J., concurring).

[24]387 U.S. at 47.

[25]Fleming, *supra* note 1, at 182.

[26]W. Wirtz, "Due Process of Arbitration," in *The Arbitrator and the Parties*, Proceedings of the Eleventh Annual Meeting, National Academy of Arbitrators (BNA Books, 1958), 19.

[27]See, e.g., *Safeway Stores, Inc.*, 55 LA 1195 (Jacobs, 1971) (confession not credited when evidence of mental duress demonstrated); *Kroger Co.*, 12 LA 1065 (Blair, 1949) ("confessions" given to private detective not credited where inducements, commitments, and threats were made by investigators); *Thrifty Drug Stores*, 50 LA 1253 (Jones, 1968) (statements elicited regarded with "skepticism" and given weight only when other corroborating evidence present in situations where interrogations occur without presence of union representation and discipline likely); *Armco Steel Corp.*, 48 LA 132 (Cahn, 1967) (discharge reversed where confessions unreliable); *Eastern Airlines, Inc.*, 46 LA 549 (Seidenberg, 1965) (confession not invalidated absent duress and coercion; no infirmity found where grievant freely admitted employer representative who secured confession and resignation). See generally, Fairweather, *supra* note 14, at 243–53; Fleming, *supra* note 1, at 181–86; Elkouri & Elkouri, *How Arbitration Works* (BNA Books, 1973), 287–88.

[28]*Safeway Stores*, 55 LA 1195, 1201 (Jacobs, 1971).

[29]50 LA 1253 (Jones, 1968).

[30]*Id.* at 1262.

[31]For an excellent discussion of the cooperation problem, see Fairweather, "The Interaction of Rules Against Self-Incrimination and the Employer's Duty to Cooperate in an Investigation of Misconduct," *supra* note 14, at 247.

[32]*Exact Weight Scale Co.*, 50 LA 8, 8–9 (McCoy, 1967).

[33]50 LA 103 (Kates, 1968). Arbitrator Kates, in *Weirton Steel*, reasoned: "I do not subscribe to the doctrine that purity must always envelop those engaged in attempting to ascertain the truth, or that subterfuge or pretense is always improper in a truth-seeking endeavor. Each such case must, I believe, be judged upon its own facts." *Id.* at 105.

[34]*Lucky Stores*, 53 LA 1274, 1277 (Eaton, 1969).

[35]The West Coast Tripartite Committee has observed:

"It seems . . . foreseeable, even probable, given the federal trend to strengthen labor arbitration as a tribunal, coincident with the federal strengthening of the privilege against self-incrimination, that arbitrators may be required to be at least as observant as judges of the dictates of that privilege, perhaps even more so, and this at the expense of vacation of an award where failure to observe the privilege may reasonably be concluded to vitiate its reasoning. . . .
    . . .
"In any event, arbitrators will have to become more knowledgeable in regard to privileges than they generally are now. Suffice here to observe that they may well find themselves deemed to be conservators of legal privileges, like it or not, and that failure so to function may jeopardize the validity of their awards." *Problems of Proof in Arbitration,* Proceedings of the Nineteenth Annual Meeting, National Academy of Arbitrators (BNA Books, 1967), 200–201.

[36]See, e.g. *Kroger Co.,* 25 LA 906 (Smith, 1955) ("Misconduct of kind which carries stigma of general social disapproval as well as disapproval under accepted canons of plant discipline . . . should be clearly and convincingly established by the evidence. Reasonable doubts raised by proofs should be resolved in favor of accused."); *Amelia Earhart Luggage Co.,* 11 LA 301 (Lesser, 1948) ("a decision against the individual would have more far reaching results than breaking plant rules, in that it would brand her for the rest of her life as an ordinary thief before associates, friends and neighbors. Considering the gravity of the consequences, it follows logically to my mind that the evidence should not leave the shadow of reasonable doubt."). But see *Southern Greyhound Lines, Inc.,* 43 LA 113 (Black, 1964) ("If I were on a jury and this were a criminal case, I would not convict grievant of the charges made by the Company; proof would then have to be beyond a shadow of a doubt, and I have shadows of doubt about the guilt of the grievant. . . . However, this is not a criminal case. I must sustain the discharge here if I am reasonably satisfied from the evidence that the Company in the context of circumstances had good cause to discharge the grievant."). See also, *American Division, ACF Industries, Inc.,* 72-2 ARB ¶ 8720 (Sinicropi, 1973) (no per se rule concerning quantum of proof).

[37]*Supra* note 35, at 205.

[38]*Id.*

[39]Wigmore, *Evidence* Sec. 2183 (McNaughton rev. ed., 1961), 7.

[40]232 U.S. 383 (1914).

[41]The object of the Fourth Amendment is to protect "people from unreasonable government intrusions into their legitimate expectations of privacy." *U.S. v. Chadwick,* ___ U.S. ___, 97 S.Ct. 2476 (1977).

[42]367 U.S. 643 (1961).

[43]See, *Lucky Stores, Inc.,* 53 LA 1274, 1276 (Eaton, 1969) (exclusionary rules of *Miranda* not applicable to private investigations where there is not an agent of state present); *International Nickel Co.,* 68-1 ARB ¶ 8229 (Shister, 1967) (no authority to consider constitutional implications of search of employee's lockers; arbitration board, which derived authority from contract, could only look to agreement in determining propriety of employer action); *United Packinghouse Workers of America,* 62-2 ARB ¶ 8544 (Kelliher, 1962) (federal substantive law not controlling in arbitration proceeding where arbitrator required to construe language of contract by application of

recognized maxims of contract interpretation). Cf. *U.S. Postal Service*, 241 NLRB No. 18, 100 LRRM 1520 (1979).

[44]See, e.g., Fleming, *supra* note 1, at 189. In *Holodnak v. Avco*, 387 F.Supp. 191, 87 LRRM 2337 (D.C. Conn. 1974), a federal district court queried whether the First Amendment can be used to bypass the tight restrictions on judicial review of a labor arbitrator's award. In addition, the court postulated that since the arbitrator is an instrument of national labor policy, he is not a mere "private person," but rather one acting on behalf of the Government who must take into account First Amendment rights. Closely related to this argument, noted the court, is the argument that the labor laws express a public policy encouraging free association and communication among employees and that courts are free to review and vacate an award which conflicts with this policy. *Id.* at 2347 n.12.

[45]Fleming, *supra* note 1, at 189.

[46]See *Campbell Soup Co.*, 2 LA 27 (Lohman, 1946).

[47]*Id.* at 31.

[48]*Imperial Glass Corp.*, 61 LA 1180 (Gibson, 1973). See also *Anchor Hocking Corp.*, 66 LA 480 (Emerson, 1976) (discharge improper where employer searched lunch boxes of 75 employees and discovered company-owned quart jars, lids, and rings worth $1.28, since employer failed to comply with *Miranda* requirements pertaining to right to counsel and also invaded employees' right to privacy).

[49]Remarks of Philip V. Carter, Seyfarth, Shaw, Fairweather & Geraldson, Workshop on Chicago Tripartite Committee, in *Problems of Proof in Arbitration*, *supra* note 35, at 134. In *Rocky Mountain Arsenal*, 64 LA 894 (1975), Arbitrator John Murphy held that the Army-employer did not violate the agreement by unilaterally conducting a search of employees' lockers in the arsenal area following a protective equipment shortage that threatened to shut down production lines.

[50]*Hennis Freight Lines*, 44 LA 711, 713 (McGury, 1964). See also *Weirton Steel Co.*, 68-1 ARB ¶ 8249 (Kates, 1968) (strict rules applicable under criminal investigations not necessarily operative to private investigations by an employer into conduct of an employee); *United States Steel Corp.*, 49 LA 101 (Dybeck, 1967) (employee's rights to be determined under agreement; claim that failure of company to afford grievant equivalent of constitutional right to legal counsel rejected).

[51]*Aldens, Inc.*, 61 LA 663, 664–65 (Dolnick, 1973).

[52]60 LA 1260 (1973).

[53]*Id.* at 1262–63.

[54]Fleming, *supra* note 1, at 189. Fleming declares that there is a difference of opinion as to the use of evidence of this type when the employee's personal property is searched without his consent, but without the necessity for entering by force. In this same regard, see *Scott Paper Co.*, 52 LA 57 (Williams, 1969) (order to employee to empty pockets improper and grievant within rights to refuse request); *Dow Chemical Co.*, 65 LA 1295 (Lipson, 1976) ("while constitutional limitations on unlawful searches are normally construed as restraints on government authorities, and are not usually applicable to contractual disputes between private parties, nevertheless the rights to privacy and personal dignity are so fundamentally a part of the American tradition that they should at least be given consideration by a labor arbitrator in passing on search problems in plants"), *id.* at 1298; *contra, International*

Nickel Co., 68-1 ARB ¶ 8229 (Shister, 1967) (employer did not violate personal rights of employee by searching part of company's property which had been designated to the employee for personal use); *Champion Spark Plug Co.*, 68 LA 702 (Casselman, 1977) (order to grievant to unbutton sweater with steward present proper where probable cause that serious plant rule [use of alcohol] existed; inappropriate to attempt to establish exact parallel between rights of citizens on street and employees in plant); *Smith's Food King*, 66 LA 619 (Ross, 1976) ("arbitrator believes that the constitutional protection against unreasonable searches and seizures does not apply against a private company to prevent their searching an employee at his place of employment under suspicious circumstances"). *Id.* at 625.

[55]See, e.g., *Colonial Baking Co.*, 62 LA 586 (Elson, 1974) (closed-circuit television in high crime area to improve security); *Ford Motor of Canada*, 57 LA 914 (Weatherill, 1971) (closed-circuit television cameras at plant gates); *Hobart Manufacturing Co.*, 62 LA 1285 (Kabaker, 1974) (video tape equipment for time studies); *Cooper Carton Corp.*, 61 LA 697 (Kelliher, 1973) (employer permitted to install two television cameras to observe production operations where contract gives employer exclusive direction of working force); *contra, Electronic Instrument Co., Inc.*, 44 LA 563 (Delany, 1965) (installation of cameras contract violation where agreement contained clause that guaranteed employees "beneficial conditions of employment" unless good cause was shown for withdrawal).

[56]46 LA 335 (1966).

[57]*Id.* at 338.

[58]See, e.g., *Los Angeles Transit Lines*, 25 LA 740 (Hildebrand, 1955); *Nat'l Distillers & Chemical Corp.*, 62 LA 339 (Geissinger, 1974); H. Black, "Surveillance and the Labor Arbitration Process" in *Arbitration and the Expanding Role of Neutrals*, Proceedings of the Twenty-Third Meeting, National Academy of Arbitrators (BNA Books, 1970).

[59]57 LA 725 (1971).

[60]31 LA 191 (Marcus, 1958). See also *Walton Mfg. Co.*, 124 NLRB 1331, 45 LRRM 1007 (1959) (transcriptions of employer's anti-union speech from dictaphone tapes admissible as accurate reproductions of speeches); *Duro Fittings Co.*, 130 NLRB 653, 47 LRRM 1363 (1961) (trial examiner did not err in refusing to admit tape recordings of numerous bargaining conferences held between employer and union where tapes of two sessions were admittedly garbled). In *Needham Packing Co.*, 44 LA 1057 (1965), Arbitrator Davey held inadmissible the recordings of telephone conversations between a union officer and the employer's attorney on the ground that the conversations were recorded without the knowledge and consent of the union.

[61]Report of the West Coast Tripartite Committee, *supra* note 35, at 204. In *NLRB v. Plasterers, Local 90*, 606 F.2d 189, 102 LRRM 2482 (7th Cir. 1979), the Court of Appeals for the Seventh Circuit held that the NLRB did not err in admitting into evidence telephone conversations between a job applicant and a union official that were recorded by the applicant, notwithstanding that use of recording devices during the telephone conversations was in violation of an Illinois statute and that Illinois courts would not admit these recordings as evidence at trial. Section 10 (b) of the NLRA states that hearings "shall, so far as practicable, be considered in accordance with the rules of evidence applicable in the district courts." *Id.* at 2484. The Seventh Circuit concluded that federal and not state law governs admission of evidence in federal proceedings.

In *Carpenter Sprinkler Corp.* v. *NLRB*, ____ F.2d ____, 102 LRRM 2199 (2d Cir. 1979), the Court of Appeals for the Second Circuit held that the Board was within its discretion in fashioning a rule that surreptitiously prepared tape recordings are inadmissible as evidence in an unfair labor practice proceeding. In reaching this conclusion, the Second Circuit stated:

"Negotiations in the labor relations field are often a delicate matter. Courts must balance the interests of an employer against the possibility of coercing or intimidating employees in the exercise of their rights under the Act, and harming the collective bargaining process. . . . The rulings of the Board in this case specifically referred to the 'significant problems' which might result [inhibiting the expression of the parties] from allowing tape recordings of contract negotiations into evidence."
(Citations omitted.) *Id.* at 2202.

In another decision the Second Circuit held that a defendant in a union disciplinary proceeding has the right, under Section 101 of the Labor-Management Reporting and Disclosure Act, to record the proceeding at his own expense, electronically or stenographically, when the union does not do so. In rejecting the argument that disciplinary proceedings should be treated like collective bargaining sessions (which are usually not recorded), the court stated that such an argument overlooks the significant difference between the two proceedings:

"Because negotiation of contract terms and grievances requires each party to compromise some or all of its interests in order to achieve a settlement best for the group as a whole, negotiators realize that the bargaining process could easily be stymied if each of the multiple, heterogeneous constituencies they represent are apprised of the details of the process. Experience teaches that labor contracts, like international treaties, cannot openly be arrived at. . . . Union disciplinary proceedings, in contrast, are comparable in several important respects to a criminal trial, where credibility is crucial and secrecy is utterly foreign to our concepts of fairness. As in criminal trials, witnesses in union disciplinary proceedings are more likely to conduct themselves properly if they know that an accurate record of their testimony can be scrutinized by others than if the sole record consists of sketchy notes made by a union official sympathetic to the union management." *Rosario* v. *ILGWU*, 605 F.2d 1228, 101 LRRM 2958 (2d Cir. 1979) at 2967.

[62]Report of the West Coast Tripartite Committee, *supra* note 35, at 201.

[63]380 U.S. 609, 85 S.Ct. 1229 (1965).

[64]*Id.* at 613.

[65]68-2 ARB ¶ 8591, at 5045 (1968).

[66]43 LA 400 (1964).

[67]40 LA 598 (1963).

[68]26 LA 742 (1956).

[69]*Id.* at 746.

[70]*Southern Bell Telephone & Telegraph Co.*, 25 LA 270, 273 (McCoy, 1955).

[71]51 LA 177 (1968).

[72]*Id.* at 181. See also *Grocers Supply Co.*, 59 LA 1280 (Taylor, 1972) ("Grievant has no right to refuse to testify in this matter if called by the

Company. If the Grievant did so refuse, there is no doubt that the Arbitrator could find such a refusal to be indicative of his guilt"). *Id.* at 1281.

[73]Wirtz, *supra* note 26, at 20.

[74]29 LA 442 (1957).

[75]Fleming, *supra* note 1, at 182.

[76]Smith, "The Search for Truth," in *Truth, Lie Detectors, and Other Problems in Labor Arbitration, supra* note 1, at 54–55.

[77]Report of the West Coast Tripartite Committee, *supra* note 35, at 201.

[78]See Report of the Chicago Area Tripartite Committee, in *Problems of Proof in Arbitration, supra* note 35, at 99; Report of the New York Tripartite Committee, *id.* at 301; Report of the West Coast Tripartite Committee, *id.* at 202. See also Smith, *supra* note 76, at 46–60.

[79]Report of the New York Area Tripartite Committee, *supra* note 78.

[80]*Id.*

[81]Report of the Chicago Area Tripartite Committee, *supra* note 78.

[82]Report of the West Coast Tripartite Committee, *supra* note 78. Arbitrator Russell Smith has noted that as a practical matter, a witness called from the other side cannot be compelled to testify, since the arbitrator has no contempt powers and can at most issue a subpoena which can be enforced only through separate judicial proceedings. Smith, *supra* note 76, at 55.

[83]37 LA 807 (Autrey, 1961).

[84]*Id.* at 809–10.

[85]Wirtz, *supra* note 26, at 18.

[86]Smith, *supra* note 76, at 55–56.

[87]See, e.g., *Tracy & Avery, Inc.*, 74-2 ARB ¶ 8357 (Feldman, 1974); *Bangor Products Corp.*, 74-2 ARB ¶ 8358 (McLeod, 1974); *Minnesota Mining & Manufacturing Co.*, 71-1 ARB ¶ 8250 (Jacobs, 1971) (affidavit not previously submitted to a union for inspection could not be admitted as evidence at an arbitration since union must have opportunity to examine and test for validity and prepare defense).

Rule 29 of the *Voluntary Labor Arbitration Rules*, American Arbitration Association (1979), in relevant part, provides: "The Arbitrator may receive and consider the evidence of witnesses by affidavit, but shall give it only such weight as he deems proper after consideration of any objections made to its admission."

[88]67 LA 163 (1976).

[89]68 LA 581 (1977).

[90]67 LA 861 (1976).

[91]65 LRRM 2647 (N.J. Super. 1967).

[92]*Id.* at 2649.

[93]See, *"New Evidence and the Arbitral Process" infra* p. 109.

[94]6 LA 31 (1947).

[95]*Id.* at 43; see also, *Ciba-Geigy Corp.*, 61 LA 438 (Jaffee, 1973) (employer producing toxic chemicals obligated to furnish union generic or common names of all chemical substances it manufactures); *Weyerhaeuser Co.*, 64 LA 874 (Barnhart, 1975) (backpay dispute resolved against employer where information not disclosed); *Weyerhaeuser Co.*, 64 LA 869 (Barnhart, 1975) (employer obligated to furnish personnel data that union demanded to substantiate job-discrimination claim).

[96]21 LA 367 (1953).

[97]"Since the authority of the arbitrator is not clearly set out, we shall refer to certain rules of the Voluntary Labor Arbitration Rules of the Ameri-

can Arbitration Association, since these rules are part of the arbitration agreement and apply to the conduct of the hearing." *Id.* at 370.

[98]*Id.* at 371.

[99]8 LA 713 (1947).

[100]*Mobil Oil Corp.*, 63 LA 263 (Sinclitico, 1974).

[101]135 N.J. Super. 552, 90 LRRM 2191 (1975).

[102]It is noteworthy that the decision of the lower court was reversed and remanded by an appellate court. *Teamsters v. ABAD*, 93 LRRM 2791 (1976). The appellate court found that there was nothing in the record to suggest that the employer itself knew that the records were incomplete. Furthermore, the court found that the circumstances surrounding the supervisor's affidavit were such to cast doubt upon its reliability. As such, the court held it error for the trial judge to enter judgment for the plaintiff without a plenary hearing. Accordingly, it remanded the case for further proceedings.

[103]In *Max Factor & Co.*, 61 LA 886 (1973), Arbitrator Edgar Jones held that a union was not entitled (until after the start of the arbitration hearing) to obtain the name and address of a former employee who was a company witness where it was demonstrated that threats were made against the witness.

[104]48 LA 373 (1967).

[105]*Id.* at 376.

[106]21 LA 367 (1953).

[107]*Id.* at 370.

[108]*Id.*

[109]24 LA 44 (1954).

[110]*Id.* at 47; but see *University of California*, 63 LA 314 (Jacobs, 1974) (arbitrator without authority to issue subpoena *duces tecum* where arbitration not conducted pursuant to Voluntary Labor Arbitration Rules of the American Arbitration Association; authority of hearing officer derives solely from Staff Personnel Policy and Policy does not authorize arbitrator to issue subpoena).

[111]See, Fairweather, "The Subpoena of Documents and Other Evidence," *supra* note 14, at 132.

[112]Title 9, U.S.C. §4 provides:

"A party aggrieved by the alleged failure, neglect, or refusal of another to arbitrate under a written agreement for arbitration may petition any United States district court . . . for an order directing such arbitration proceed in the manner provided for in such agreement."

The same Act prescribes in 9 U.S.C. §7:

"The arbitrators selected . . . may summon in writing any person to attend before them or any of them as a witness and in a proper case to bring with him or them any book, record, document or paper which may be deemed material as evidence in the case. The fees for such attendance shall be the same as the fees of any witness before masters of the United States courts. Said summons shall issue in the name of the arbitrator . . . and shall be directed to the said person and shall be served in the same manner as subpoenas to appear and testify before the court; . . ."

9 U.S.C. §1 provides:

"[N]othing herein contained shall apply to contracts of employment of seamen, railroad employees, or any other class of workers engaged in foreign or interstate commerce."

The federal courts have been in disagreement concerning the applicability of the statute to arbitration provisions contained in collective bargaining agreements. *Compare Signal-Stat Corp.* v. *Local 475, United Electrical Workers*, 235 F.2d 298, 38 LRRM 2378 (2d Cir. 1956), *cert. denied*, 354 U.S. 911, 40 LRRM 2200 (1957) (statute applicable to suits upon collective bargaining agreements), *with Local 205, United Electrical Workers* v. *General Electric Co.*, 233 F.2d 85, 98-100, 38 LRRM 2019 (1st Cir, 1956), *aff'd on other grounds*, 353 U.S. 547, 40 LRRM 2119 (1957). The issue has not been resolved by the Supreme Court except by negative implication in *Textile Workers* v. *Lincoln Mills*, 353 U.S. 448 (1957).

[113]Section 301(a), 29 U.S.C. §185, of the LMRA provides:

"Suits for violation of contracts between an employer and a labor organization representing employees in an industry affecting commerce as defined in this chapter, or between any such labor organizations, may be brought in any district court of the United States having jurisdiction of the parties, without respect to the amount in controversy or with regard to the citizenship of the parties."

[114]363 F.Supp. 1351, 84 LRRM 2514 (E.D.Mich. 1973).

[115]329 F.Supp. 283, 77 LRRM 2596 (D. Conn. 1971).

[116]*Supra* note 112.

[117]*Local Lodge 1746* v. *United Aircraft Corp.*, *supra* note 115, at 2599.

[118]29 U.S.C. §158(a)(5).

[119]"Sec. 8(a). It shall be an unfair labor practice for an employer—
. . .

"(5) to refuse to bargain collectively with the representatives of his employees, subject to the provisions of section 9(a) . . .
. . .

"(d) For the purpose of this section, to bargain collectively is the performance of the mutual obligation of the employer and the representative of the employees to meet at reasonable times and confer in good faith with respect to wages, hours, and other terms and conditions of employment, or the negotiation of an agreement, or any question arising thereunder, and the execution of a written contract incorporating any agreement reached if requested by either party, but such obligation does not compel either party to agree to a proposal or require the making of a concession . . .
. . .

"Sec. 9(a). Representatives designated or selected for the purposes of collective bargaining by the majority of the employees in a unit appropriate for such purposes, shall be the exclusive representatives of all the employees in such a unit for the purposes of collective bargaining in respect to rates of pay, wages, hours of employment, or other conditions of employment."

[120]___ U.S. ___, 100 LRRM 2728 (1979).

[121]*Id.* at 2733.

[122]351 U.S. 149, 38 LRRM 2042 (1956).

[123]385 U.S. 432, 64 LRRM 2069 (1967).

[124]*Id.* at 2070.

[125]*Id.* at 2071.

[126]*Detroit Edison Co.* v. *NLRB*, *supra* note 120, at 2737 n.5, citing *NLRB* v. *Acme Industrial Co.*, *supra* note 123, at 437.

[127]233 NLRB 694, 97 LRRM 1204 (1977).

[128]*Id.*

[129]237 NLRB No. 146, 99 LRRM 1174 (1978).

[130]437 U.S. 214, 98 LRRM 2617 (1978) (held: Freedom of Information Act, 5 U.S.C. §552, does not require Board to disclose, prior to hearing on an unfair labor practice complaint, statements of witnesses whom Board intends to call at hearing).

[131]*Anheuser-Busch, Inc.*, supra note 129, at 1177.

[132]*Id.*

[133]See, e.g., *United Aircraft Corp.*, 192 NLRB 382, 77 LRRM 1785 (1971) (medical records).

[134]*Supra* note 120.

[135]*Id.* at 2734.

[136]See Reports on Case-Handling Developments at NLRB, *Labor Relations Yearbook—1979* (BNA Books, 1980), 303.

[137]Fleming, *supra* note 1, at 175.

[138]See, e.g., Iowa Code Ann. §68.A.7(10)–(11) (West 1973) (regulating disclosure of confidential employee information).

[139]5 U.S.C. §552a (1976).

[140]*Local 2047, Am. Federation of Government Employees* v. *Defense General Supply Center*, 573 F.2d 184, 97 LRRM 3207 (4th Cir. 1978).

Chapter 9

[1]Report of the West Coast Area Tripartite Committee, in *Problems of Proof in Arbitration*, Proceedings of the Nineteenth Annual Meeting, National Academy of Arbitrators (BNA Books, 1967), 207. For an excellent discussion of credibility issues, see Mittenthal, "Credibility-A Will-O'-the-Wisp," in *Truth, Lie Detectors, and Other Problems in Labor Arbitration*, Proceedings of the Thirty-First Annual Meeting, National Academy of Arbitrators (BNA Books, 1979), 64–74.

[2]*Id.* at 207–208.

[3]See Mittenthal, *supra* note 1, at 63.

[4]*National Food Stores of Louisiana, Inc.*, 74-2 ARB ¶ 8512 (Marlatt, 1974).

[5]*George A. Hormel & Co.*, 65-2 ARB ¶ 8562 (Boles, 1965).

[6]*Gordon Pride, Inc.*, 68 LA 1232 (Jaffee, 1977).

[7]Mittenthal, *supra* note 1, at 63.

[8]Arbitrator Mittenthal notes that the typical arbitration is heard without the benefit of transcript. Since the arbitrator spends a considerable amount of time taking notes and recording testimony, he has little time to observe the witness's expressions and "body language." In addition, the busy arbitrator may hear several cases before the opinion is drafted. Thus, he may have problems recalling the faces of the witnesses, much less their demeanor. See Mittenthal, *supra* note 1, at 64.

[9]79 LRRM 2709 (E.D. Pa. 1972).

[10]See, e.g., *The International Nickel Co.*, 66-1 ARB ¶ 8318 (Duff, 1966); *American Air Filter Co.*, 1975 ARB ¶ 8024 (Hilpert, 1975).

[11]*Harvey Aluminum, Inc.*, 67-1 ARB ¶ 8085 (Prasow, 1967); see also *Cameron Iron Works*, 73 LA 878 (Marlatt, 1979) ("[grievant's] story is so patently absurd that I will not dignify it by categorizing it as a lie; it hardly even rises to the level of bullshit, and if the union officials believe it, they also believe in Santa Claus and the Tooth Fairy"). *Id.* at 879.

[11a]E. Cleary, *McCormick on Evidence* (West Publishing Co., 1972), 20.

[12]*South Penn Oil Co.*, 29 LA 718 (Duff, 1957). In *Exhibitors Film Delivery & Service, Inc.*, 67 LA 982 (1976), Arbitrator Gerald Cohen, in holding

that testimony of an auditor could not be credited, cited perception and memory considerations:

"I do not doubt that [the] witness was sincere. But while accepting his sincerity, I do not necessarily concede his accuracy.

"He was on the job for only a short time. He knew none of the employees prior to that day. Being new on the job, he would be unlikely to spend too much time doing anything but his job. As the general manager's grandson, he would be even more likely to be extremely attentive to his work.

"In addition, the whole incident was of short duration, given little chance for short observation. Further, his attention would not necessarily have been called to the incident immediately, given the need for a new employee to concentrate on an unfamiliar task.

"My willingness to accept [the] identification is further weakened by the fact there was a lapse of time of several days before he was called upon to make his identification. This resulted in discrepancies of identification as to details of hair color, etc." *Id.* at 985.

[13]29 LA 718. See also Mittenthal, *supra* note 1, at 65.

[14]29 LA 718.

[15]The Federal Rules of Evidence have limited the uses of specific instances of conduct for the purpose of attacking or supporting credibility. *Fed. R. Evid.* 608 provides:

"(a) *Opinion and reputation evidence of character.* The credibility of a witness may be attacked or supported by evidence in the form of opinion or reputation, but subject to these limitations: (1) the evidence may refer only to character for truthfulness or untruthfulness, and (2) evidence of truthful character is admissible only after the character of the witness for truthfulness has been attacked by opinion or reputation evidence or otherwise.

"(b) *Specific instances of conduct.* Specific instances of the conduct of a witness, for the purpose of attacking or supporting his credibility, other than conviction of crime as provided in Rule 609, may not be proved by extrinsic evidence. They may, however, in the discretion of the court, if probative of truthfulness or untruthfulness, be inquired into on cross-examination of the witness (1) concerning his character for truthfulness or untruthfulness, or (2) concerning the character for truthfulness or untruthfulness of another witness as to which character the witness being cross-examined has testified."

See also Rules 404 & 405.

[16]66-1 ARB ¶ 8318 (1966).

[17]68-2 ARB ¶ 8515 (1968).

[18]66-3 ARB ¶ 8969 (1966).

[19]*Imperial Glass Corp.*, 61 LA 1180, 1184 (Gibson, 1973).

[20]*South Penn Oil Co.*, 29 LA 718 (Duff, 1957).

[21]*Id.*

[22]*American Smelting & Refining Co.*, 67-2 ARB ¶ 8409 (Leonard, 1967).

[23]*The International Nickel Co.*, 66-1 ARB ¶ 8318 (Duff, 1966).

[24]*Herrud & Co.*, 77-2 ARB ¶ 8410 (Daniel, 1977).

[24a]*Lake Orion Community Schools*, 73 LA 707 (Roumell, 1979).

[25]Mittenthal, *supra* note 1, at 70. See also, *Commodity Warehousing Corp.*, 60 LA 1260 (Doppelt, 1973) ("while it is true that the grievant has a greater self-interest in this case than L- , it should not lightly be presumed that he is lying. A man is presumed innocent from the outset, and a person will deny a theft because of his true innocence as well as from self-interest. It

is just as fair to presume that grievant denied his complicity in the theft because he was innocent thereof, as it is to presume that he perjured himself out of self interest"). *Id.* at 1264.

Some arbitrators have taken the position that they should not try to reconcile or choose between contradictory and conflicting testimony, but rather should resolve the case only on the basis of whether the employer's conduct was based on substantial evidence. See, e.g., *Parkview-Gem, Inc.*, 59 LA 429 (Dugan, 1972).

[26]*Ready-Mix Concrete Co.*, 73-1 ARB ¶ 8082 (Mulhall, 1973).

[27]*American Air Filter, Co.*, 1975 ARB ¶ 8024 (Hilpert, 1975).

[28]*International Nickel Co.*, 66-1 ARB ¶ 8318 (Duff, 1966).

[29]*National Food Stores of Louisiana*, 74-2 ARB ¶ 8512 (Marlatt, 1974) ("[B]ut one must take into consideration that he [the grievant] was obviously a man of little education. He had great difficulty in understanding even the simplest questions put to him on cross-examination, asking that almost all of them be repeated.").

[30]See Mittenthal, *supra* note 1, at 66-67 ("Does the witness's inconsistency concern mere detail or the crucial matters in dispute? At what point does inconsistency of detail become substantial enough to discredit a man? Does the particular inconsistency indicate just slovenliness of mind and eye? Can consistency itself become suspect where the witness has repeated his story in great detail many times without the slightest variation"?).

[30a]For an excellent application of this principle, see *State of New York*, 66 LA 633 (Kornblum, 1976), 636-37.

[31]*Campbell Wyant & Cannon*, 70-1 ARB ¶ 8106 (Keefe, 1969); see also, *Koenig Trucking Co.*, 60 LA 899 (Howlett, 1973) (filing of false report with Michigan Employment Securities Commission is admission against interest by employer and raises questions concerning credibility of employer's officers who testified at arbitration hearing); *Southern Iron & Equipment Co.*, 65 LA 694 (Rutherford, 1975) ("It is well established that a witness's credibility can be impeached by prior inconsistent statements. This method of impeaching a witness is not dependent upon whether or not the witness has been reminded of his prior inconsistent statement before the hearing. Such a requirement would be ludicrous."). *Id.* at 699. *Commodity Warehousing Corp.*, 60 LA 1260 (Doppelt, 1973) ("L-, by his own admission, has committed a dishonest act. He has stolen from his employer on several occasions. This gives rise to questions concerning his basic credibility."). *Id.* at 1265.

[32]This is not to assert that no limits are imposed. For example, in *Friden Calculating Machine Co.*, 27 LA 496 (1956), Arbitrator Justin found that "personal invectives" used by the union in a posthearing brief for the purpose of attacking the credibility of a company witness went beyond the latitude generally accorded the parties in challenging credibility.

[33]Arbitrator Edgar Jones cited some cases noted by Judge Jerome Frank in *Courts on Trial* (1949): "Occasionally there are astonishing revelations of absurd rules-of-thumb some trial judges use, such as these: A witness is lying if, when testifying, he throws his head back; or if he raises his right heel from the floor; or if he shifts his gaze rapidly; or if he bites his lip. . . . Not very long ago, a federal trial judge, toward the end of his long career on the bench, publicly revealed for the first time that he had always counted as a liar any witness who rubbed his hands while testifying. That judge must have decided hundreds of cases in which he arrived at his findings of fact by applying that asinine test for detecting falsehoods." Jones, " 'Truth' When the

Polygraph Operator Sits as Arbitrator (or Judge): The Deception of 'Detection' in the 'Diagnosis of Truth and Deception,' " in *Truth, Lie Detectors, and Other Problems in Labor Arbitration,* Proceedings of the Thirty-First Annual Meeting, National Academy of Arbitrators (BNA Books, 1979), 130 n.107.

Chapter 10

[1]385 U.S. 432, 64 LRRM 2069 (1967).

[2]*Id.* at 438, 2071.

[3]See, e.g., Fairweather, *Practice and Procedure in Labor Arbitration* (BNA Books, 1973), 93–98; Elkouri & Elkouri, *How Arbitration Works* (BNA Books, 1973), especially Chapter 5; Wirtz, "Due Process of Arbitration," *The Arbitrators and the Parties,* Proceedings of the Eleventh Annual Meeting, National Academy of Arbitrators (BNA Books, 1958), 14.

[4]Fleming, "Some Problems of Due Process and Fair Procedure in Labor Arbitration," 13 *Stanford Law Review* 235 (1961).

[5]See, e.g., *Price Brothers Co.,* 61 LA 587 (Howlett, 1973) (employer precluded from presenting evidence of alleged offenses where union not notified of charges until third step of grievance procedure; argument that evidence not discovered until third step not credited); *Thompson City Delivery,* 74-2 ARB ¶ 8696 (Ross, 1975) (discharge must stand or fall on the reasons given at time of discharge; record may not be subsequently augmented by supplementary reasons where information known to employer at time of discharge); *Purex Corp.,* 62-3 ARB ¶ 8919 (Doyle, 1962) (arbitrator credits new evidence where party had not sought to enlarge or create new grievance).

[6]35 LA 205 (1960).

[7]*Id.* at 209.

[8]24 LA 353 (1955). See also *Wagner Electrical Corp.,* 61 LA 363 (Ray, 1973) (employer may sustain discharge on ground which is different from that initially relied upon where employer abandoned initial ground as basis for discharge and both union and employee advised).

[9]See generally, Smith, Merrifield & Rothschild, *Collective Bargaining and Labor Arbitration* (Bobbs-Merrill Co., 1970), 274; Elkouri & Elkouri, *supra* note 3, at 258-61; Fairweather, *supra* note 3, at 229-31.

[10]*Bethlehem Steel Co.,* 18 LA 367 (Feinberg, 1951).

[11]1975 ARB ¶ 8068 (1975).

[12]*Id.* at 3286-87.

[13]64 LA 107 (1975).

[14]65 LA 694 (1975).

[15]*Id.* at 698.

[16]60 LA 536 (1973).

[17]*Id.* at 537 n.1.

[17a]62 LA 616 (1974).

[17b]*Id.* at 620.

[17c]67 LA 1005 (1976).

[17d]It is noteworthy that there is authority to the contrary. For example, in *Mobil Chemical Co.,* 64 LA 10 (1974), Arbitrator Douglas Naehring, in allowing an employer to assert an arbitrability defense for the first time at the hearing, cited the analysis of Arbitrator Sam Kagel:

"Some arbitrators have held that the parties must raise the issue of arbitrability at one of the grievance procedure steps prior to the arbitration hearing. If this is required, it may hamper efforts to settle the grievance through negotiation. Rather than run the risk of losing the right to raise the issue of arbitrability after negotiations have failed (if they do fail), the parties would feel compelled to argue this technicality early in negotiations, thus possibly interfering with genuine attempts to settle the dispute without resorting to arbitration.

"Other arbitrators, following what seems to be the better view permit the issue of arbitrability to be raised for the first time at the hearing. Because this issue is critical only if the parties do, in fact, resort to arbitration, the right to raise it for the first time at the hearing places neither party at a disadvantage and yet has the positive value of freeing the negotiation steps from unnecessary technicalities."

Id. at 11, citing Kagel, Anatomy of Labor Arbitration (Washington, D.C.: BNA Books, 1961) at 10-11.

[18]See, e.g., Elkouri & Elkouri, supra note 3, at 258-61.

[19]Report of the New York Tripartite Committee, in Problems of Proof in Arbitration, Proceedings of the Nineteenth Annual Meeting, National Academy of Arbitrators (BNA Books, 1967), 302-303.

[20]48 LA 585 (1967).

[21]Elkouri & Elkouri, supra note 3, at 229.

[22]67 LA 328 (1976).

[23]33 LA 303 (1959).

[24]Id. at 307.

[25]18 LA 78 (1952).

[26]Id. at 81.

[27]61-3 ARB ¶ 8639 (1961).

[28]Id. at 5927.

[29]See, Fairweather, supra note 3, at 329. The Code of Professional Responsibility for Arbitrators of Labor-Management Disputes provides: "An arbitrator must not consider a post hearing brief or submission that has not been provided to the other party." See Appendix B, p. 145.

[30]61–2 ARB ¶ 8429 (1961).

[31]Id. at 5038.

[32]60 LA 572 (1973); contra: Mason & Hanger, Silas Mason Co., 60 LA 1270 (Fox, 1973) (employer entitled to include prior arbitration award under existing contract notwithstanding fact that award not introduced into evidence at hearing; citation and discussion of precedents along with expanded discussion regarding interpretation of agreement acceptable).

[33]66 LA 357 (1975).

[34]Id. at 363–64.

[35]17 LA 183 (1951).

[36]Id. at 185–86.

[37]American Arbitration Association, Voluntary Labor Arbitration Rules (1979), Rule 35.

[38]Gross error or mistake is an accepted common law ground for setting aside an arbitration award. For example, in Northwest Airlines v. ALPA, 530 F.2d 1048, 91 LRRM 2304 (D.C. Cir. 1976), a federal court held that a lower court erred in refusing to set aside an arbitration award where it was predicated on a dispositive mistake of fact. The court stated that the policies which mandate deference to substantive decisions by arbitrators are in-

applicable if a mistake of fact has led the arbitrator not to resolve the issue tendered. *Id.* at 2306. See also *Electronics Corp. of America* v. *Electrical Workers, IUE, Local 272*, 492 F.2d 1255, 85 LRRM 2534 (1st Cir. 1974) (award vacated where central fact underlying arbitrator's decision erroneous); *District 65* v. *Franklin Textile, Inc.*, 100 LRRM 2076 (N.Y. S.Ct. 1978) (award may be reviewed where decision completely irrational and holding in effect creates new contract).

[39]Section 301 of the Labor Management Relations Act, 29 U.S.C. §185, provides for suits in the federal district courts for violations of collective bargaining contracts between labor organizations and employers without regard to the amount in controversy. This section also contemplates suits by and against individual employees, and even encompasses suits to seek uniquely personal rights such as wages, hours, overtime pay, and wrongful discharge. *Smith* v. *Evening News Ass'n*, 371 U.S. 195, 51 LRRM 2646 (1962). Under federal law, an employee cannot bring a 301 action in federal court unless he first attempts to utilize the contractual procedures for settling his dispute with his employer. To ultimately prevail against the employer in a 301 suit, an individual must demonstrate that the union breached its duty of fair representation. See *Vaca* v. *Sipes*, 386 U.S. 171, 64 LRRM 2369 (1967); *Hines* v. *Anchor Motor Freight, Inc.*, 424 U.S. 554, 91 LRRM 2481 (1976).

[40]See *Steelworkers* v. *American Manufacturing Co.*, 363 U.S. 564 (1960); *Steelworkers* v. *Warrior & Gulf Navigation Co.*, 363 U.S. 574 (1960); *Steelworkers* v. *Enterprise Wheel & Car Corp.*, 363 U.S. 593 (1960). But see *General Drivers Local 89* v. *Hays & Nicoulin, Inc.*, 594 F.2d 1093 (6th Cir. 1979).

[41]424 U.S. 554, 91 LRRM 2481 (1976).

[41a]485 F. Supp. 511, 104 LRRM 2326 (D.C. Utah, 1980).

[41b]*Id.* at 2328.

[41c]*Id.* at 2329.

[42]Wirtz, "Due Process of Arbitration," *supra* note 3, at 14–15.

[43]54 LRRM 2660 (E.D. Pa. 1963).

[44]236 N.W. 2d 231, 91 LRRM 2890 (Wisc. S.Ct. 1975).

[45]350 F.Supp. 1221, 82 LRRM 2107 (E.D. Pa. 1972).

[46]*Id.* at 2109.

[47]See e.g., *Borden Co.* (Morvant, 1959).

Chapter 11

[1]William E. Simken, Conference on Training of Law Students in Labor Relations, Vol. III, Transcript of Proceedings at 636, 637, as cited in Smith, Merrifield, and Rothschild, *Collective Bargaining and Labor Arbitration* (Bobbs-Merrill, 1970), 214.

[2]Cox, "The Place of Law in Labor Arbitration," in *The Profession of Labor Arbitration*, Selected Papers From the First Seven Annual Meetings of the National Academy of Arbitrators, 1948-1954 (BNA Books, 1957), 86.

Table of Cases

Index

A

Abernethy, Byron R.   54–55
Adversary party, evidence from (see Due process)
Affidavits as hearsay evidence   91
Alexander, Gabriel   111
Altieri, James   86
American Arbitration Association
  Voluntary Labor Arbitration Rules   20, 58, 95–96
  text   123–30
Arbitration
  in absence of one party   23
  discovery in   97–99
  judicial proceedings compared   65–66, 114–15
  as means of obtaining information in possession of other party   96
  search or seizure rights under   78, 83
  self-incrimination protection, application to arbitral process   74–75
  voluntary nature of   84–85
Arbitration awards (see Awards)
Arbitrators, authority of
  consideration of new evidence, courts' deference to   119–20
  disclosure of evidence, ordering of   95–97, 99–100
  interrogation of witnesses   21–22
  order of witness presentation, regulation of   20, 92–93
  reopening of hearing prior to making award   117–18
  subpoena power   96–97, 99
Awards
  prior awards, evidentiary value of   40–42
  refusal of courts to review   15–16, 117–18

B

Belkin, Louis   37–38
Best-evidence rule   28–29

"Beyond a reasonable doubt"   10–13
Block, Howard   10–11, 62
Bowles, George E.   49–50
Briefs, post-hearing   116–17
Burden of proof
  definition   13
  imposition on management or labor, arbitrators' opinions on   13–15
  usefulness in arbitration process   16

C

Caraway, John F.   112
Carmichael, Peter   70
Chicago Area Tripartite Committee report
  cross-examination, scope of   19
  grievant as initial witness   90
  leading questions   18–19
  negotiations prior to arbitration, exclusion of as evidence   56–57
  parole evidence rule   55
  rules of evidence, usefulness of   2
  search and seizure rights in arbitral process   80
  written medical statements   30
Circumstantial evidence   4–6
Cleary, E.   19, 24, 42
Closed-circuit television, admissibility of evidence obtained by   83–84
Code of Professional Responsibility for Arbitrators of Labor-Management Disputes   21, 58
  text   131–46
Collateral estoppel
  collateral criminal proceedings   64–67
  definition   60
  findings of industrial unemployment compensation boards   61–64
  res judicata distinguished from   61
  results from collateral proceedings, use of   67–68

197

About the Authors

Marvin Hill, Jr., currently Associate Professor of Labor and Industrial Relations at the College of Business Administration, Northern Illinois University, is a member of the Iowa Bar Association. He is actively engaged in labor arbitration through the Offices of the American Arbitration Association, the Federal Mediation and Conciliation Service, the Iowa Public Employment Relations Board, and the Wisconsin Employment Relations Commission, and serves on arbitration panels for the Illinois Department of Personnel and the Illinois Board of Education. He has contributed articles to *The Arbitration Journal*, *The Labor Law Journal*, *Indiana Law Review*, and the *Public Employment Relations Library*.

Anthony V. Sinicropi is John F. Murray Professor of Industrial Relations at the University of Iowa, and Chairman of the Department of Industrial Relations and Human Resources in the College of Business Administration. He is also Director of the Industrial Relations Institute. He has served as a consultant for several government organizations, as an arbitrator and umpire, and as a mediator and fact finder in the public sector. He is a member of the Board of Governors of the National Academy of Arbitrators and President of the Society of Professionals in Dispute Resolution. Among his publications are *Iowa Labor Laws*, "The Legal Status of Supervisors in Public Sector Labor Relations," "The Legal Framework of Public Sector Dispute Resolution," "Excluding Discrimination Grievances from Grievance and Arbitration Procedures: A Legal Analysis," and "Subcontracting in Labor Arbitration."